PAST & PRESENT

MOSCOW

Opposite: This early photograph shows a Grand Army of the Republic parade in front of the Moscow Brewery at the corner of A and Main Streets. Otto Fries opened the Moscow Brewery in 1882. In 1908, the wooden structure burned down, and a brick and concrete building replaced the original. The Corner Club bar opened at that location in 1948, although part of the building was demolished to accommodate the highway rerouting couplet in 1981. The bar is still in operation in 2024. (Courtesy of the Latah County Historical Society.)

PAST & PRESENT

MOSCOW

Latah County Historical Society

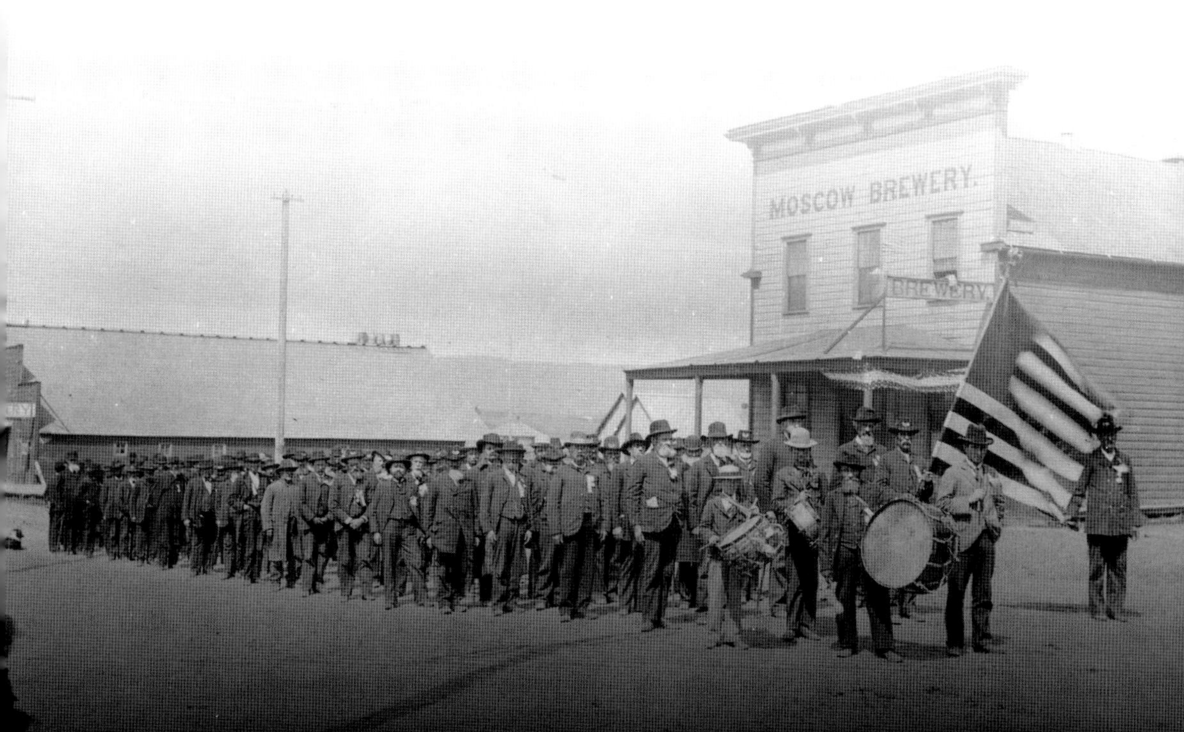

ISBN 978-1-4671-6237-1

Library of Congress Control Number: 2024949696

Published by Arcadia Publishing
Charleston, South Carolina

Printed in the United States of America

For all general information, please contact Arcadia Publishing:
Telephone 843-853-2070
Fax 843-853-0044
E-mail sales@arcadiapublishing.com

Visit us on the Internet at www.arcadiapublishing.com

On the Front Cover: These photographs from the intersection of Fourth and Main Streets looking north are at the heart of Moscow's downtown. In the 1980s, Fourth Street was closed to through traffic, creating Friendship Square. Friendship Square is now the central gathering place in Moscow's downtown, hosting celebrations, protests, and events like Moscow's farmers market. Moscow's downtown historic district was listed in the National Register of Historic Places in 2005. (Courtesy of the Latah County Historical Society.)

On the Back Cover: Rick Jones took this photograph of the University of Idaho Administration Building overlooking the lawn from the current Life Sciences Building. The students in the photograph appear to be playing football. Jones attended the University of Idaho from 1952 to 1956, capturing his experience in photography. Several of his photographs appear throughout the book. (Courtesy of the Latah County Historical Society.)

Contents

Acknowledgments

The Latah County Historical Society would like to acknowledge all current and past board members, volunteers, staff, and society members. Latah County Historical Society executive director Hayley Noble relied heavily on the knowledge of Steve Talbott, Nancy Ruth Peterson, and LeNelle McInturff for their historical Moscow insights. Hayley also relied on *A Great Good Country* by Lillian W. Otness for much of this book. Thanks to our 2024 board of directors for their support of this endeavor: Joanne Westberg, Ronald Goble, Robert Lee Sappington, LeNelle McInturff, Earl Bennett, Ann Hoste, Sandra Kelly, Nancy Ruth Peterson, Murf Raquet, Zoe Stave, Steve Talbott, Denise Thomson, and Kelly Zakariasen. Additional thanks go to curator Kaitlynn Anderson for her support during this project. Office coordinator Elaina Pierson was invaluable to this project. Without her photography and expertise, this book would not have been completed.

Unless otherwise noted, all historical photographs in this book come from the Latah County Historical Society archives, with contemporary photographs by Elaina Pierson. We are thankful to the University of Idaho Special Collections and Archives, which contributed images as well. Elaina would also like to thank the following for their assistance in gaining access to locations and recreating certain historical photographs: Steve Bonnar, Ryan Watson, Beau Babcock, and Randy Smith at the University of Idaho; Chief Brian Nickerson, Alyssa Griffith, and Pam Rogers of the Moscow Volunteer Fire Department; downtown business owners Andy Kiblen and Cam Kidd; and Jim Logan at the Latah County Fairgrounds. Special thanks go to Raymond Pankopf and Amy Thompson with the Office of Architectural and Engineering Services for their encyclopedic knowledge of the University of Idaho campus. Additional gratitude goes to B.J. Swanson for donating her time and drone aerial photographs to this project.

Introduction

Like many towns in the western United States, Moscow's existence is largely tied to the railroad and to agriculture. Before railway transportation, few other than indigenous peoples set foot in what would become Moscow, Idaho, prior to the 1860s. The Palouse hills are the ancestral homelands of the Nez Perce and Coeur d'Alene tribes. Before white settlement, the tribes passed through this area as part of their seasonal migration to harvest the abundant camas that grew in this area. A scattering of Euro-American fur trappers found their way to Idaho in the 1860s, but Moscow did not see its first homesteaders until the early 1870s. The fertile land drew families to the hills to grow crops and raise livestock, and the railroad's arrival in 1885 led to rapid growth. The town of Moscow was incorporated in 1887 and became the Latah County seat in 1888.

Early players in Moscow's development were instrumental in bringing the state's land-grant institution to town. The University of Idaho was established in 1889, one year before Idaho officially became a state in 1890. By that time, the town was growing, and the oldest buildings still standing today date from the late 1880s and early 1890s. The economic growth, both in town and agriculturally, and the burgeoning university meant that Moscow saw steady growth into the late 20th century that never really slowed down. In 1920, Moscow had nearly 4,000 residents, and by 2020, that number ballooned to over 25,000 according to census data. Like most of Idaho, the town is predominantly white, harkening to the early immigration of Scandinavian families and other Euro-American Caucasian ethnic groups. Despite the very homogenous population, Native American, Asian, Latine, and African American people have all historically, and continue to, call Moscow "home." The influx of students during the school year diversifies the community and truly makes Moscow a "college town." Neighboring Washington State University, the University of Idaho, and local government are the main employers in the community, but many folks stay because of the thriving art scene, beautiful landscapes with outdoor recreation, and the interesting blend of rural small-town life coupled with the resources of two large universities nearby. Although the railroad no longer travels through town, Moscow's 137 years of history is rich and unique, setting it apart from the rest of Idaho and championing the slogan as the "heart of the arts."

CHAPTER 1

Downtown Moscow

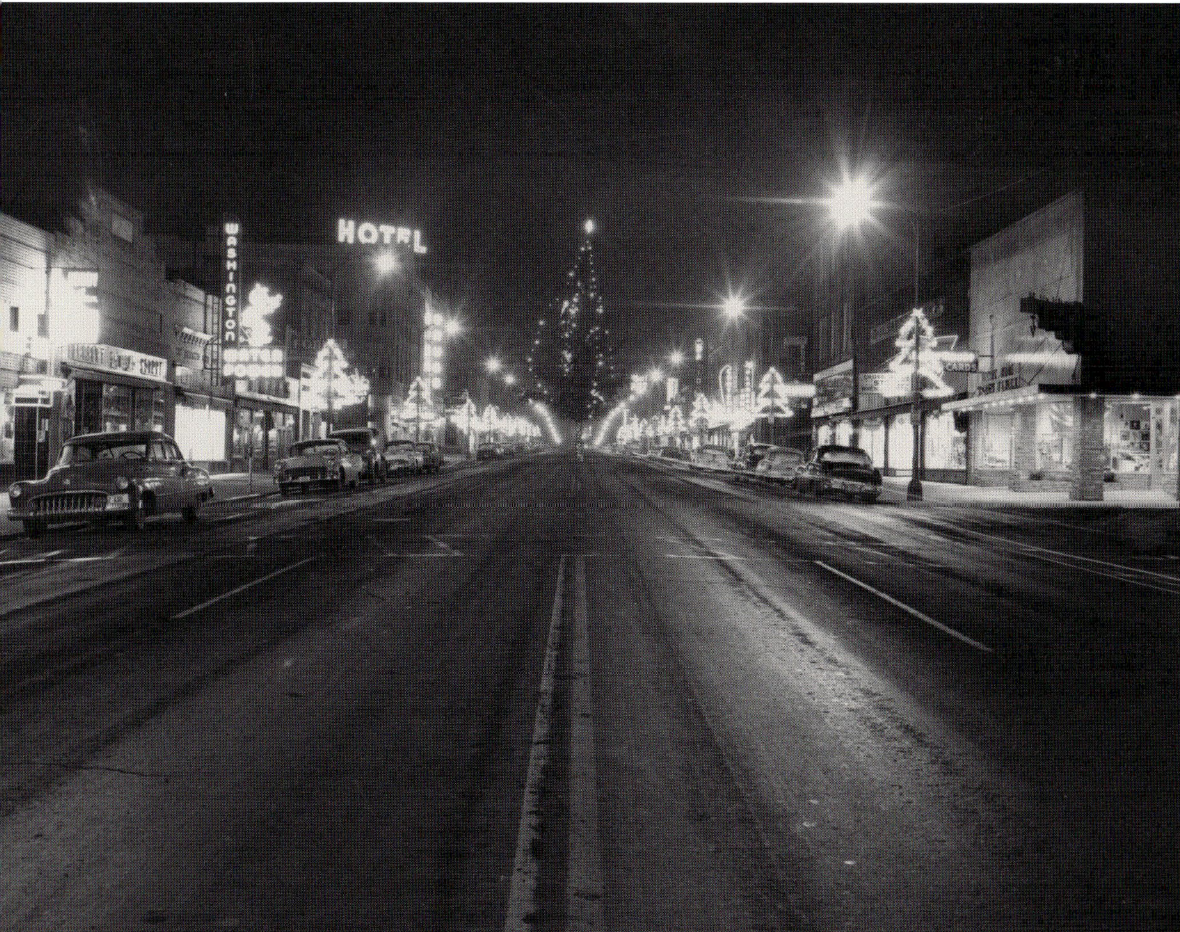

This 1950s photograph looking north along Main Street from Fifth Street shows a Christmas tree at the intersection of Third and Main Streets. While Moscow no longer has a tree in this intersection, the town continues to decorate its downtown streets with twinkling lights in the trees that line the Main Street sidewalks.

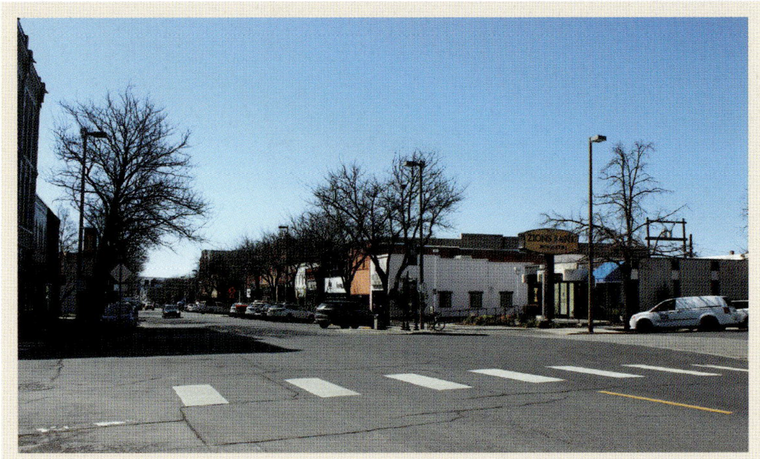

This view looking south shows the west side of Main Street beginning at First Street. Most of the block from First to Third Streets was constructed from 1890 to 1893 and held various stores and offices. This photograph from around 1920 has a Washburn-Wilson Seed Company store, Ford garage, and Pastime Poolhall. Farther down in the Smith-Dolson building in the middle of the block was Creighton's department store. Now, the corner stores no longer exist, and much of the ornamentation along the rooflines of the block has been removed.

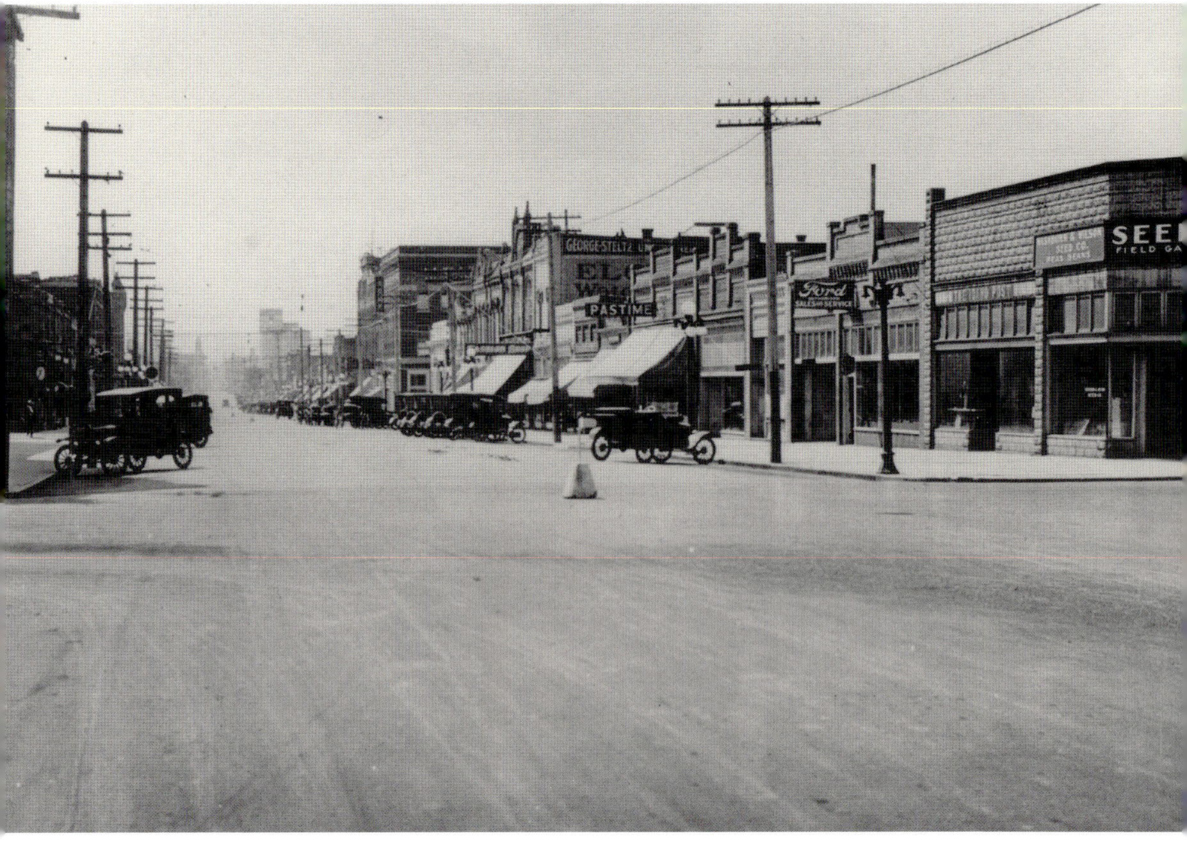

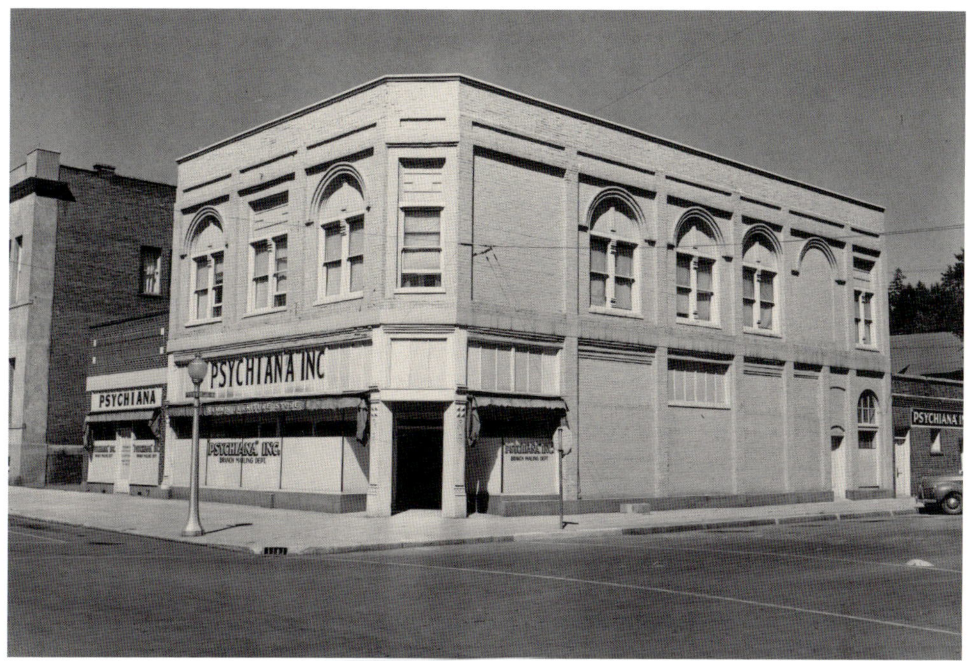

Frank White opened Moscow's first drugstore at First and Main Streets in 1885. A brick building replaced the wooden one in 1889 and was home to a general store, department store, hardware store, furniture store, and bakery. In the 1930s and 1940s, Frank B. Robinson used the space for the accounting and lesson-assembly departments of his mail-order religion and business, Psychiana. The building was partially demolished in the early 1950s and is now home to the restaurant Lodgepole.

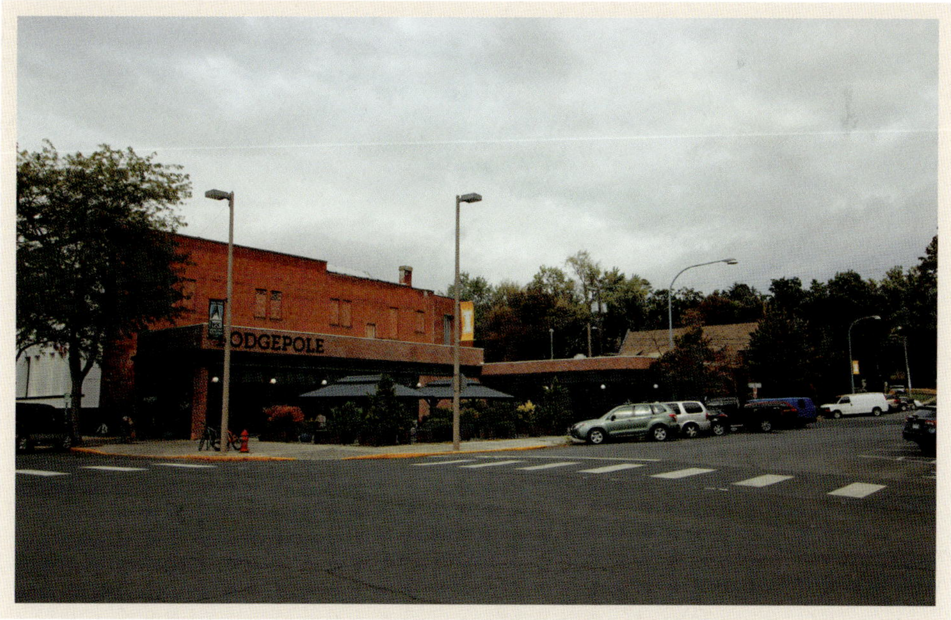

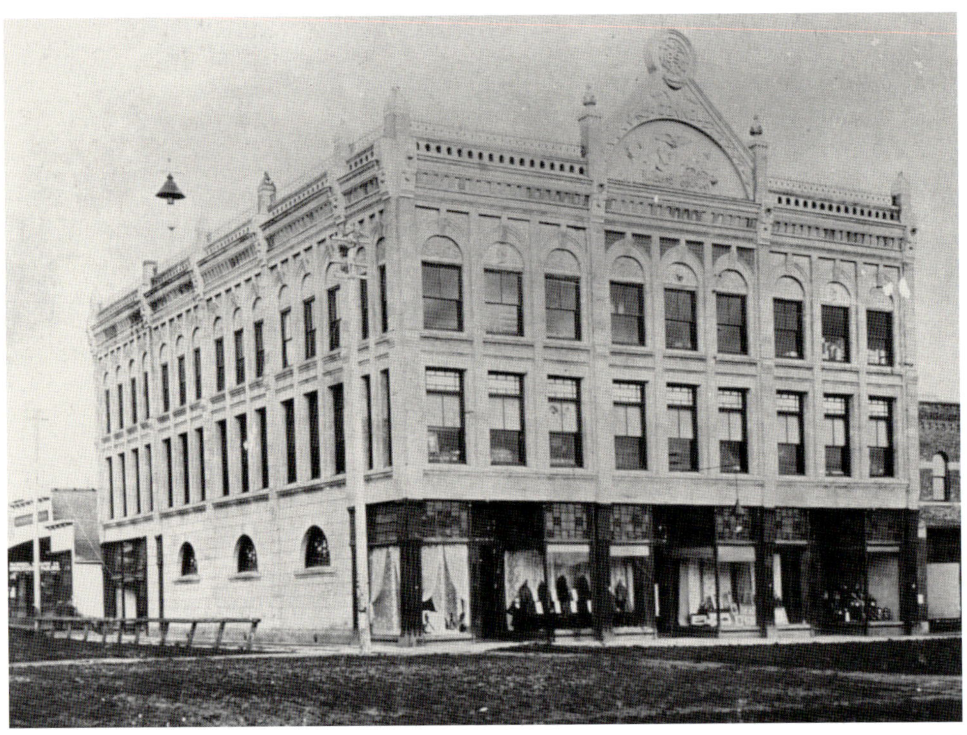

William J. McConnell and James H. Maguire constructed this building to house their general store at the corner of First and Main Streets in 1891. The McConnell Maguire store supplied furniture, clothing, jewelry, and other necessities on all three floors. An economic depression forced the store to close in 1893. From 1911 to 1919, Nathaniel Williamson operated his own store in the space. The building sat empty until the upper floors were converted into apartments in 1928. Mingles Bar and Grill currently occupies the first floor. At some point, the ornate roof ornamentations visible in early photographs were removed.

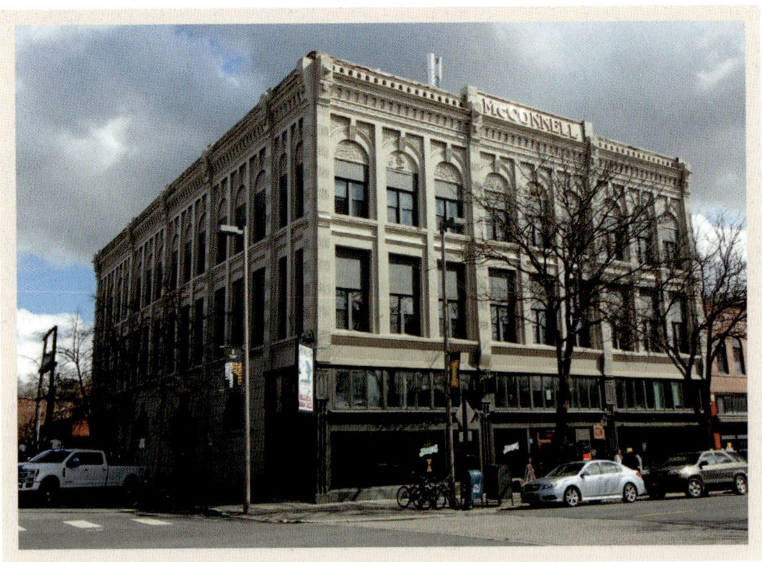

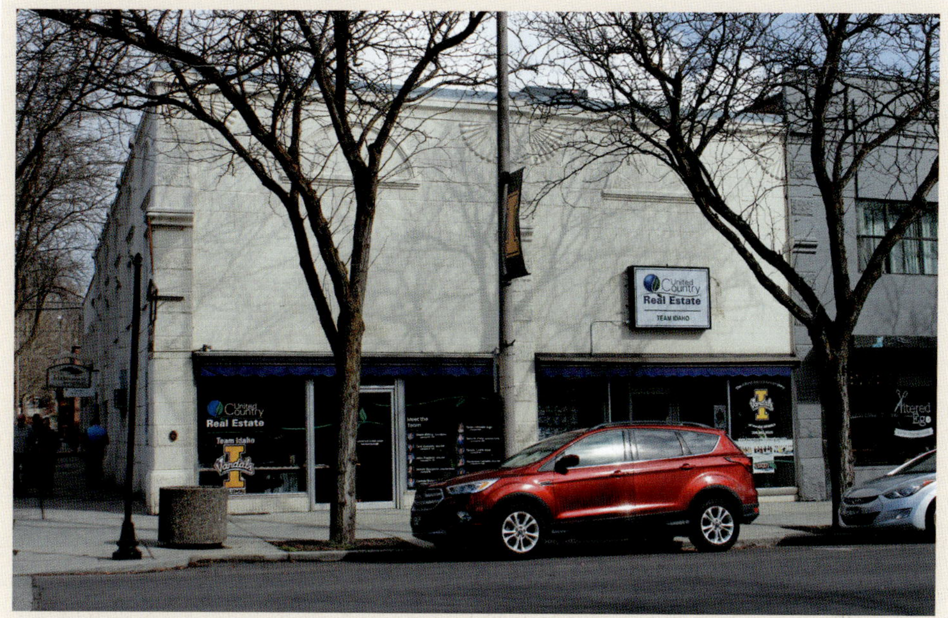

This eastern corner of Second and Main Streets has been home to many different businesses. In the early 1900s, it was a general store, then a bank, before becoming a café in the 1940s, as pictured. In 2024, a real estate office occupies this space. The exterior brick decoration is still visible under the paint, but changes to the facade have modified the windows and doors, and the roof pillars have been removed.

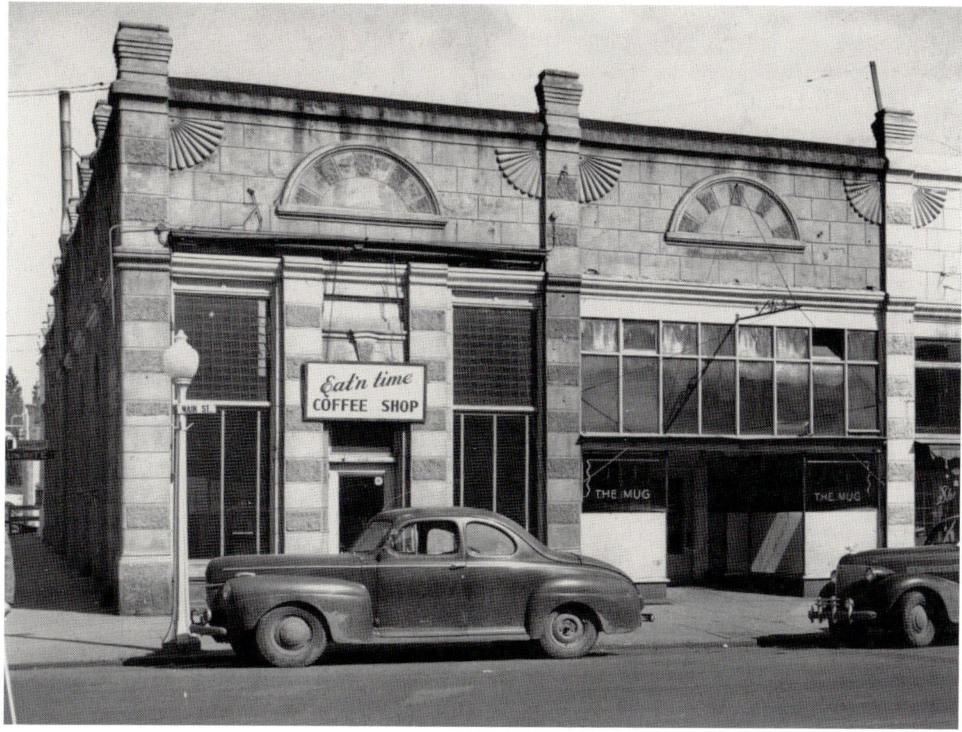

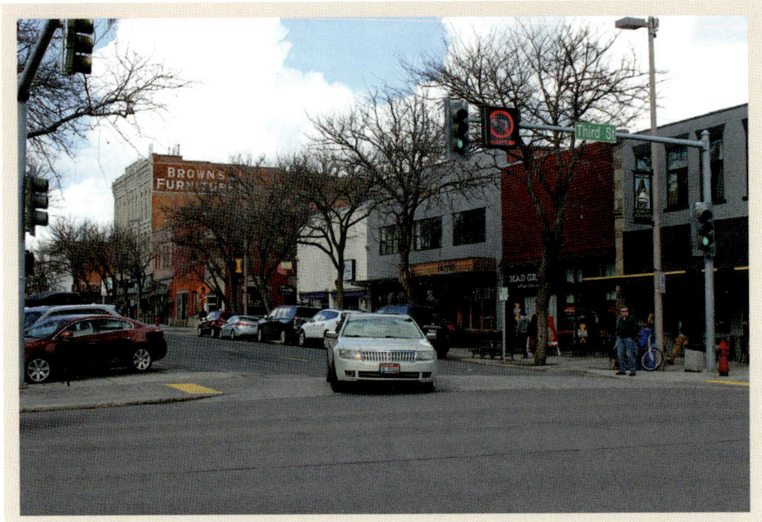

This view of Main Street north of Third Street from the early 1900s shows some of the many businesses in the Spicer Block, between Third and Second Streets, named for William H. Spicer, who constructed the block in 1898. Some of these included Shorty's Poolhall, the Vandal Café, and a jewelry store. The Moscow National Bank is also visible at the intersection of Second and Main Streets. Now, the bank is home to the Latah County Title Company, and the Spicer Block houses offices and restaurants.

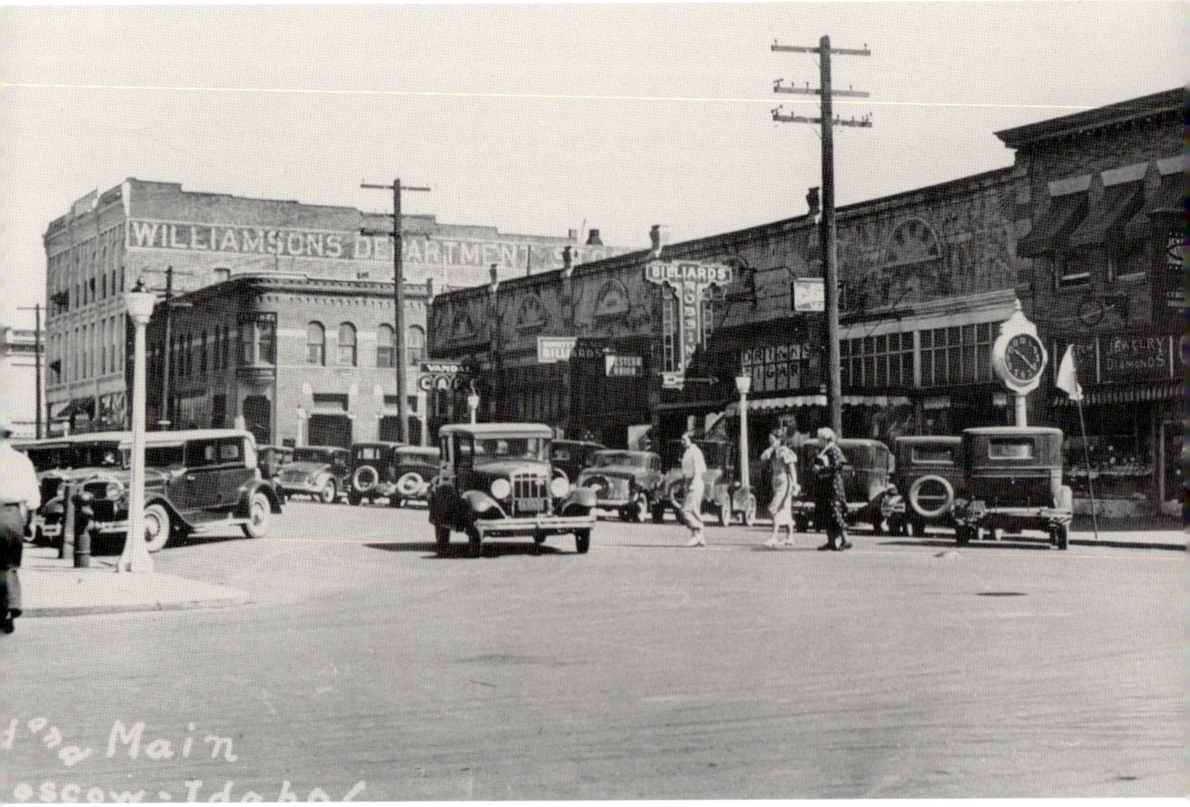

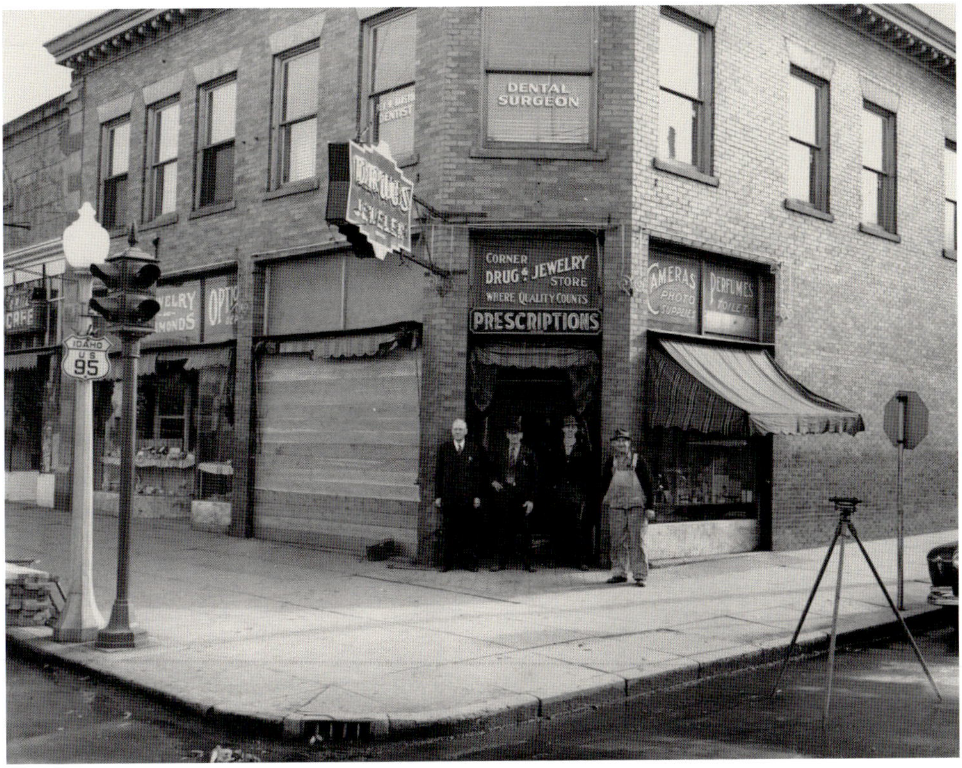

George Creighton constructed this two-story brick building in 1909 after several wooden structures stood on this spot. Charles Bolles and his business partner purchased the space in 1912 to operate the Corner Drug Store at Third and Main Streets. A fire in the 1940s forced the building's renovation. Several stores and restaurants used the space, such as Myklebust's and Sister's Brew, before its current occupant, Café Artista.

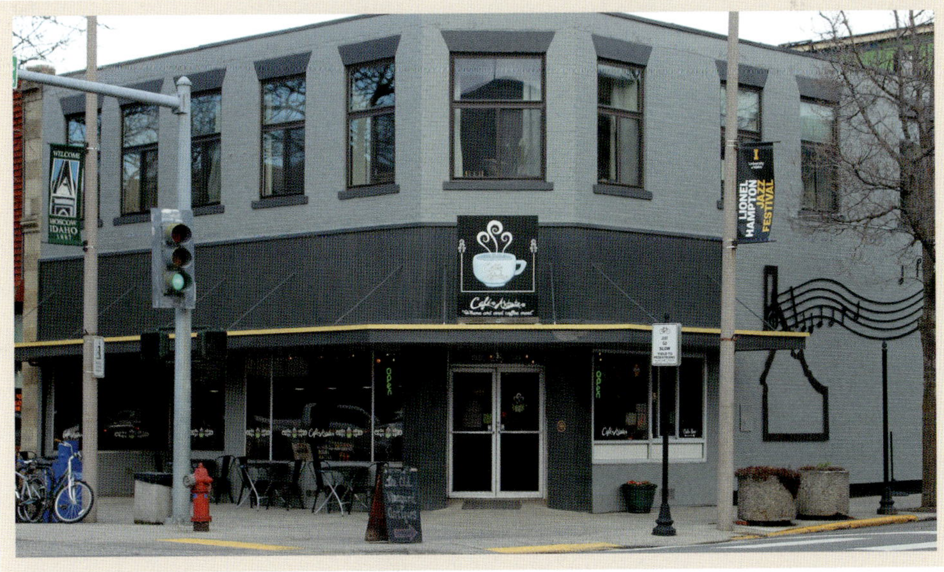

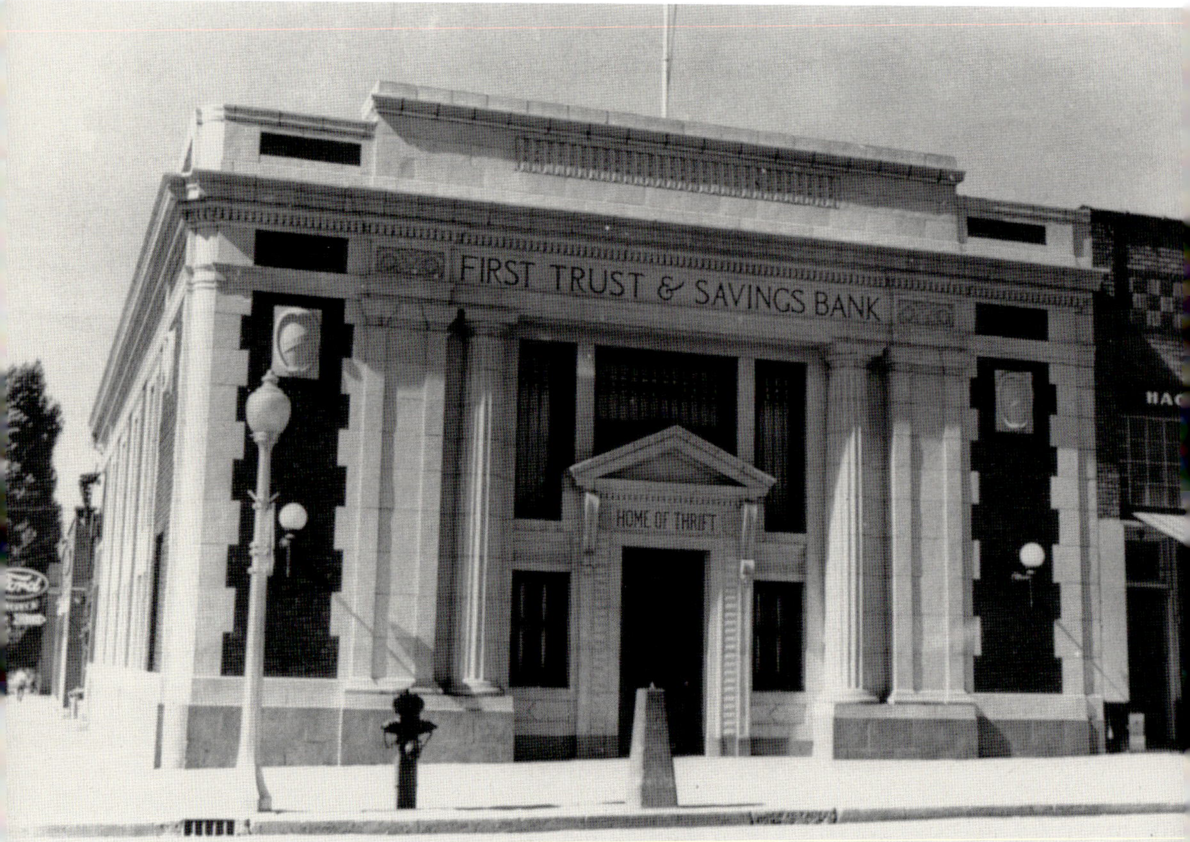

Andrew and Hawkin Melgard bought Clinton Lieuallen's store at the corner of Third and Main Streets to construct the First Trust and Savings Bank in 1921. The bank then changed hands, becoming the First Security Bank of Idaho, and was renovated with its facade changed to reflect modernizing times in 1964. In 1994, a new building incorporated the next-door space to expand the bank into what is now Wells Fargo.

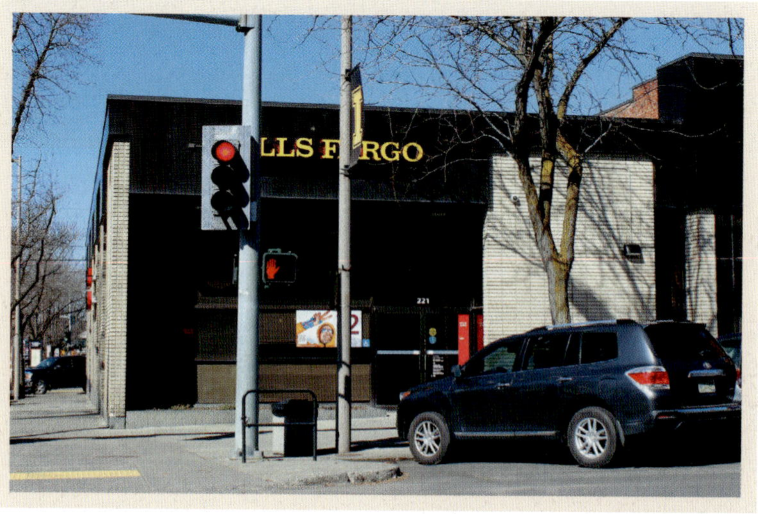

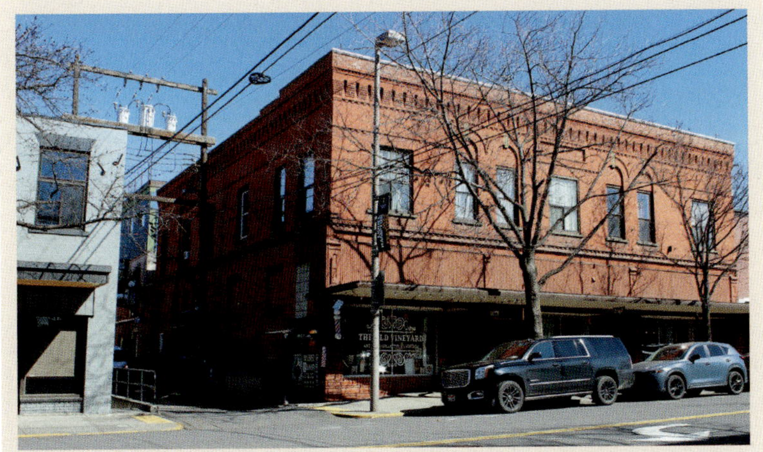

This building along Third Street between Main and Washington Streets retains much of its exterior second-floor features, although the street-level windows have changed. This building was constructed by David Urquhart around 1905 to replace wooden structures. This 1930s photograph shows the drugstore purchased by Frank Robinson when he was a pharmacist before starting his mail-order religion, Psychiana. Jerry's Ice Cream parlor is also visible across the alley. Now, the space houses shops on the corner with offices on the second story.

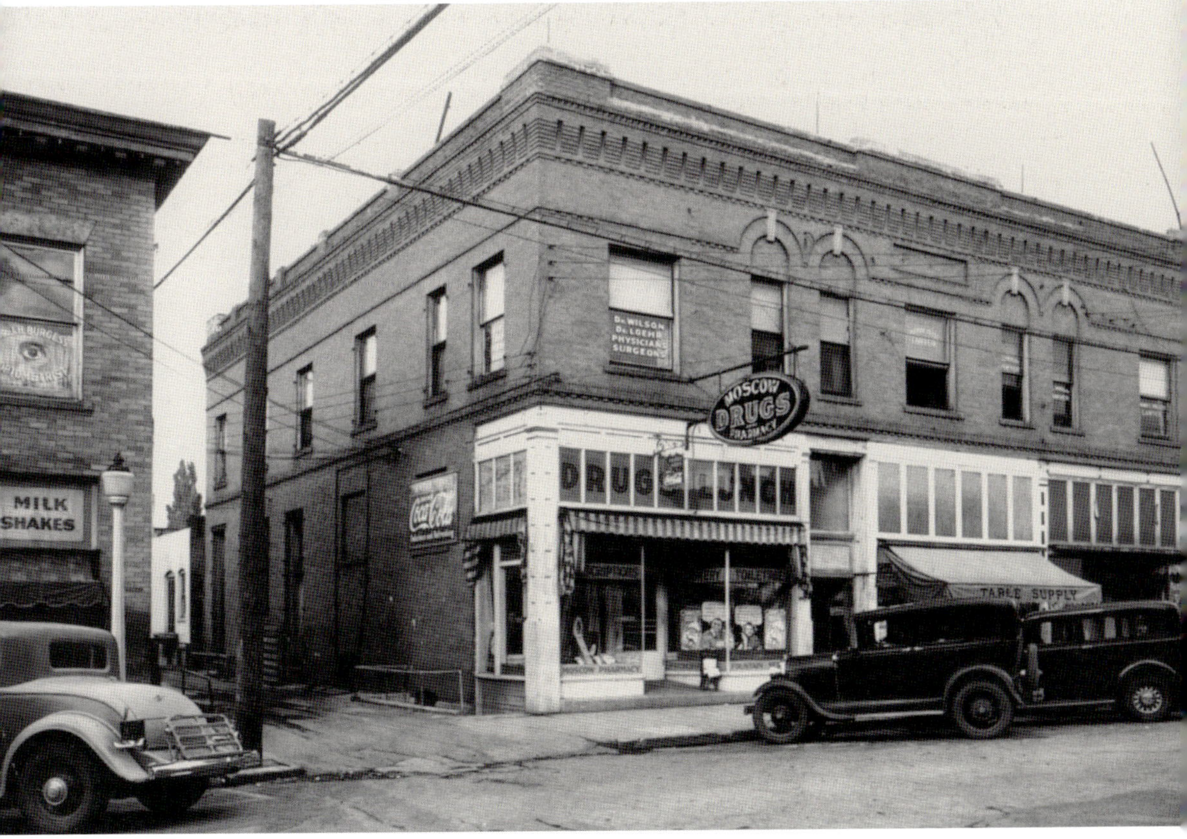

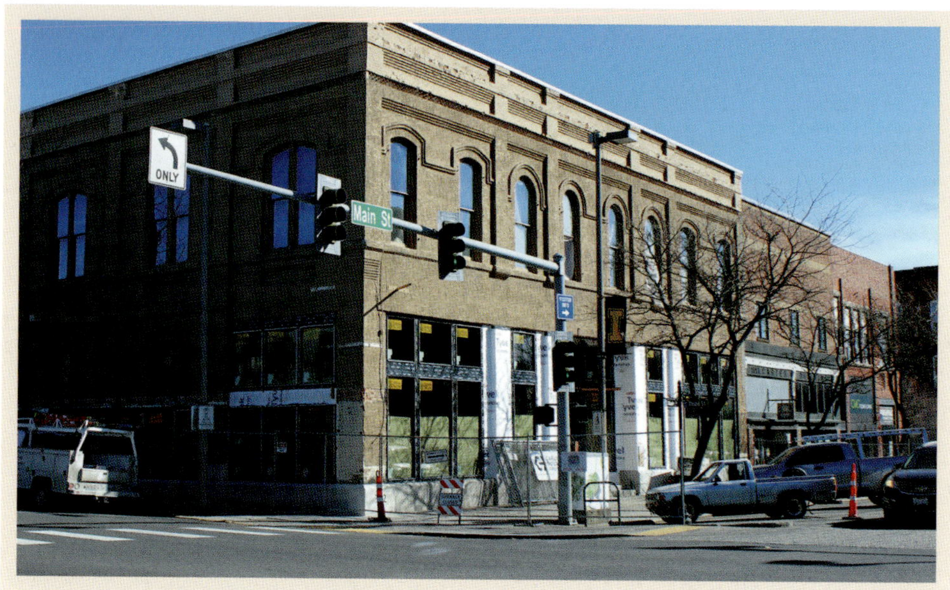

Originally constructed in 1889 for the Dernham and Kaufmann department store, Frank David and Wellington Ely bought the store for their own department store shortly after in 1889. David and Ely's department store operated until 1919, when the Davids bought the Ely share. They ran the store as Davids' until 1959 with the sale of the business. The store still operated under the same name until 1979. Since then, the building has housed multiple businesses, namely bars and nightclubs. In 2024, the building was renovated to accommodate new restaurants.

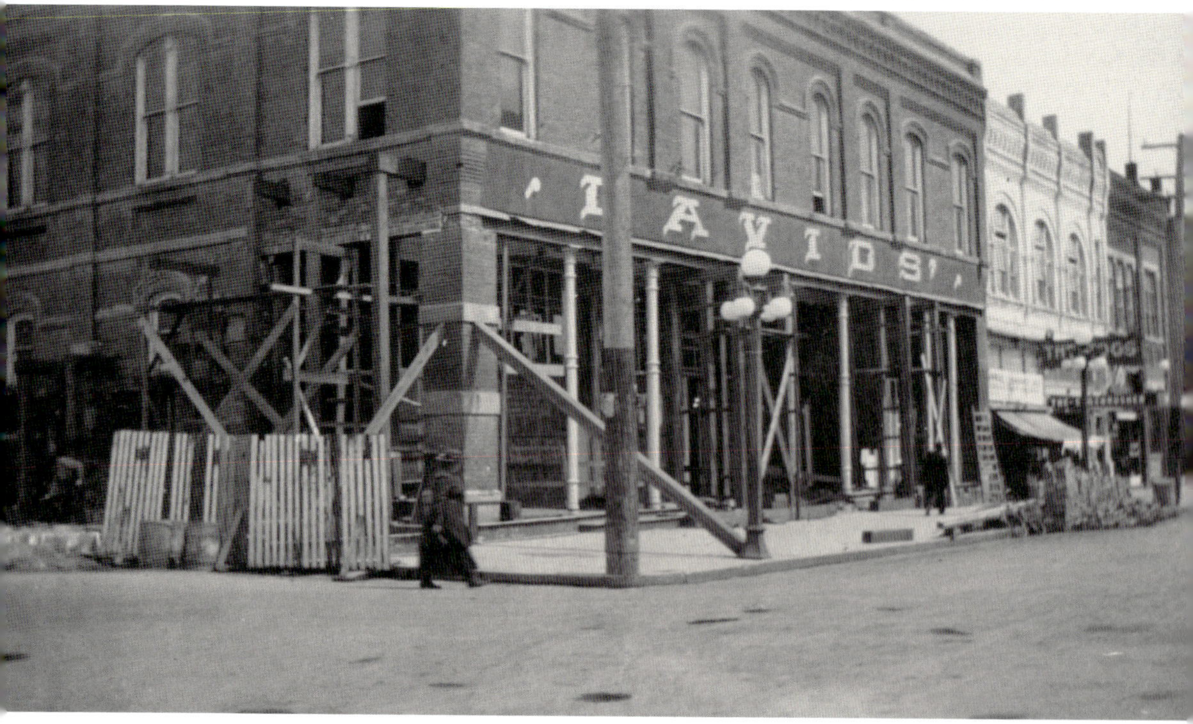

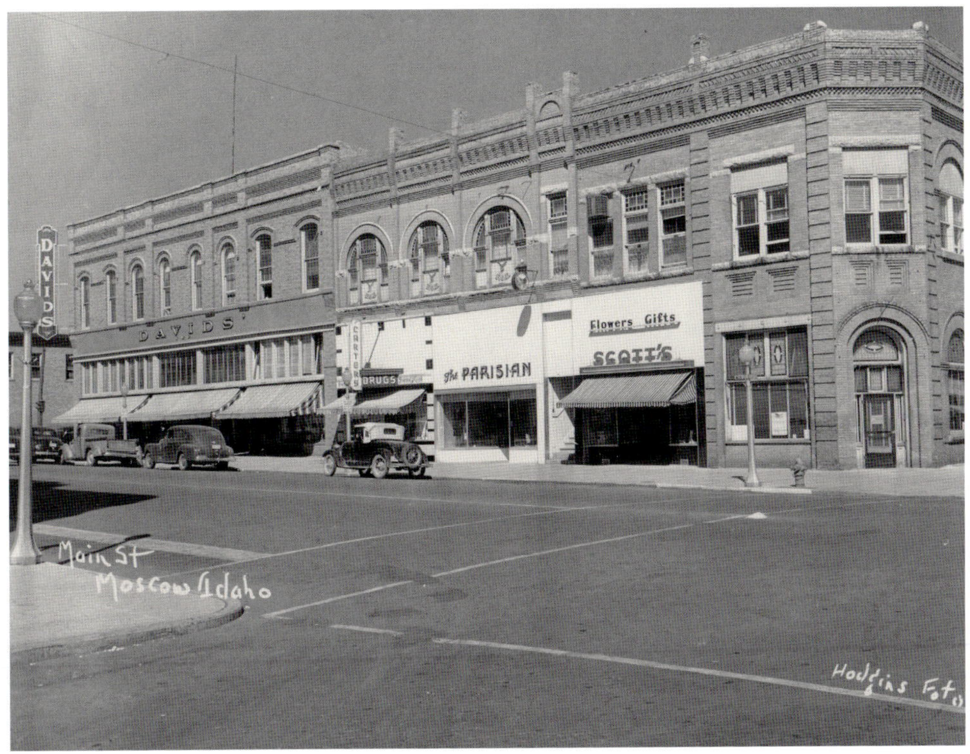

The McCartor Block is located along Main Street between Third and Fourth Streets. The first building constructed was the Dernham and Kaufmann store in 1889. Frank David and Wellington Ely bought the store shortly after. Leonidas McCartor expanded construction to fill the block, notably the Farmers Bank. In 1900, that corner space became city hall. This photograph from the 1930s shows Davids', Carter's drugstore, the Parisian, and Scott's floral store. In 2024, the building was leased as office and retail spaces, apartments, and restaurants.

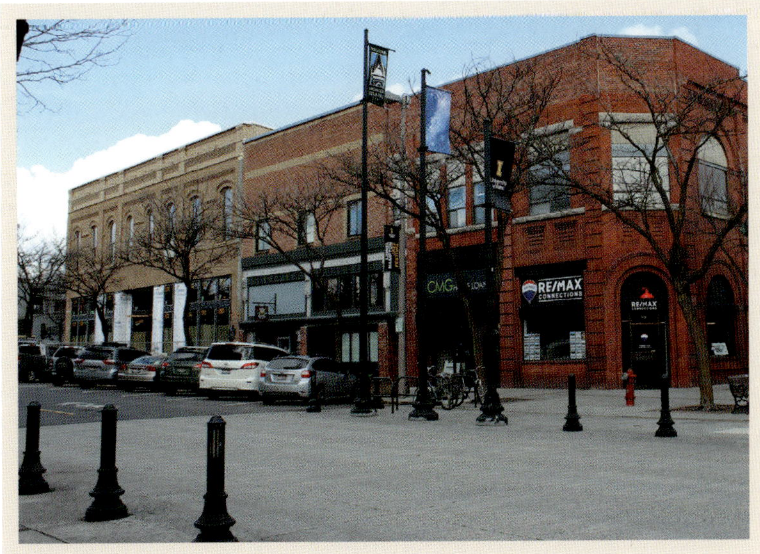

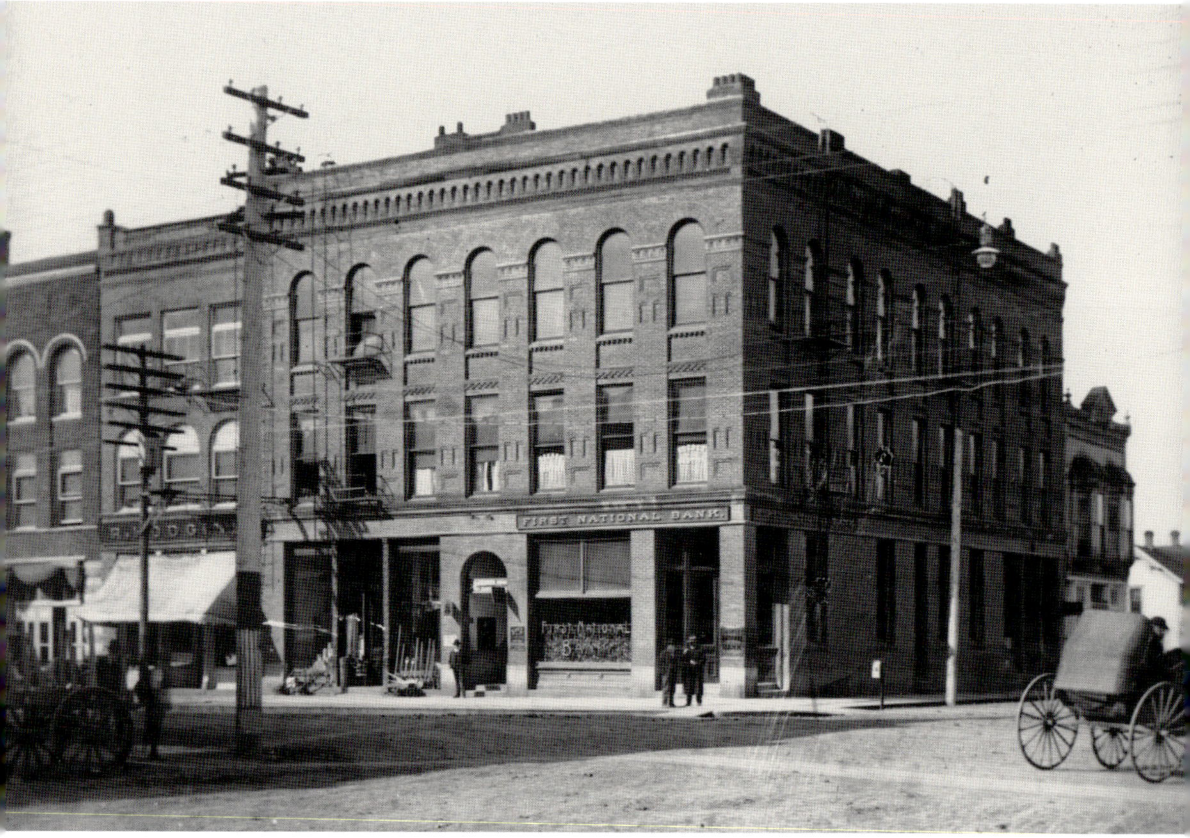

The First National Bank first occupied this corner at Third and Main Streets in 1891, sharing the ground floor with hardware stores over the years. This early-1900s photograph also shows Hodgins Drugstore next door, at the same location today. The building also housed offices, and the upper floors were used by several fraternal organizations. In 1965, the building was razed to construct a more modern building. Now, locals refer to it as the "escalator bank" because it was the first building in town with an escalator. The building is now home to offices.

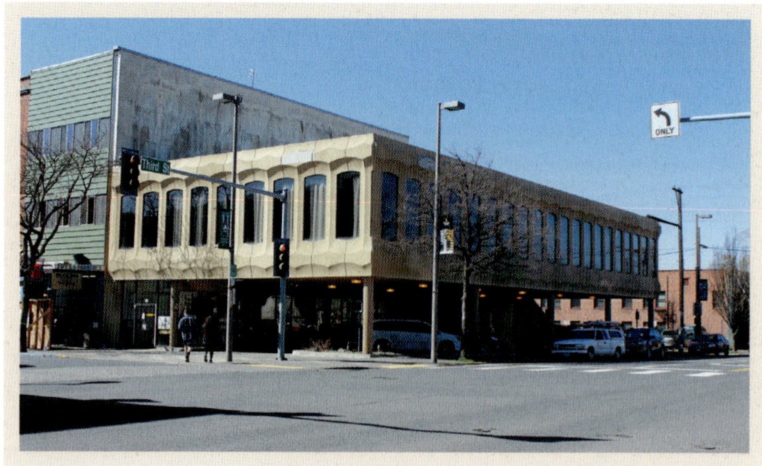

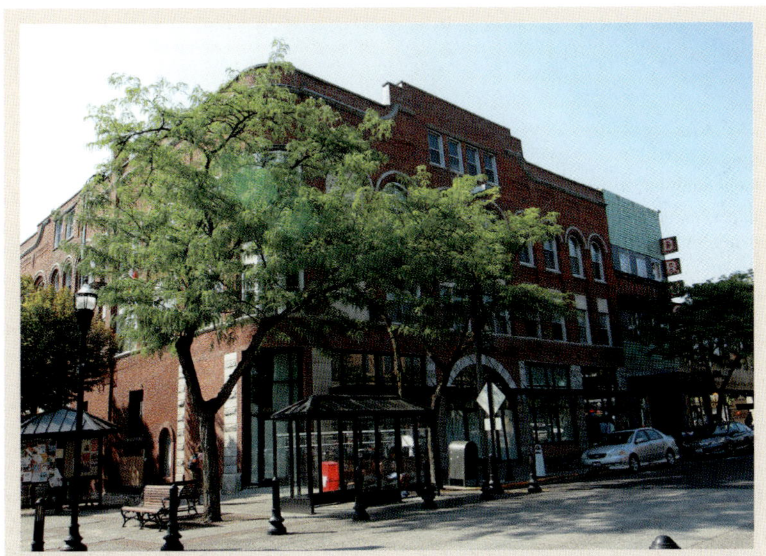

Robert H. Barton built Moscow's first hotel in 1880, but an 1890 fire destroyed the structure at Main and Fourth Streets. Barton's new hotel was finished in 1892 with retail space at street level and rooms on the floors above. The 1890s photograph shows the original Hotel Moscow corner cupola and roof ornamentation, which were later removed. Also, note the cigar store and Hodgins Drugstore. In 1927, the hotel was expanded toward Jackson Street, and eventually, the rooms were converted into apartments. In 2024, Hodgins still exists next door, and renovations are ongoing for a lounge at the street level.

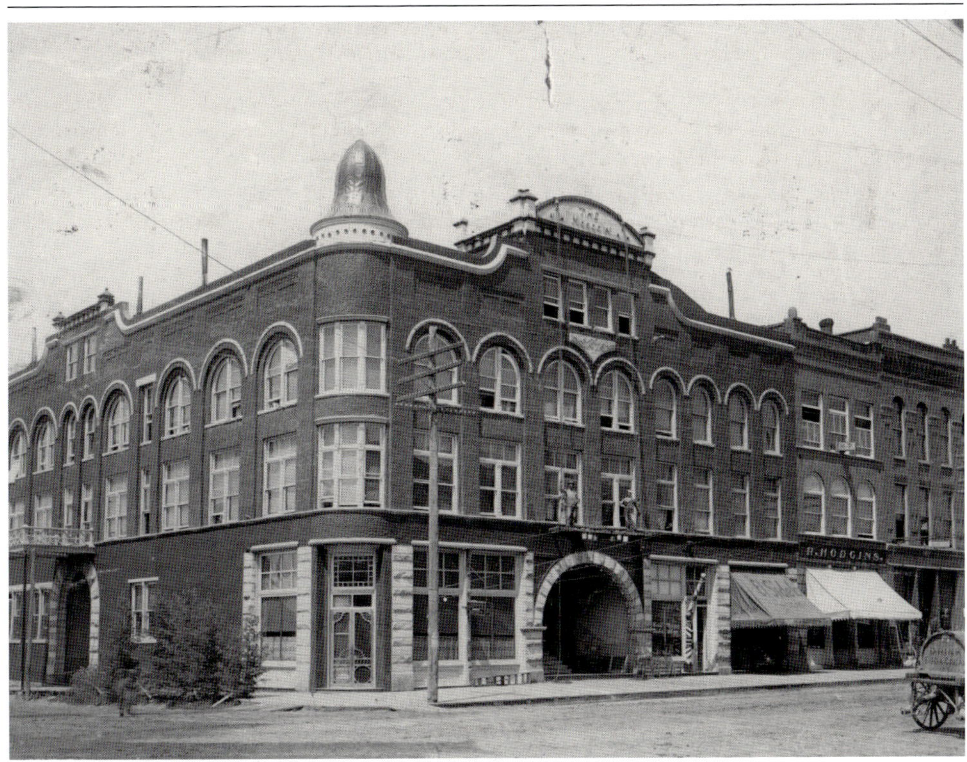

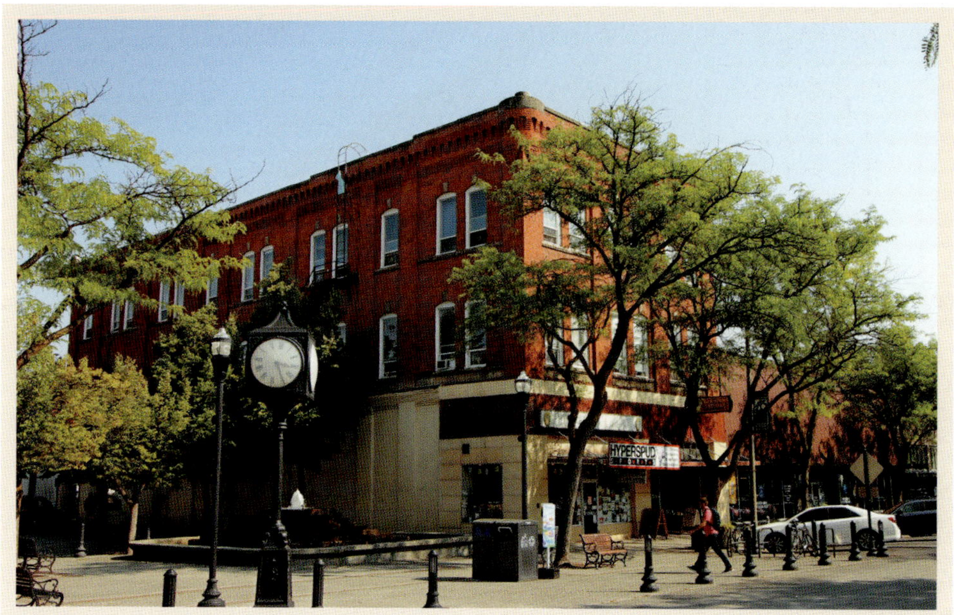

Michael J. Shields established the first three-story brick building in Moscow at the corner of Fourth and Main Streets in 1889. His hardware store soon incorporated building materials and farm and mill machinery and was restructured into a construction business. Shields's contractors were responsible for building much of Moscow and its infrastructure. The Moscow Business College utilized the upstairs rooms, and they were later inhabited as apartments. Now, the Main Street storefront is home to Hyperspud Sports, an outdoor sporting goods store.

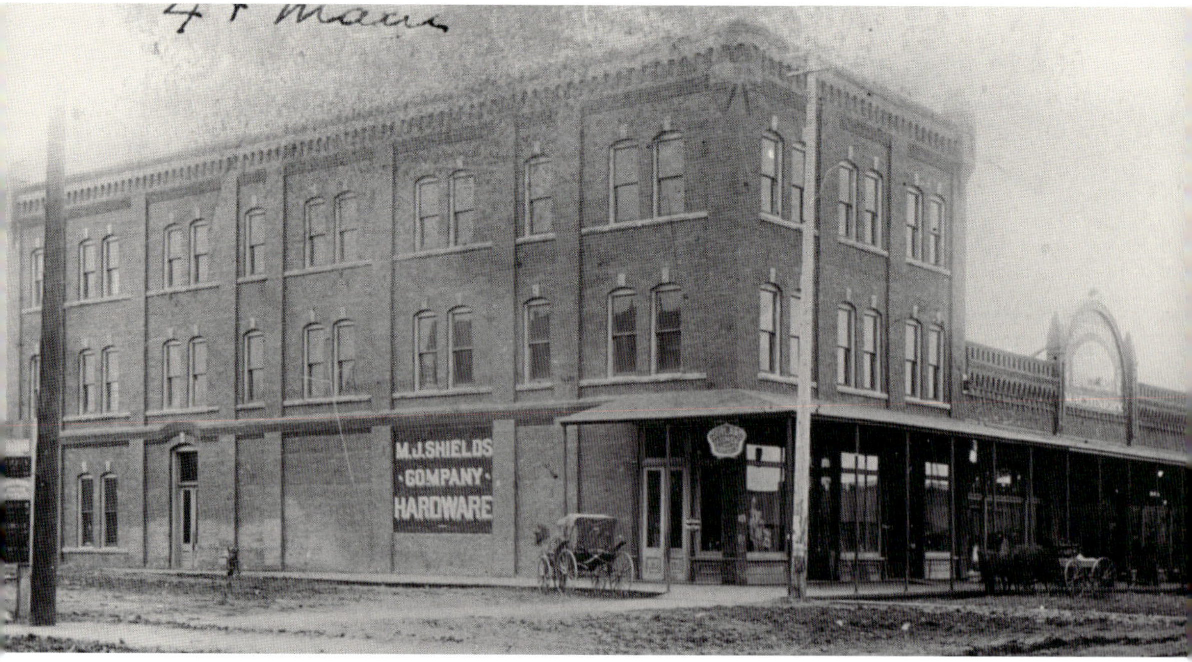

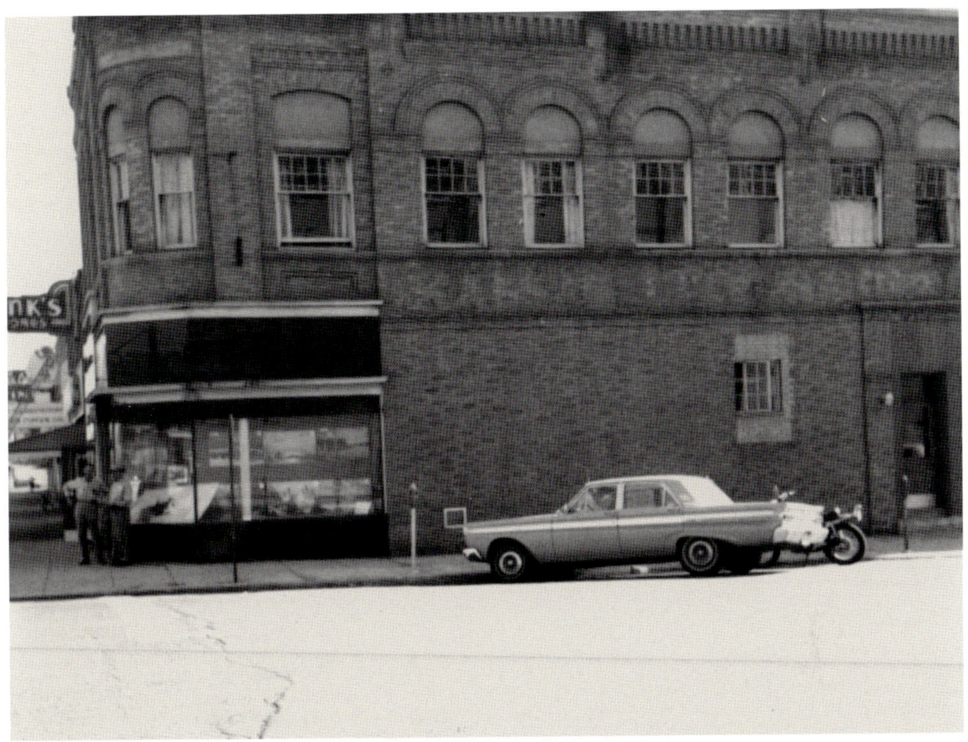

In 1891, Kenneth Skattaboe constructed this building, which housed various stores in its early years, including Shaw department store, Gem City Hardware, Jackle Jewelry, and the Hutchinson photography studio. The Inland Telephone Company purchased the building in 1925 and later took over the entire ground floor. The building's exterior has only been altered slightly after a 1966 fire and 1978 renovations. New Saint Andrews College purchased the building from the telephone company in 1994. The structure was listed in the National Register of Historic Places in 1978.

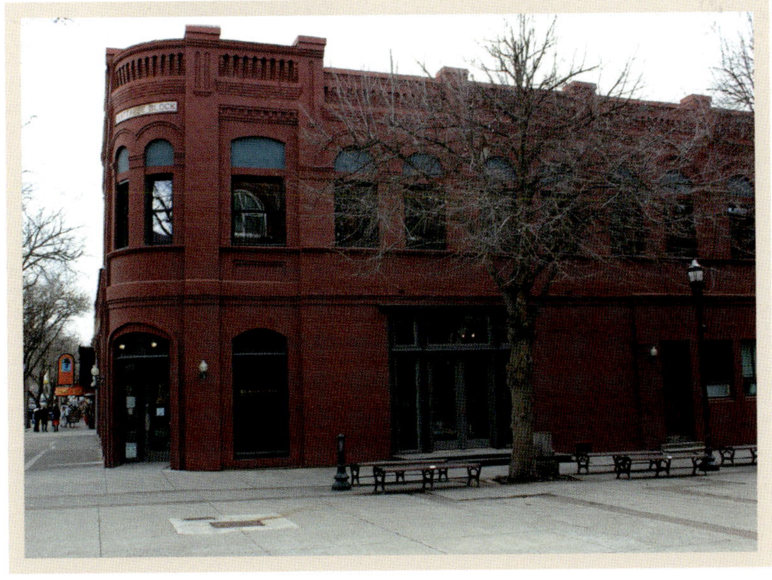

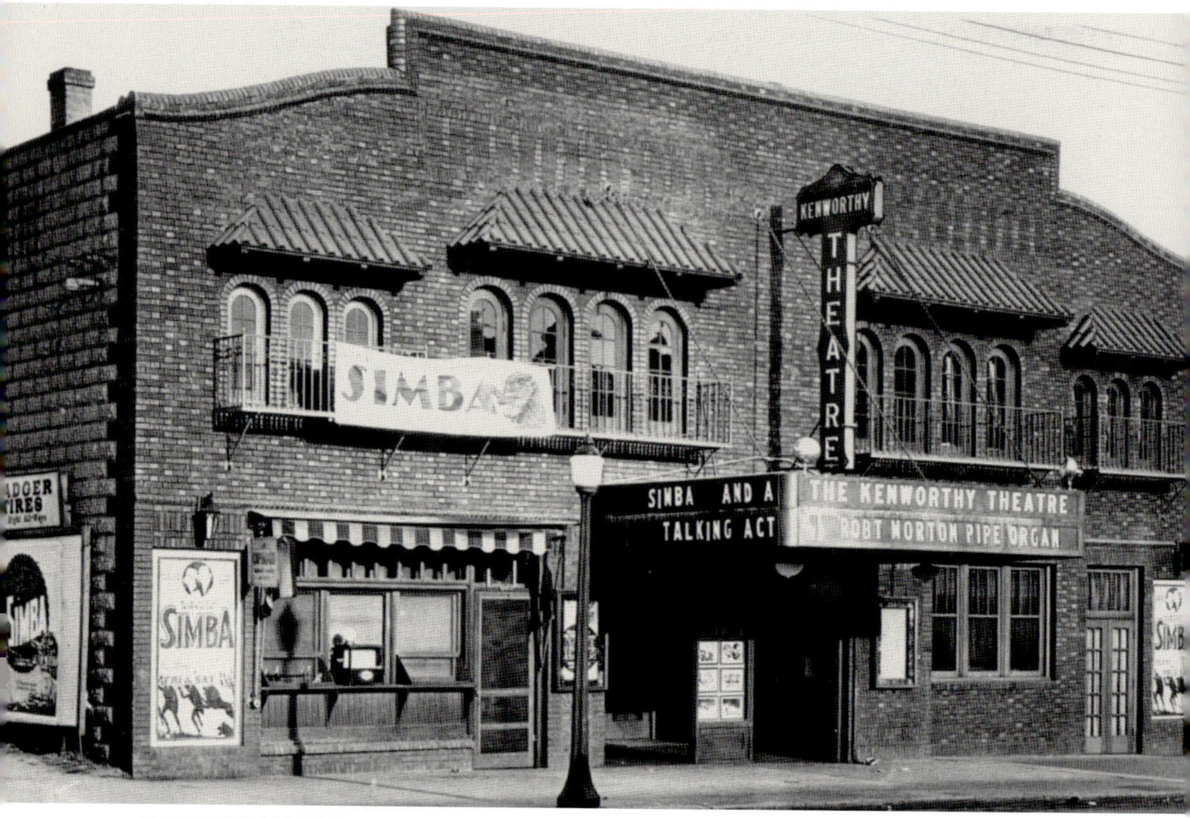

One of the first theaters in Moscow was the Crystal Theatre, which opened in the early 1900s. It functioned as an opera house and showed silent films. The Crystal closed and operated as a car garage and Neely's Hudson Dealership until 1925, when Milburn Kenworthy bought the building. After extensive remodeling and expansion, the Kenworthy Theatre opened in 1926. The new marquee and facade were updated in 1949, featuring the existing terra-cotta tile.

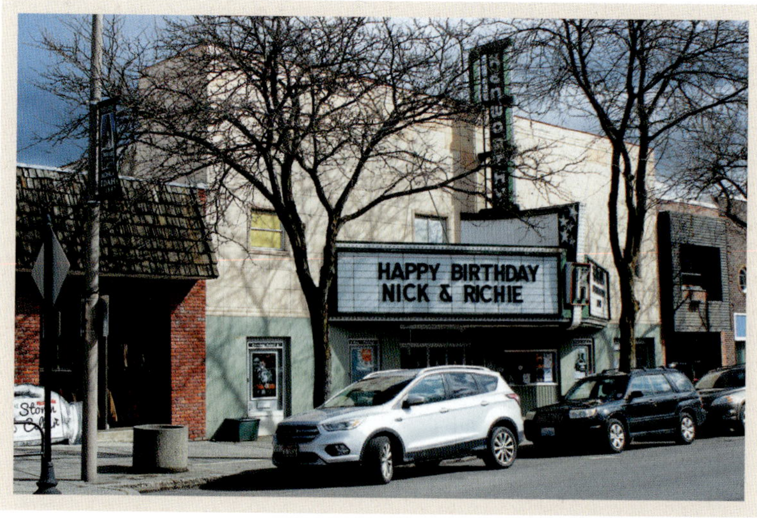

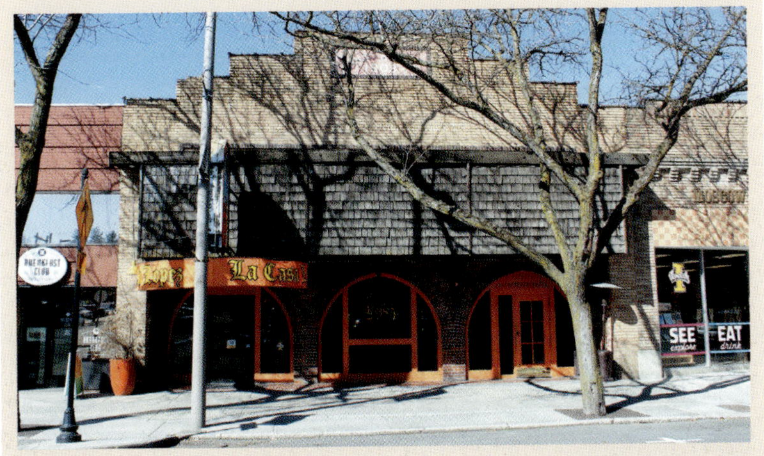

Charles B. Holt constructed this building along the west side of Main Street near the intersection of Fifth Street in 1903. This photograph of the Biscuitroot Park restaurant shows that not much has changed on the exterior since the 1970s. For many years, meat markets and grocery stores occupied this space, with signs for the Nobby Inn visible on the left. Now, La Casa Lopez Mexican restaurant is housed here, with the Breakfast Club in the former Nobby Inn space and the Moscow Chamber of Commerce and Visitor Center on the other side.

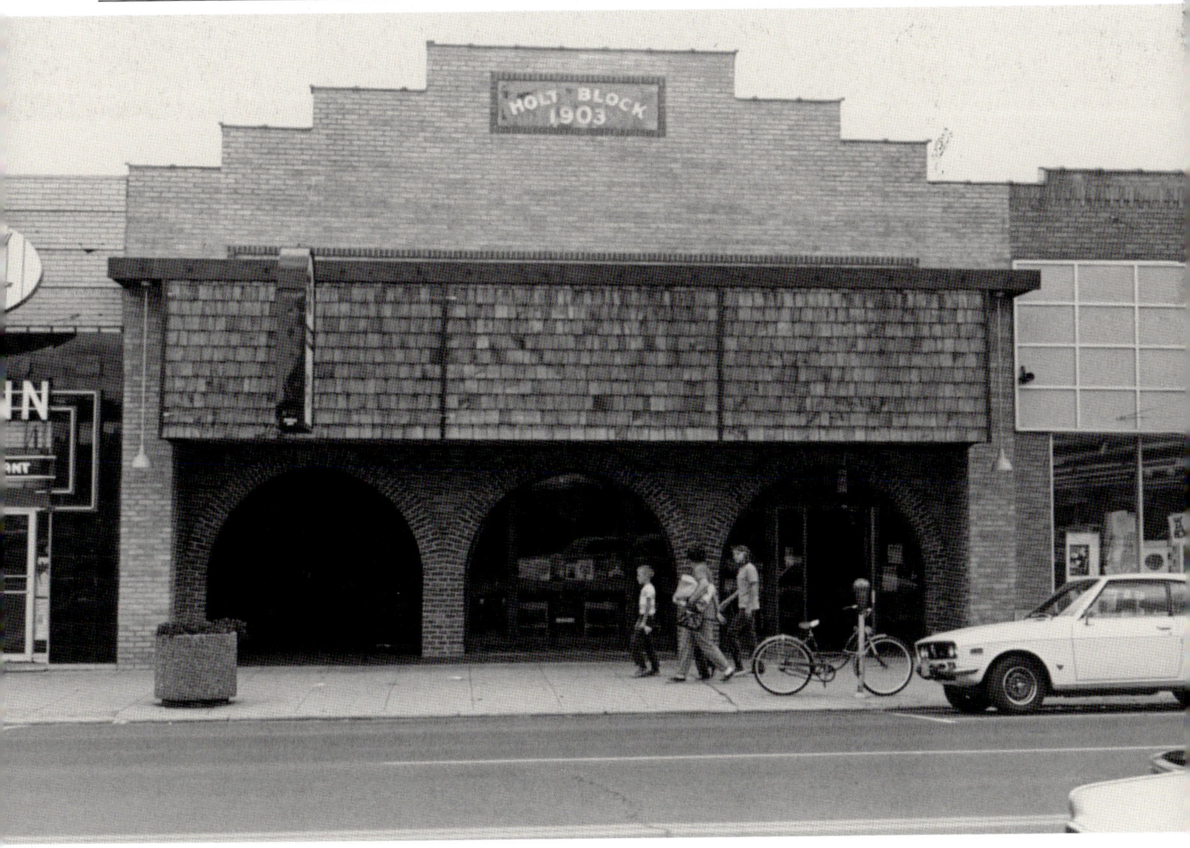

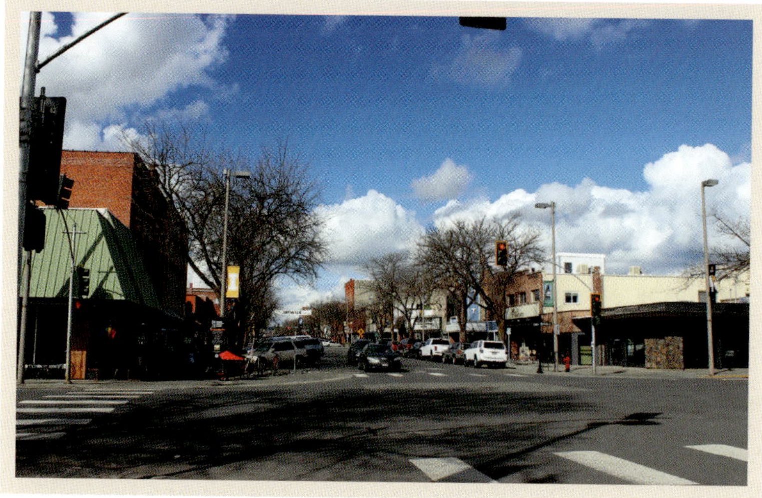

This view of downtown Moscow from Sixth and Main Streets illustrates how downtown was the commercial hub of the town. This photograph from the mid-1940s shows the Nuart Theater, restaurants, dry cleaners, a car dealership, grocery and department stores, and utility companies. Today, this stretch of Main Street is still busy but is home to more offices than retail or restaurant spaces, although many of the buildings retain their historic character.

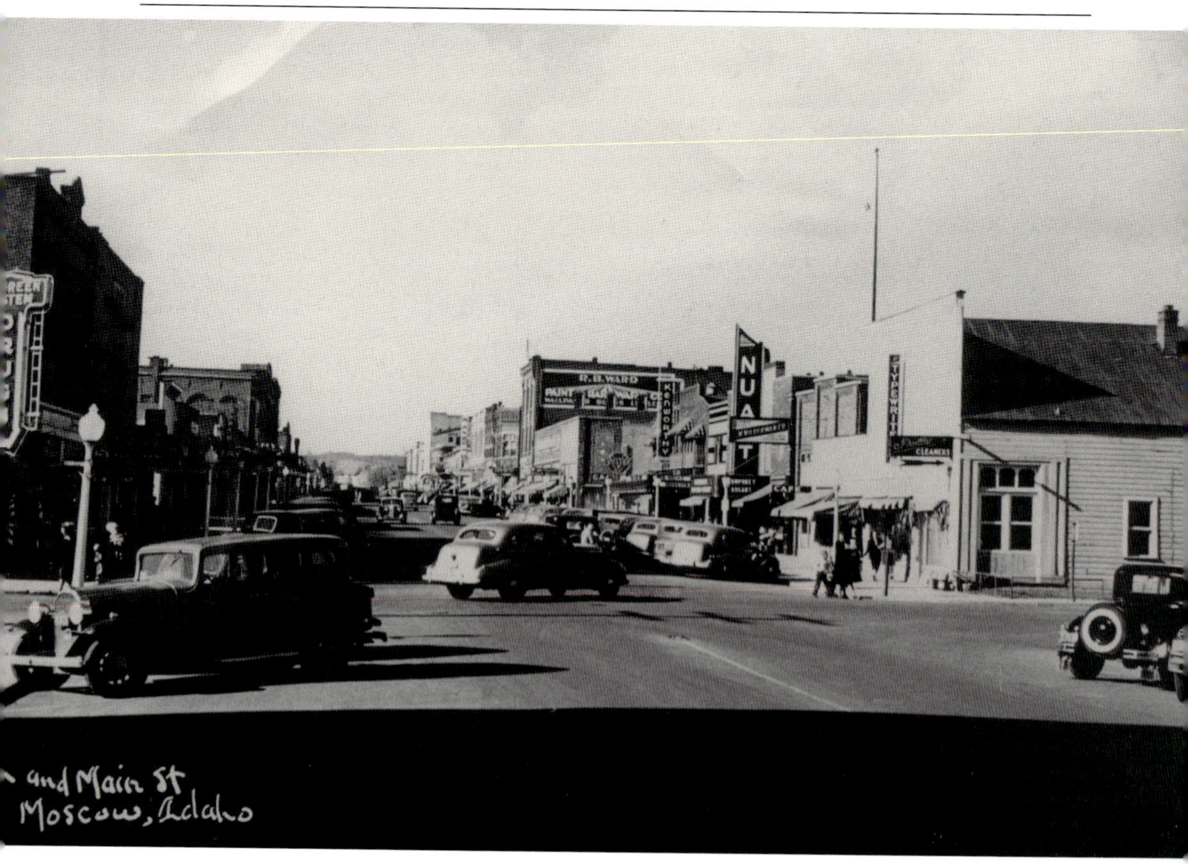

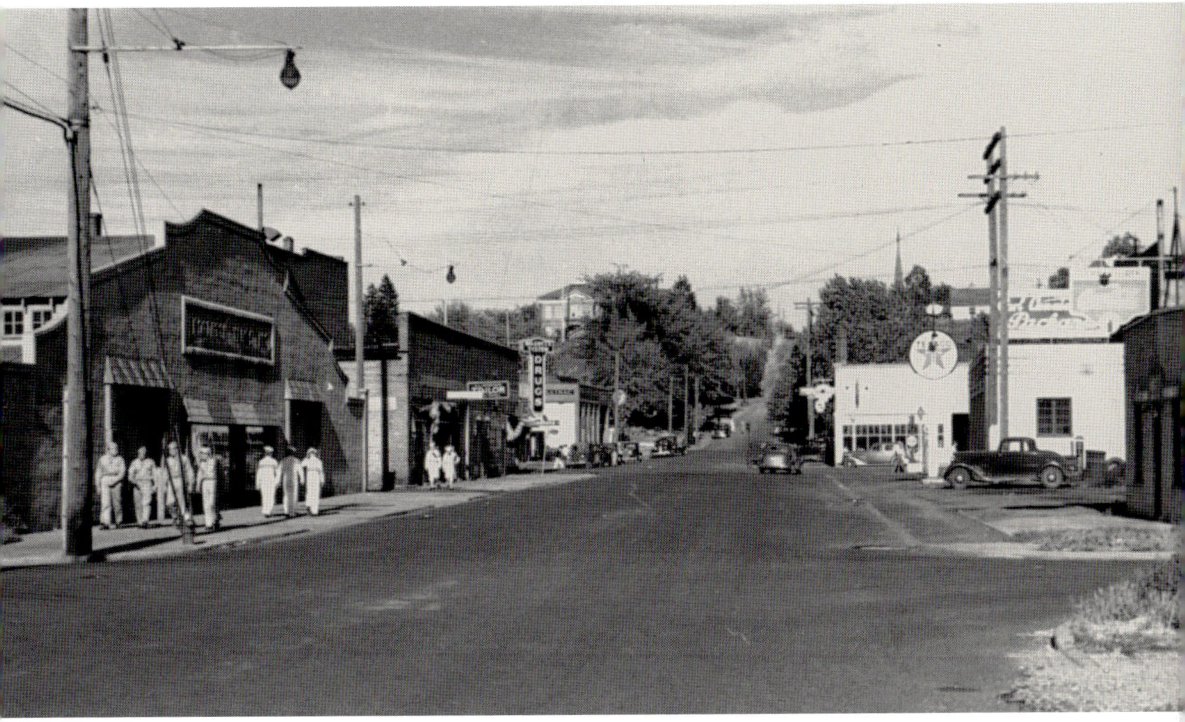

This view of the intersection at Sixth and Jackson Streets, looking east, is now home to a motel and bank. Down the street, the corner of One World Café is shown at Sixth and Main Streets. The mid-1940s photograph exhibits the town's Texaco station, Potlatch lumber warehouse, a tailor shop, and a drugstore. Up on the hill above the buildings, the original Latah County Courthouse is also visible.

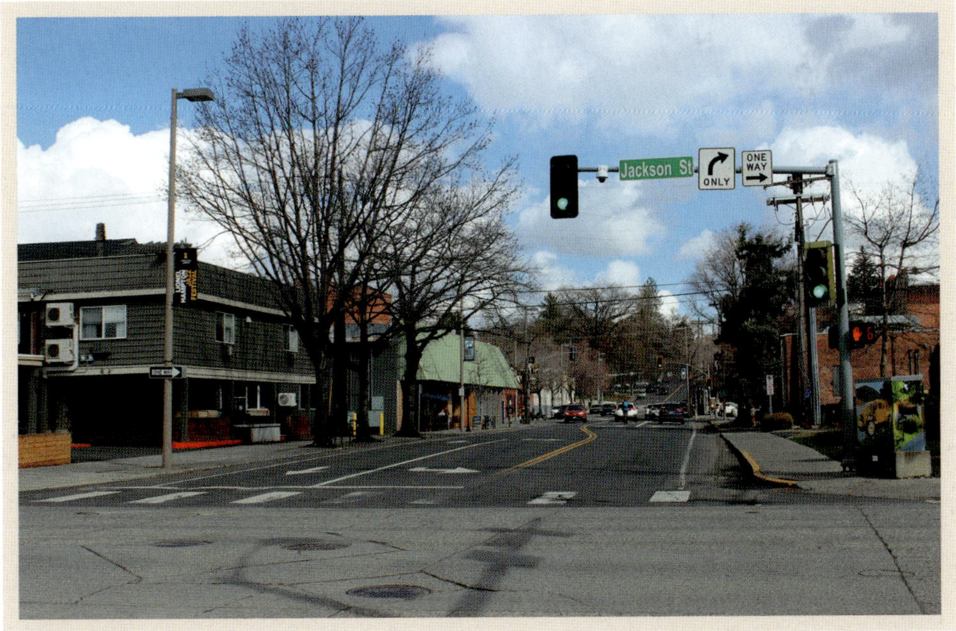

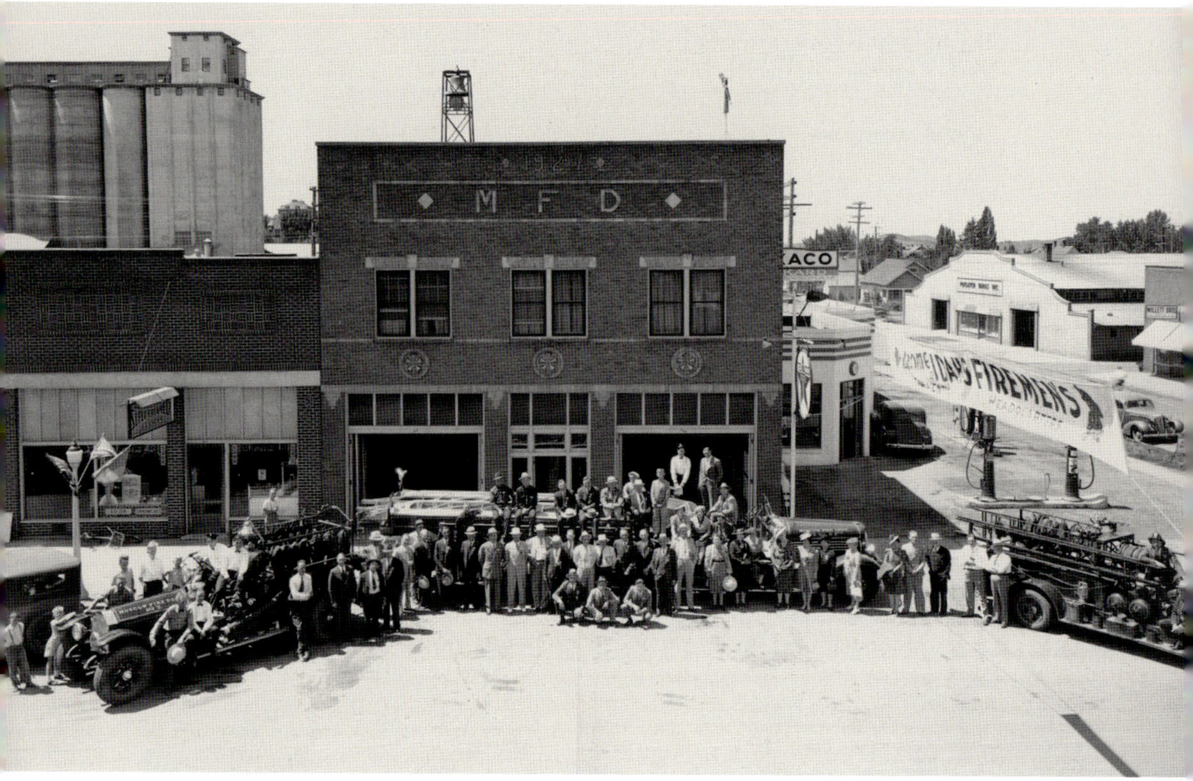

The City of Moscow established the Moscow Volunteer Fire Department in 1892. Before they occupied their current station, companies with hoses were stored throughout town. The department secured mechanized equipment in 1915 and set up temporary stations at Fourth and Washington Streets and Sixth and Main Streets. In 1927, the department secured its building at Sixth and Main Streets. A second adjacent building was constructed in 1954 to expand the department to meet the needs of the growing town.

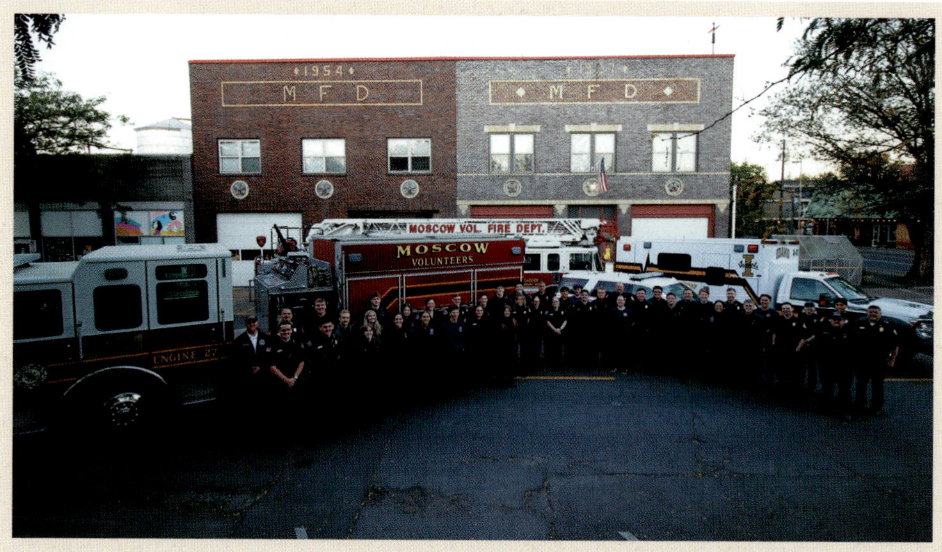

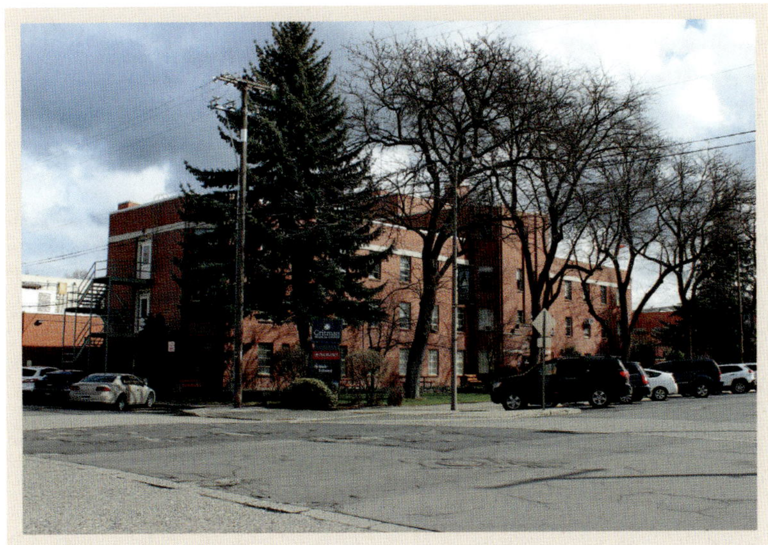

Dr. Charles Gritman began visiting patients in Latah County in 1893 and purchased the McGregor House in 1897 for use as a hospital. Dr. Gritman operated his practice at the hospital and continued to make house calls until his death in 1933. His wife, Bertie, donated the facility to Moscow under the condition that it bear Gritman's name. The McGregor House was demolished, and construction was completed in 1940, unveiling Gritman Memorial Hospital. In 1991, the name changed to Gritman Medical Center. The current campus now sits on several blocks centered around Main and Seventh Streets.

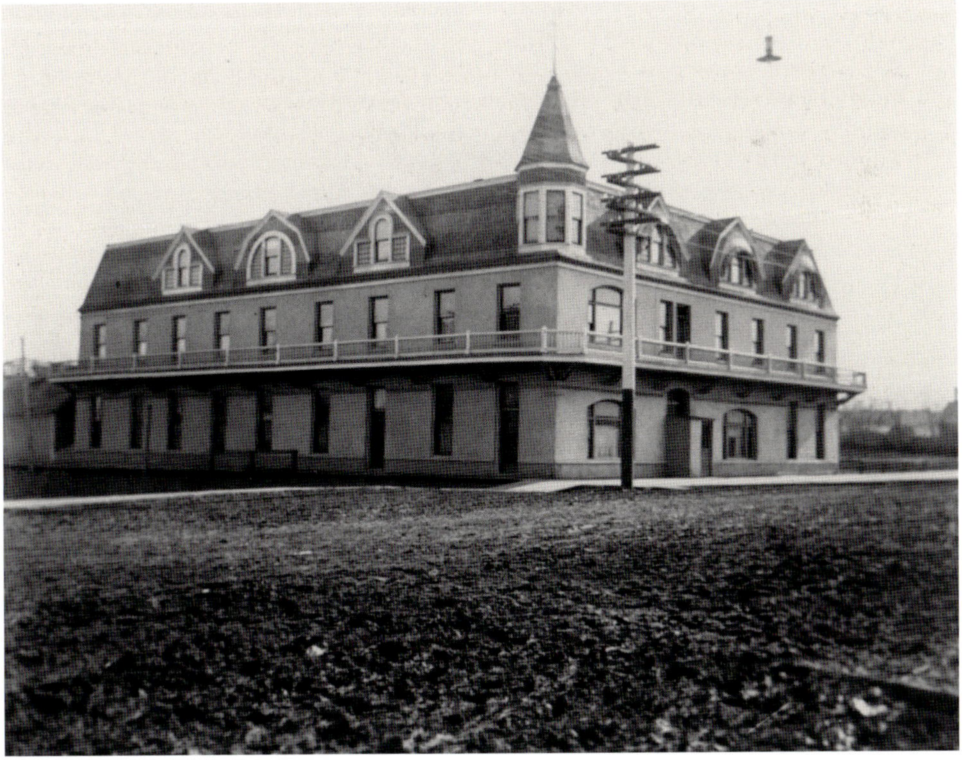

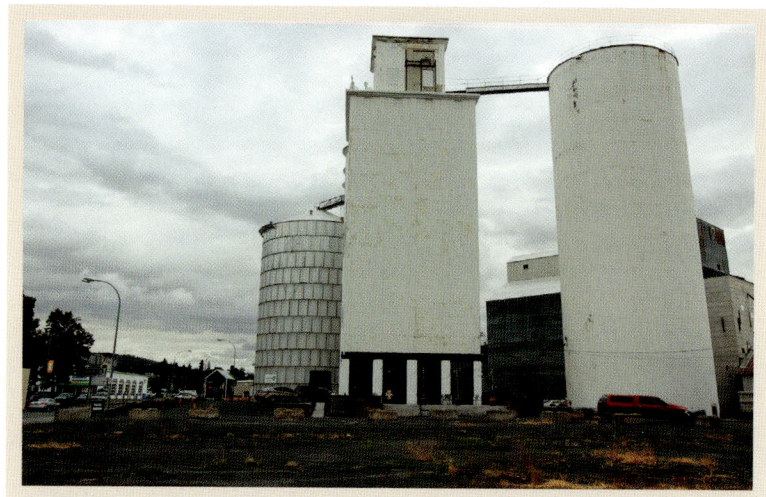

Moscow was and continues to be a large agricultural hub on the Palouse. Grain elevators such as these used by the Latah County Grain Growers span dates from the late 1890s to the 1940s. These grain elevators, constructed from concrete in the 1920s, are a symbol of agriculture's significance to the community. No longer in existence, the railroad tracks adjacent to these structures meant that crops could be transported throughout the region with relative ease. The railroad tracks were removed in the late 2000s, and some of the elevators were razed in 2008.

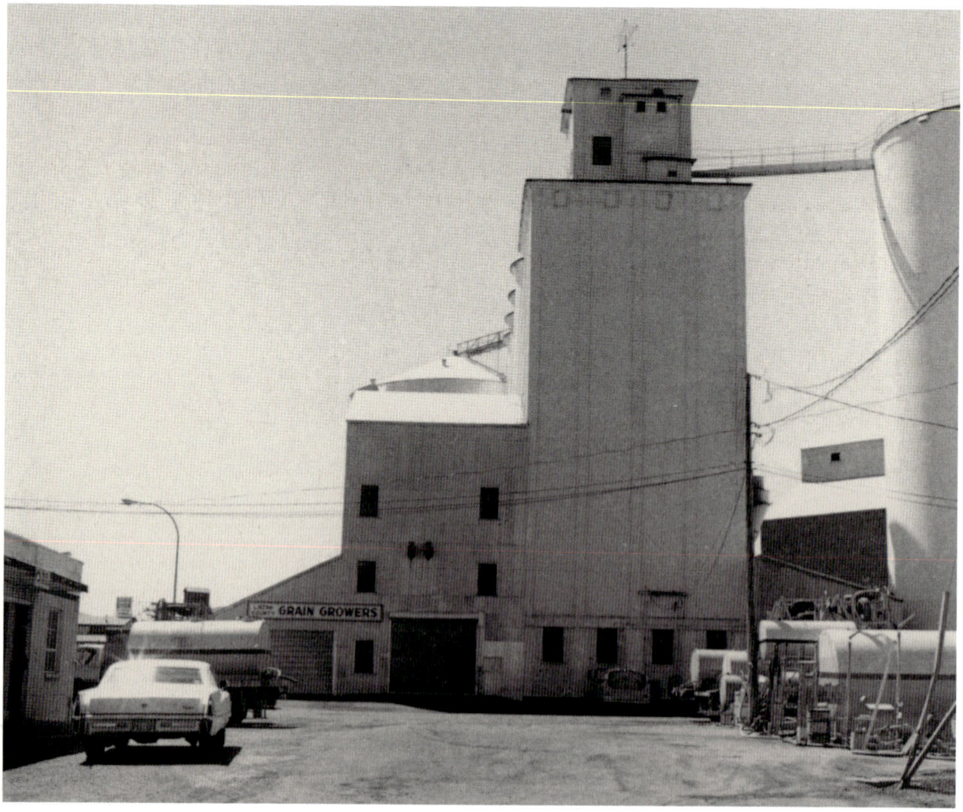

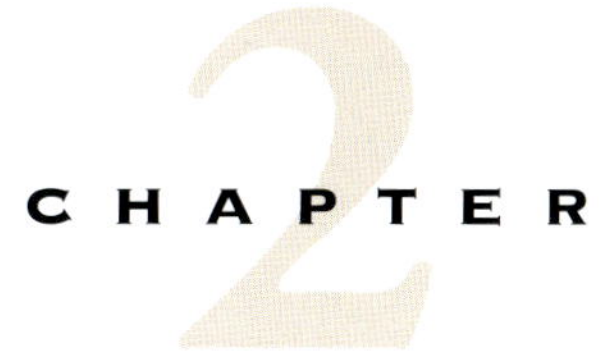

CHAPTER 2

UNIVERSITY OF IDAHO

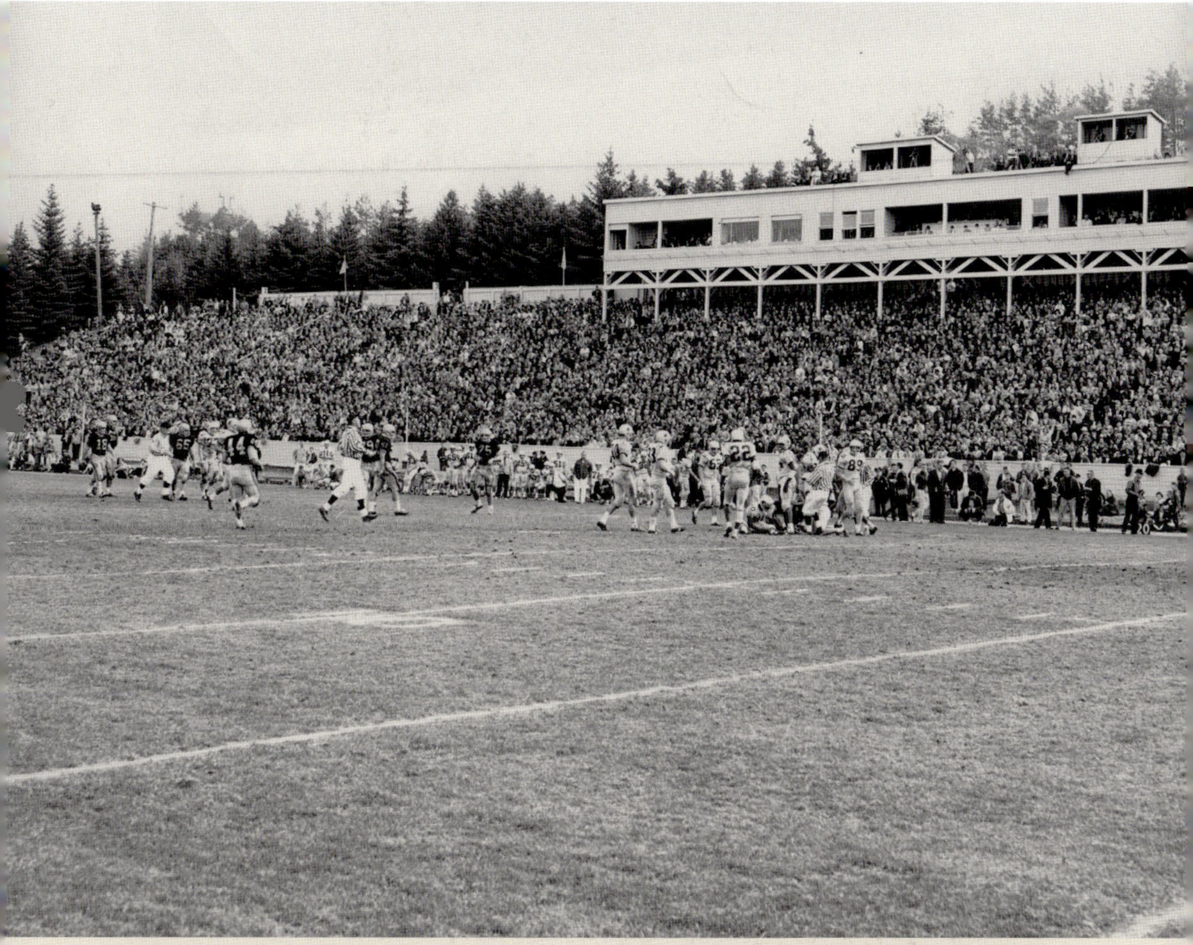

Before the Kibbie Dome, Neale Stadium hosted many of the University of Idaho's sporting events. Named after university president Mervin G. Neale, the facility was in use from 1937 to 1968. Before Neale Stadium, MacLean Field saw most university games beginning in 1914. Neale Stadium was located where the Kibbie Dome now stands.

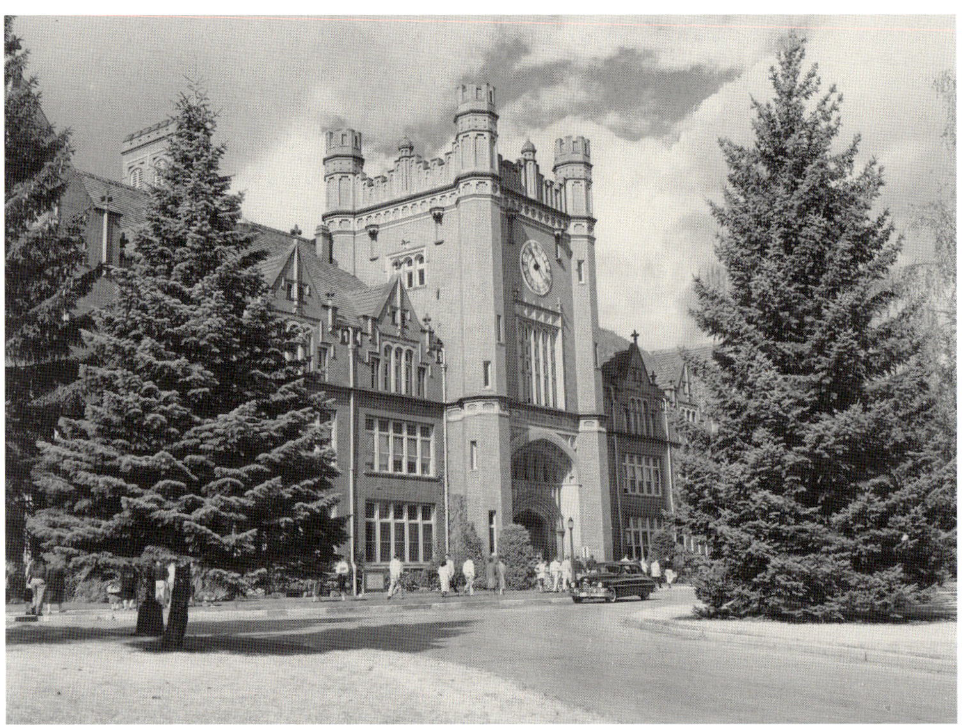

The first University of Idaho Administration Building was constructed in 1892, after the university's founding in 1889. It stood until a fire destroyed it in 1906. The current Administration Building was completed in 1909 and designed by John E. Tourtellotte. It holds an auditorium, classrooms, and administrative offices and underwent multiple renovations. The building held the library collection until a new library building was finished in 1957. The building was placed in the National Register of Historic Places in 1978.

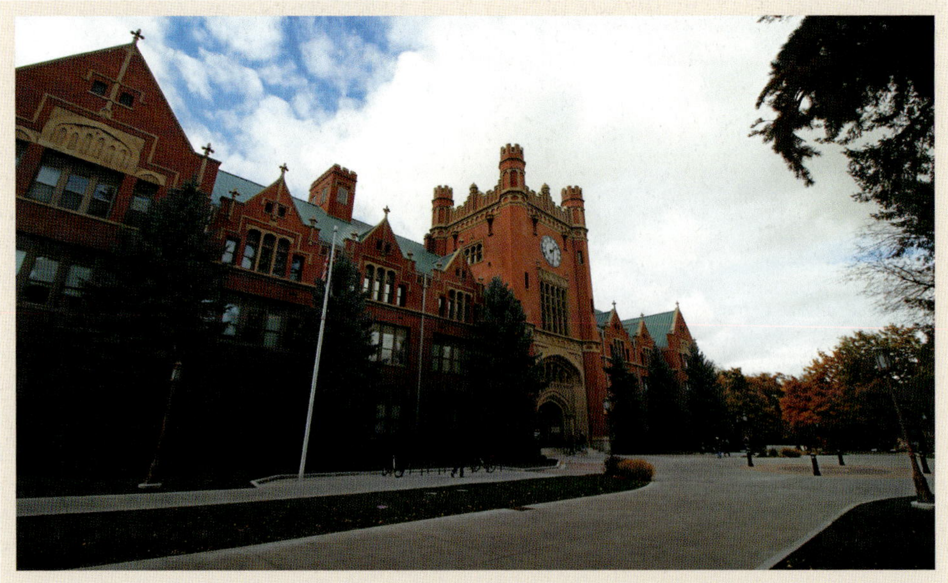

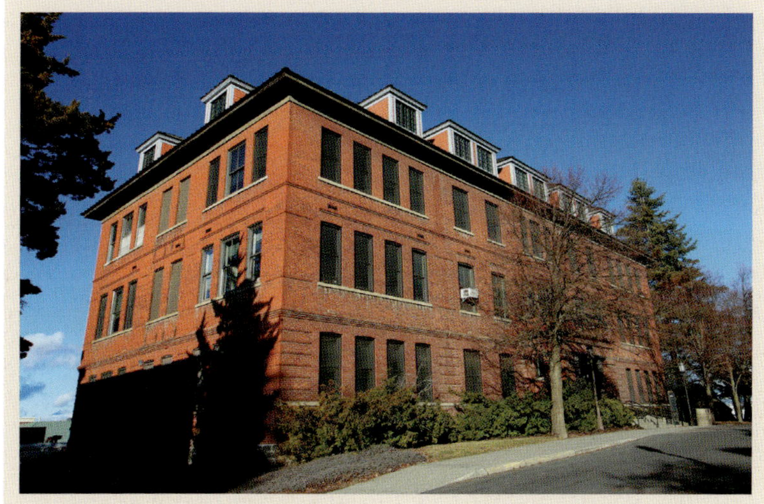

Named for the Morrill Act of 1862, which established the system of land-grant colleges, this building first housed the College of Agriculture after completion in 1906. It was constructed using insurance funds gained after the original Administration Building fire the same year. A fourth story was added in 1930, and in 1950, it became the Forestry Building. In 1972, it reverted back to Morrill Hall, and it has housed the philosophy department as well as the graduate college offices.

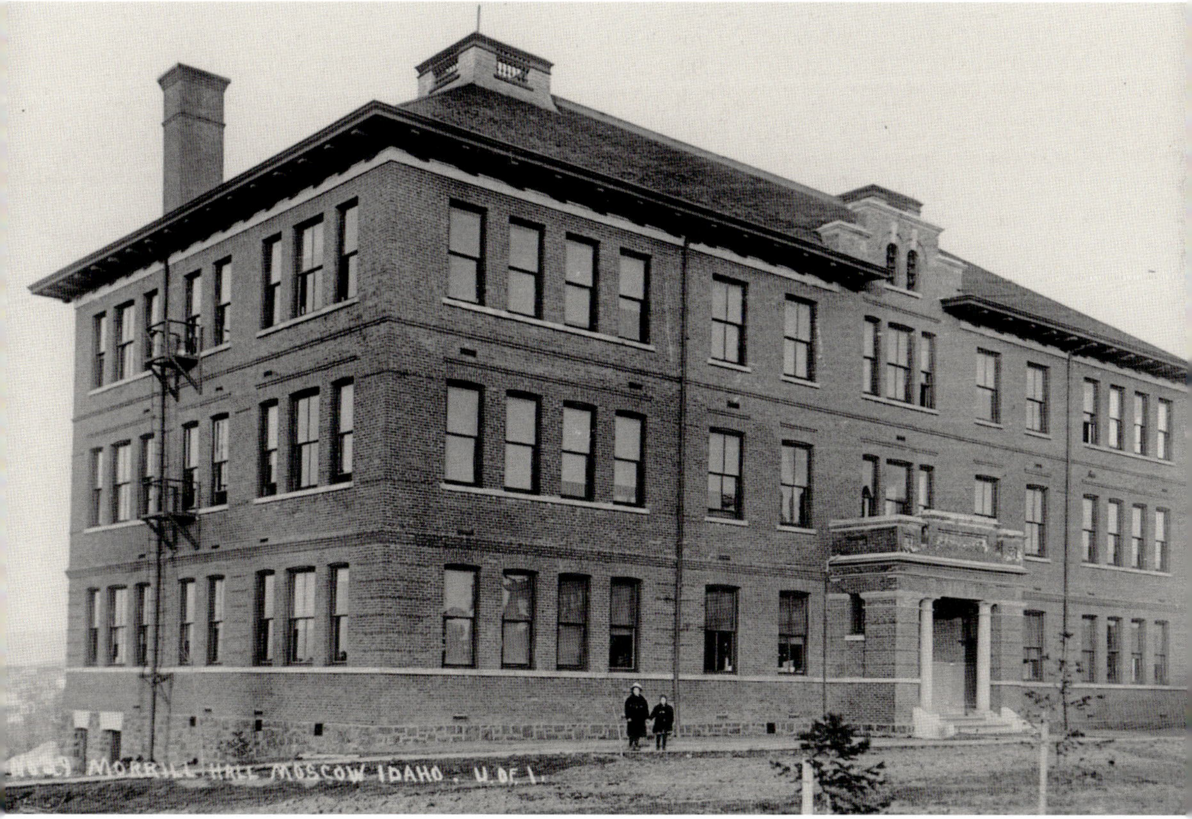

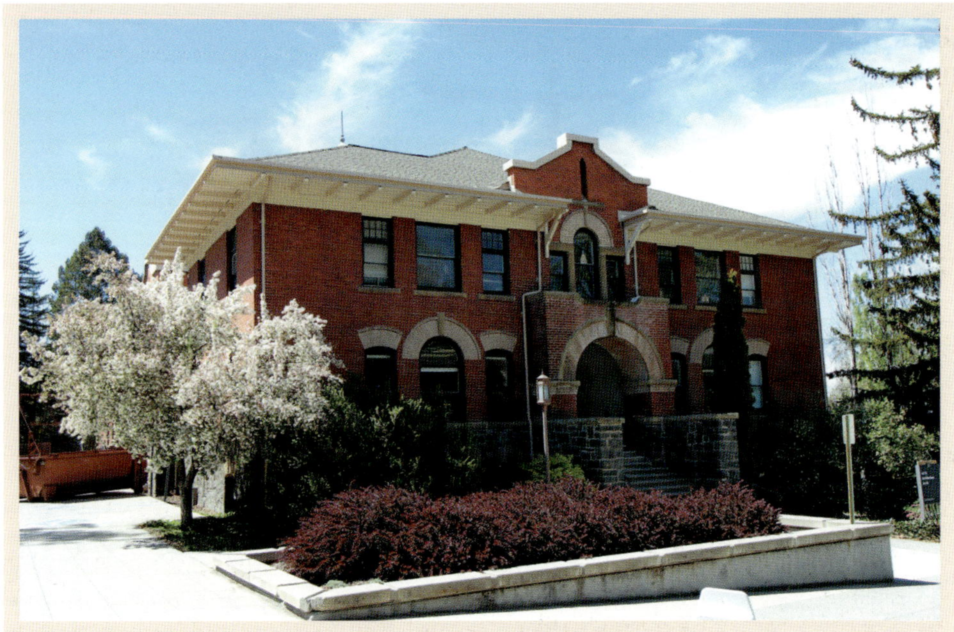

Before the Memorial Gymnasium was constructed, the Old Gymnasium and Armory was the indoor sporting center on campus. Once the Memorial Gym was finished, the old gym building served as the women's gym from 1929 to 1970. Constructed in 1904, it had also served as temporary offices, classrooms, and a library while the Administration Building was reconstructed following its 1906 fire. Now known as Art and Architecture South, the building was renovated to accommodate art studios in 1976 and added to the National Register of Historic Places in 1983.

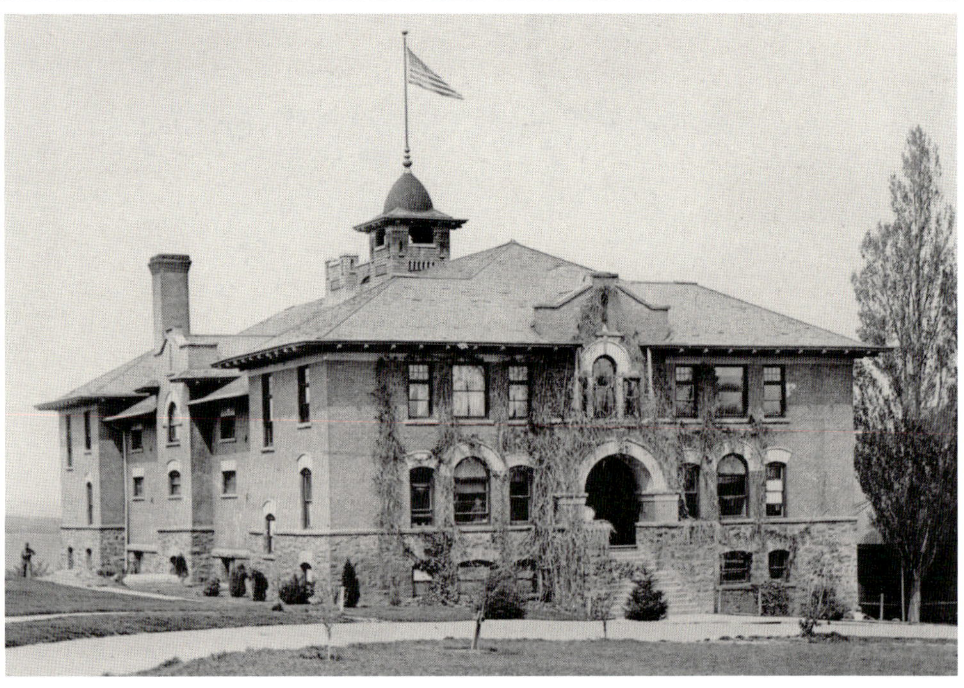

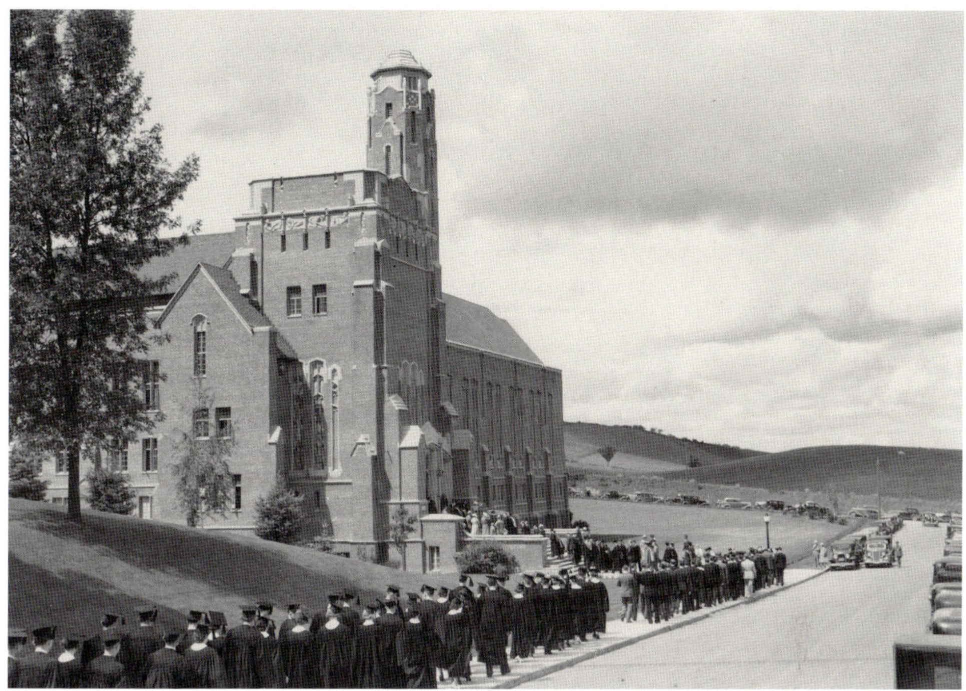

Graduation ceremonies previously took place in the Memorial Gymnasium. As graduating classes grew, the Kibbie Dome and Idaho Central Credit Union Arena hosted commencement ceremonies. In the photograph, students march to the Kibbie Dome for a spring ceremony. The Memorial Gymnasium is notable for its ornamentation, including tall stained-glass windows and football player statuary decoration. Built in 1929 and designed by faculty members, the building is a memorial to Idahoans lost in the world wars. The building was placed in the National Register of Historic Places in 1977. (Past, courtesy of the University of Idaho Special Collections and Archives.)

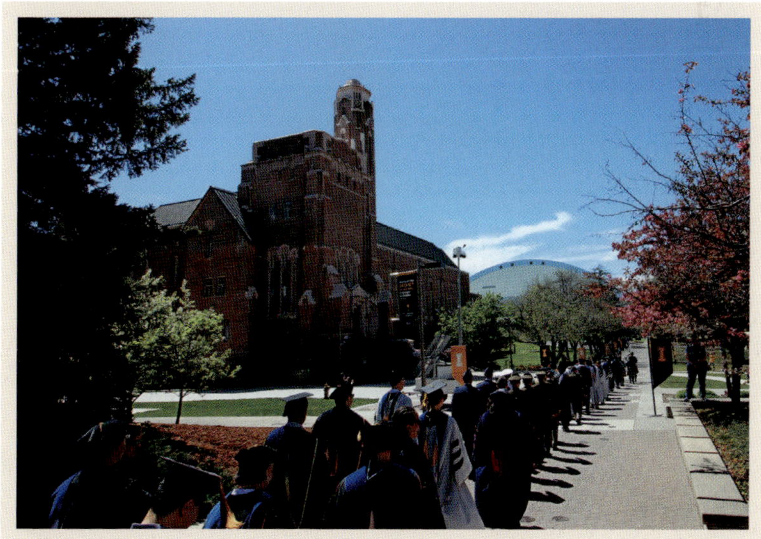

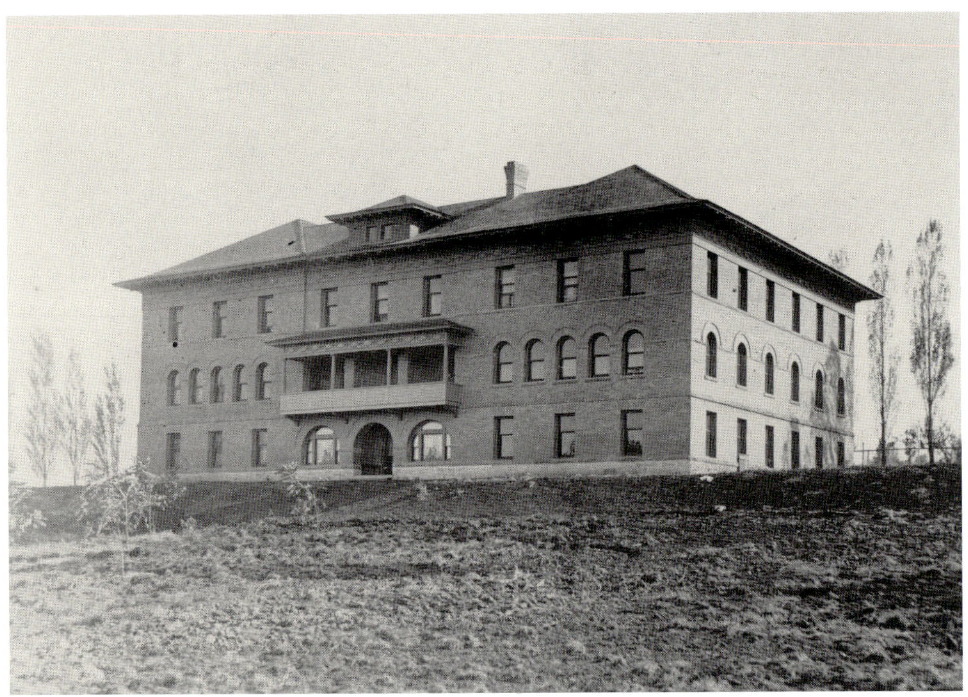

The first women's dormitory on campus was Ridenbaugh Hall, named for Mary E. Ridenbaugh, a university regent from 1901 to 1907. Constructed in 1902, the building also contained domestic science laboratories, music practice rooms, dance studios, and art gallery space throughout its history. It was placed in the National Register of Historic Places in 1977 and is the oldest brick building on the University of Idaho campus.

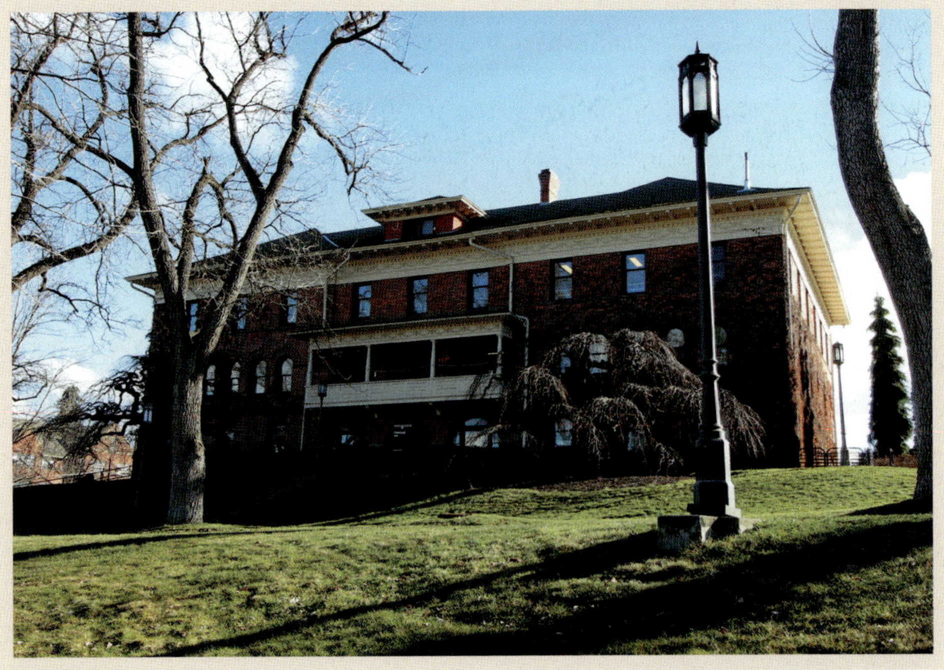

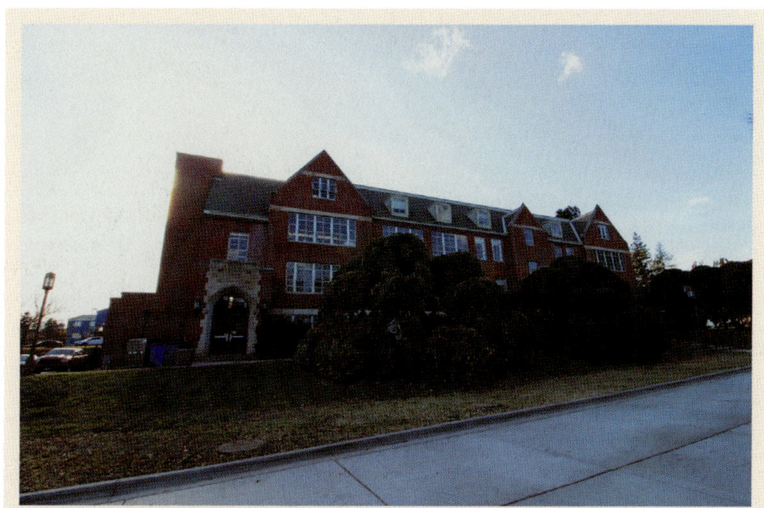

Before the Niccolls Home Economics Building, this location was home to the old Engineering Building. The Engineering Building was one of the original campus buildings completed in 1906. It housed the School of Mines, the applied sciences department, and other engineering classrooms and labs. In 1951, officials deemed the building unsafe and demolished it to make way for the current Niccolls Home Economics Building. Pieces of the old structure were placed around campus as benches and part of the Memorial Steps.

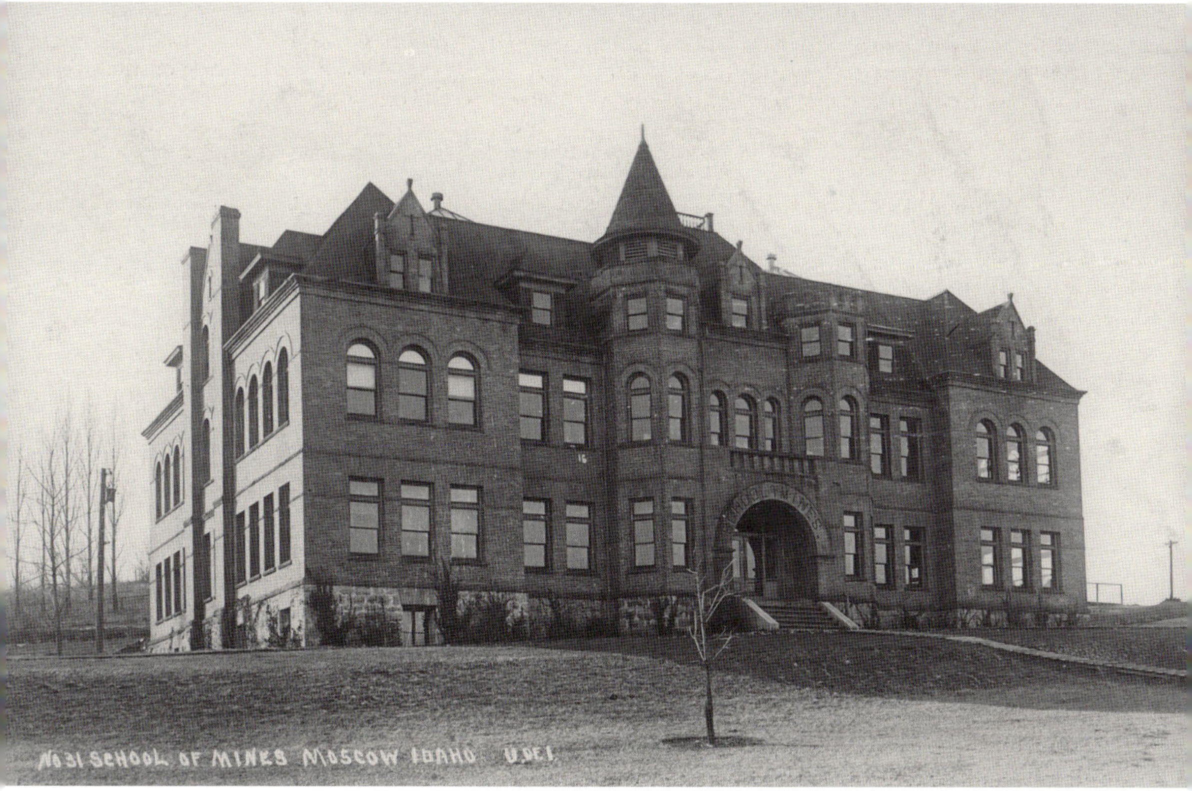

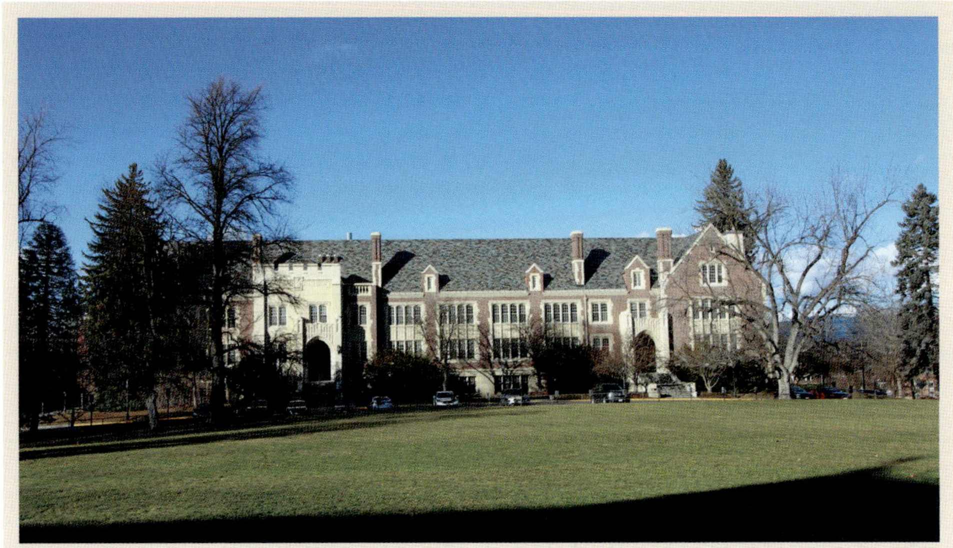

Built in 1924, the Science Hall housed classrooms and laboratories for science disciplines. Renamed the Life Sciences Building in 1964, it continues to host science classes and labs. Designed in the Tudor Gothic architectural style, it was one of the last buildings on campus built in this style. The only notable differences are more mature trees scattered along the administration lawn and an unseen 1986 addition to the building.

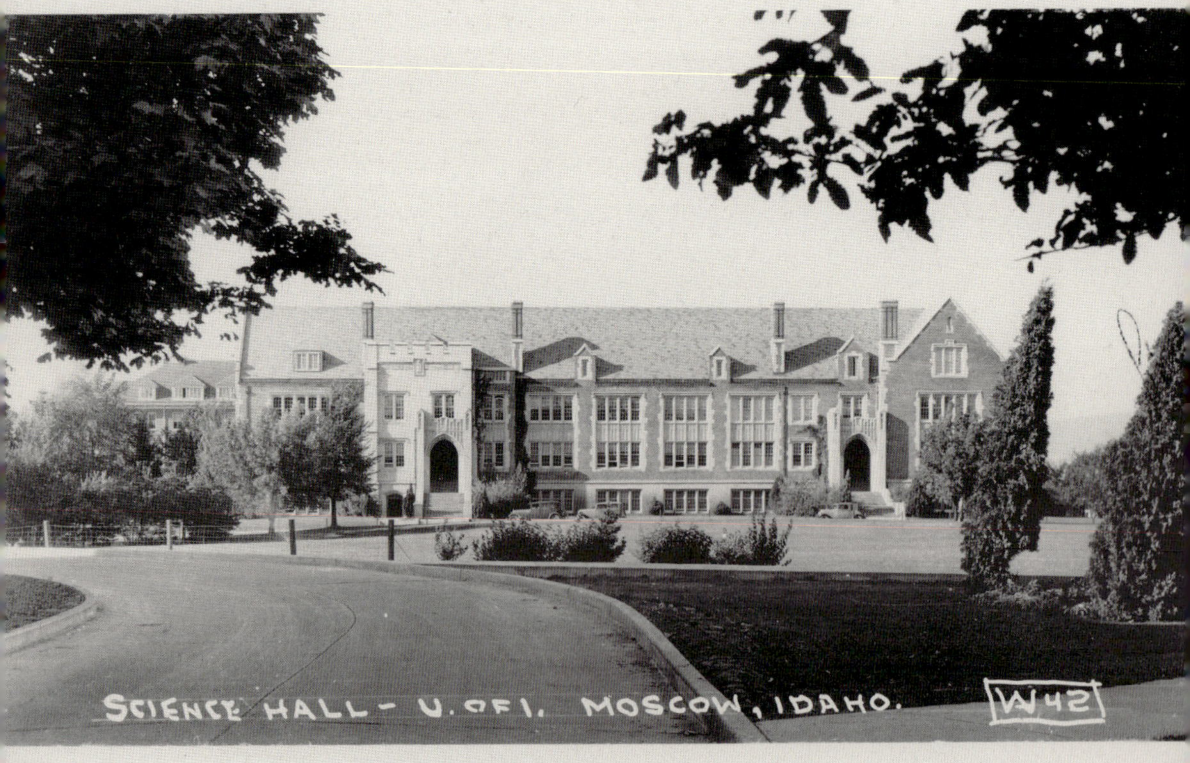

SCIENCE HALL – U. OF I. MOSCOW, IDAHO. W42

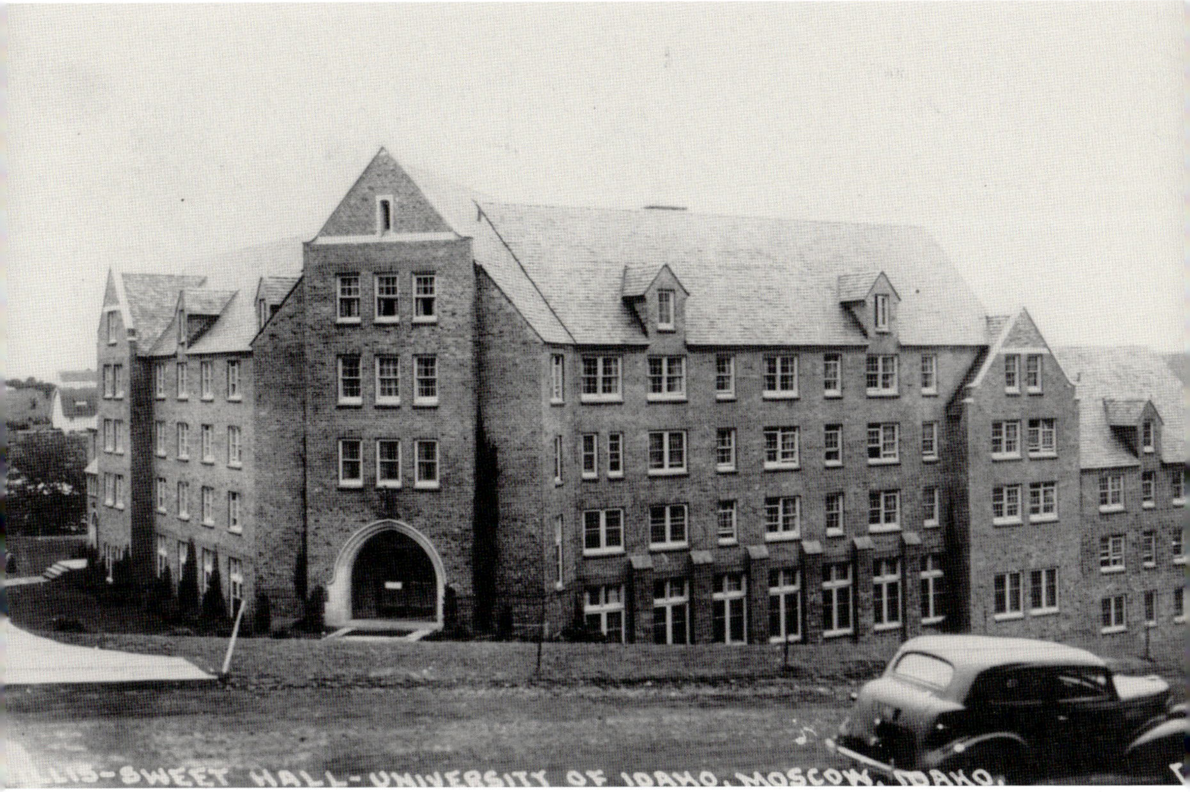

In 1936, the Willis Sweet Hall opened as a male residence hall. The honor was bestowed upon Sweet for his role in establishing the University of Idaho and serving on the first board of regents. After Idaho gained statehood in 1890, Sweet served as Idaho's representative in Congress from 1890 to 1895. Later, the building held various departmental, faculty, and graduate student offices, and it was renamed Brink Hall in the 1980s. The new name was in honor of former student and author Carol Ryrie Brink. Brink attended the university from 1914 to 1917.

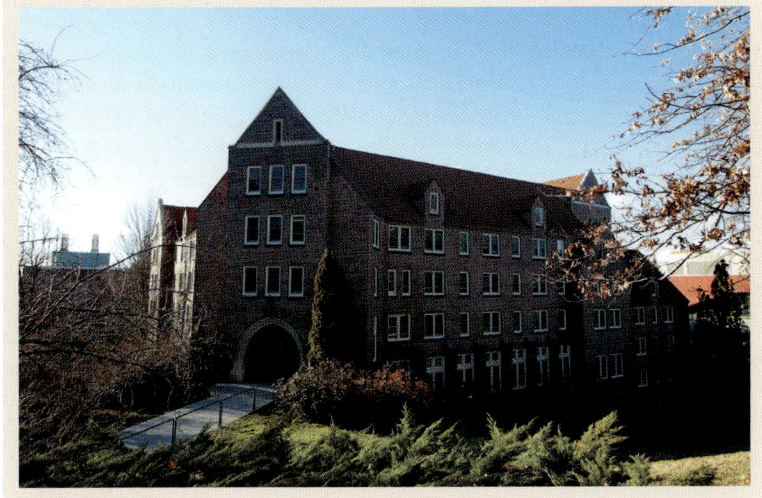

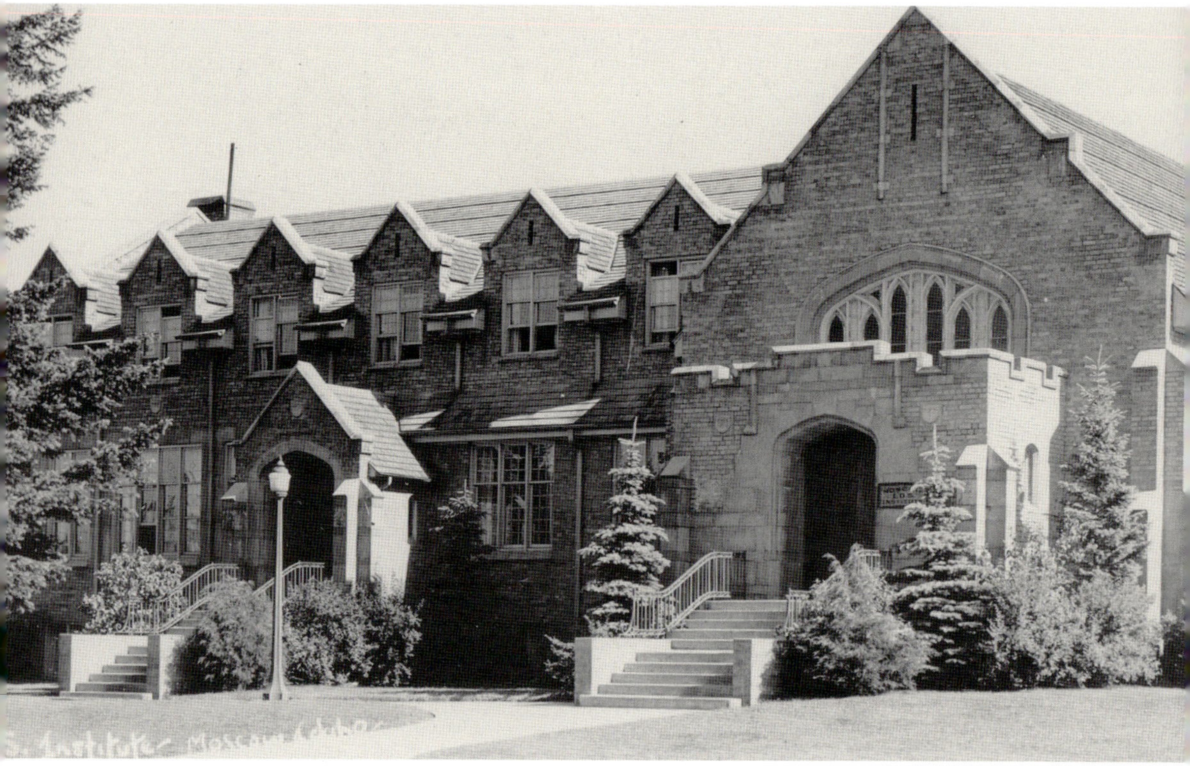

The Church of Jesus Christ of Latter-Day Saints Institute of Religion has existed on the University of Idaho campus since 1926. According to *Deseret News*, it was the first institute of religion established by the church, which now has thousands throughout the world. The original building was razed in 1967 to make way for the current building, which was finished in 1968. The institute offers classes, church services, and social gatherings.

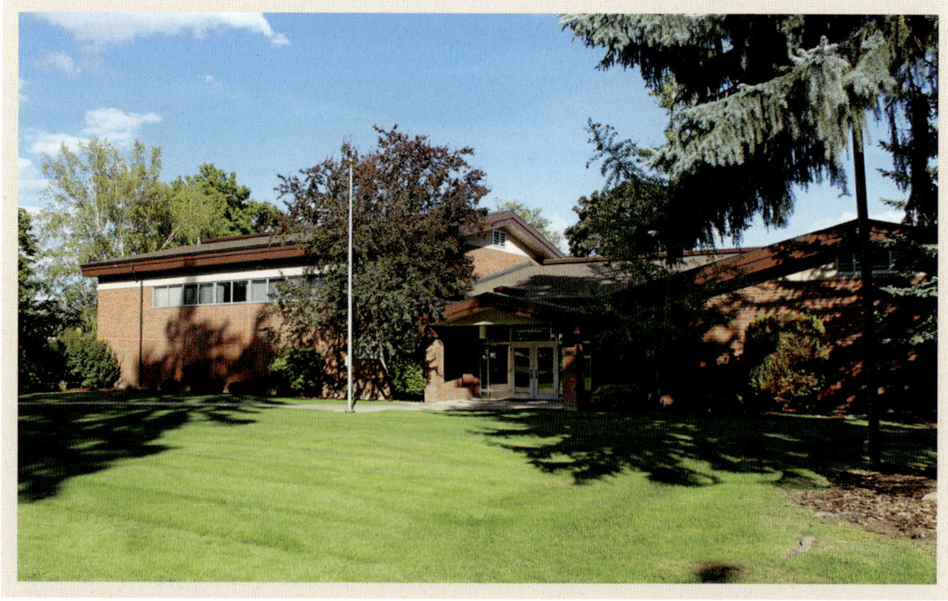

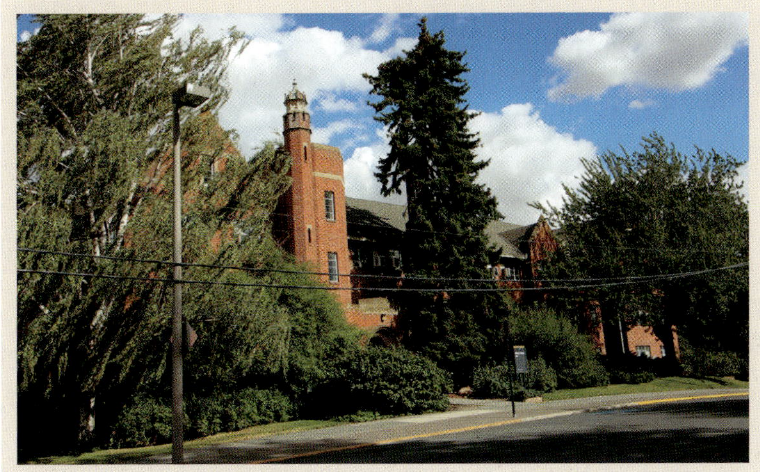

First built in 1923 in the Collegiate Gothic architectural style, Forney Hall honored Moscow woman Mary E. Forney. Wife of the first acting university president, James H. Forney, Mary actively involved herself in Moscow, serving on the first public library board raising funds to build the Carnegie Library, as an early president of the Moscow Historical Club working to develop East City Park, and getting involved with other civic endeavors. The building was first used as a women's residence hall then converted to offices.

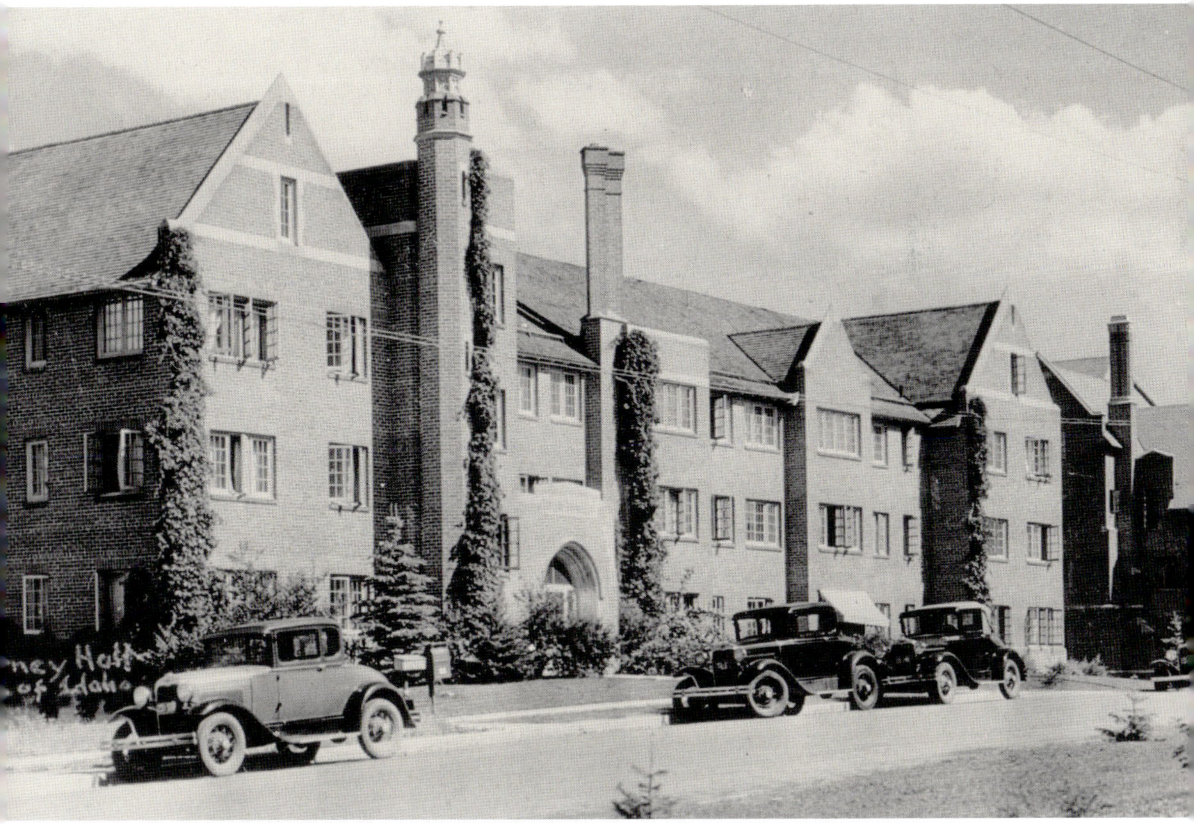

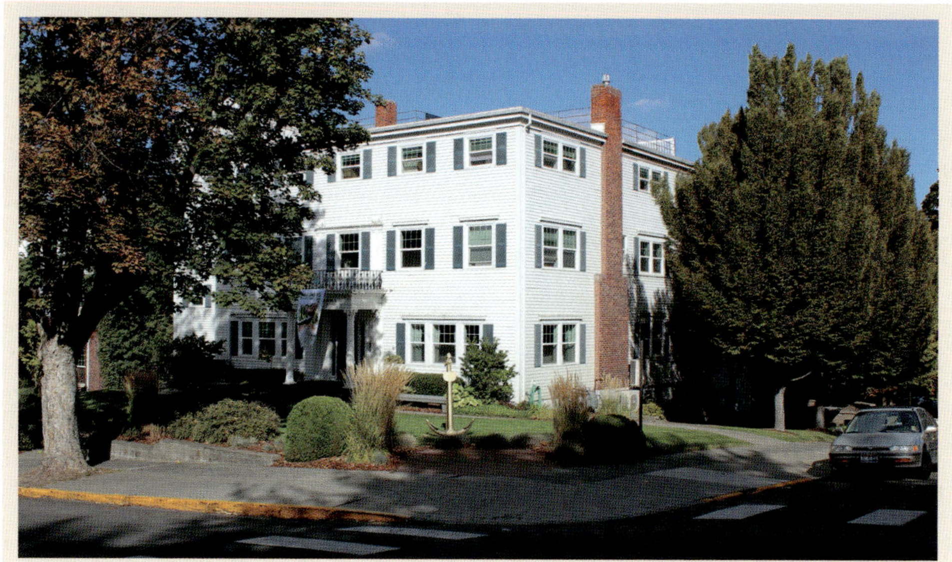

The Delta Gamma sorority was chartered on the University of Idaho campus in 1911, making it one of the oldest sororities on campus. Their house, located at the northeast corner of Idaho Avenue and Elm Street, was finished in 1914, and students moved in shortly after. Renovations to the building were completed in 1984, when notably, the third floor was expanded. The property continues to house the Delta Gamma sorority today.

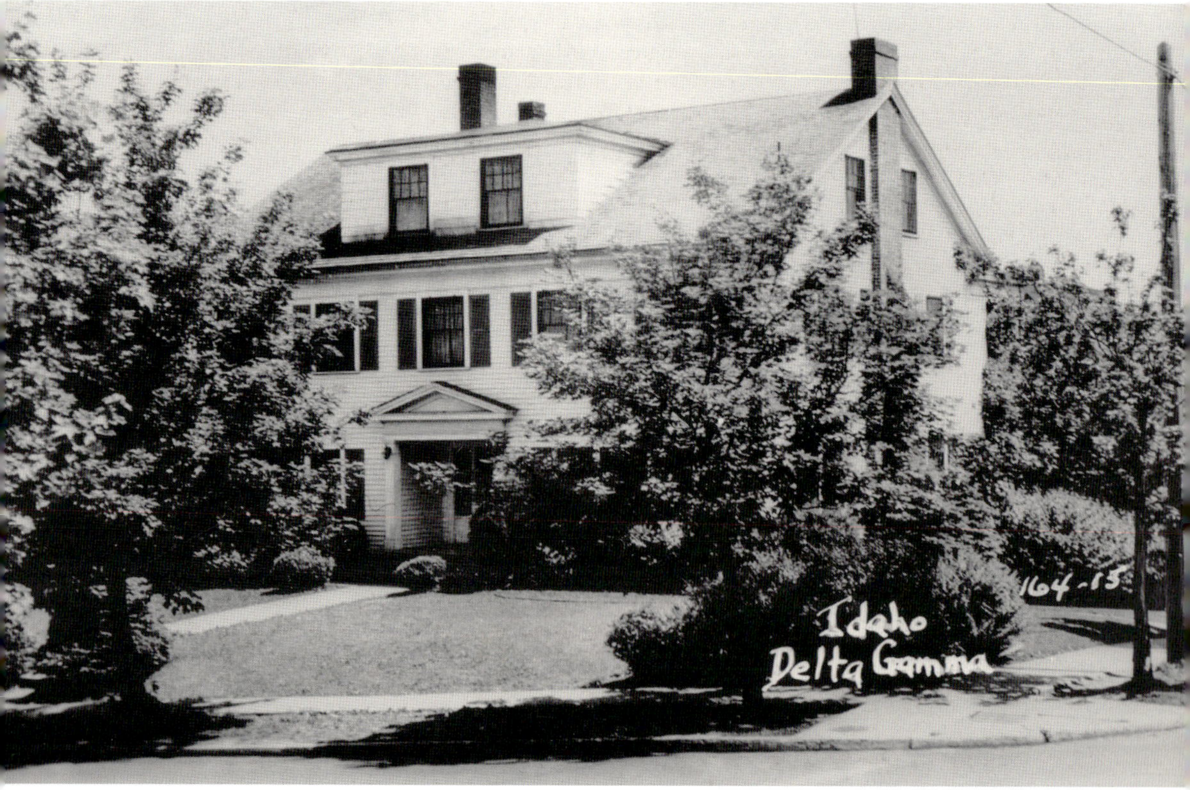

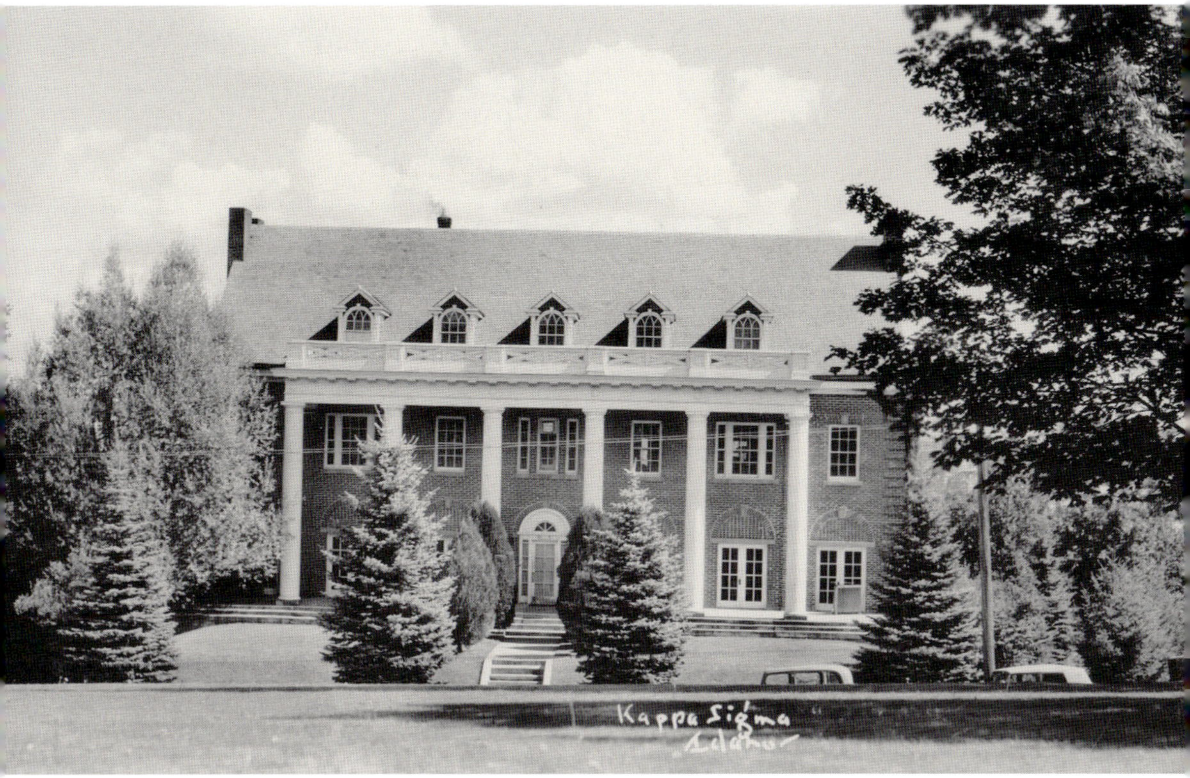

The Gamma Theta chapter of the Kappa Sigma fraternity traces its charter to 1905. In 1916, Kirkland Cutter designed the neoclassical house reminiscent of the American South. The Kappa Sigma fraternity still occupies this house. It is the oldest fraternity building on the University of Idaho campus and was placed in the National Register of Historic Places in 1996.

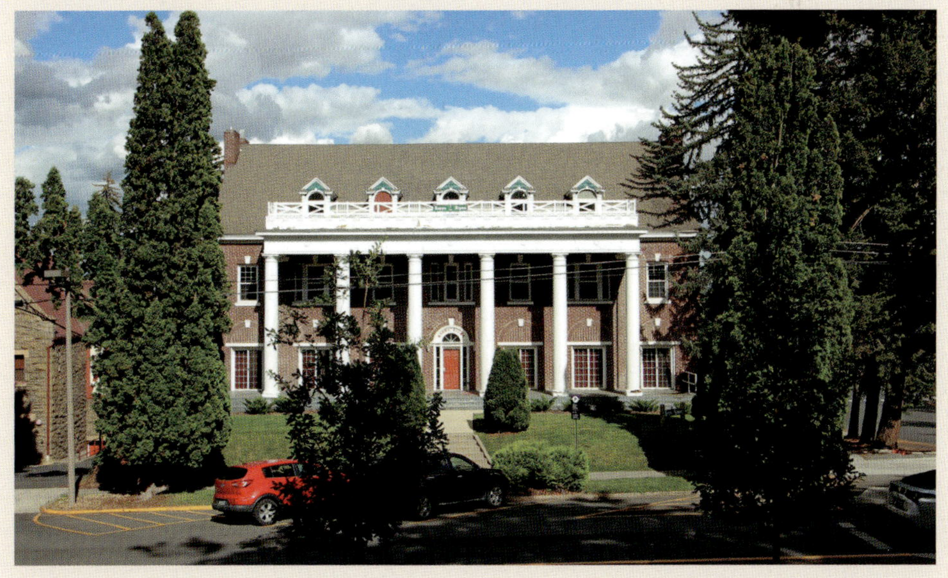

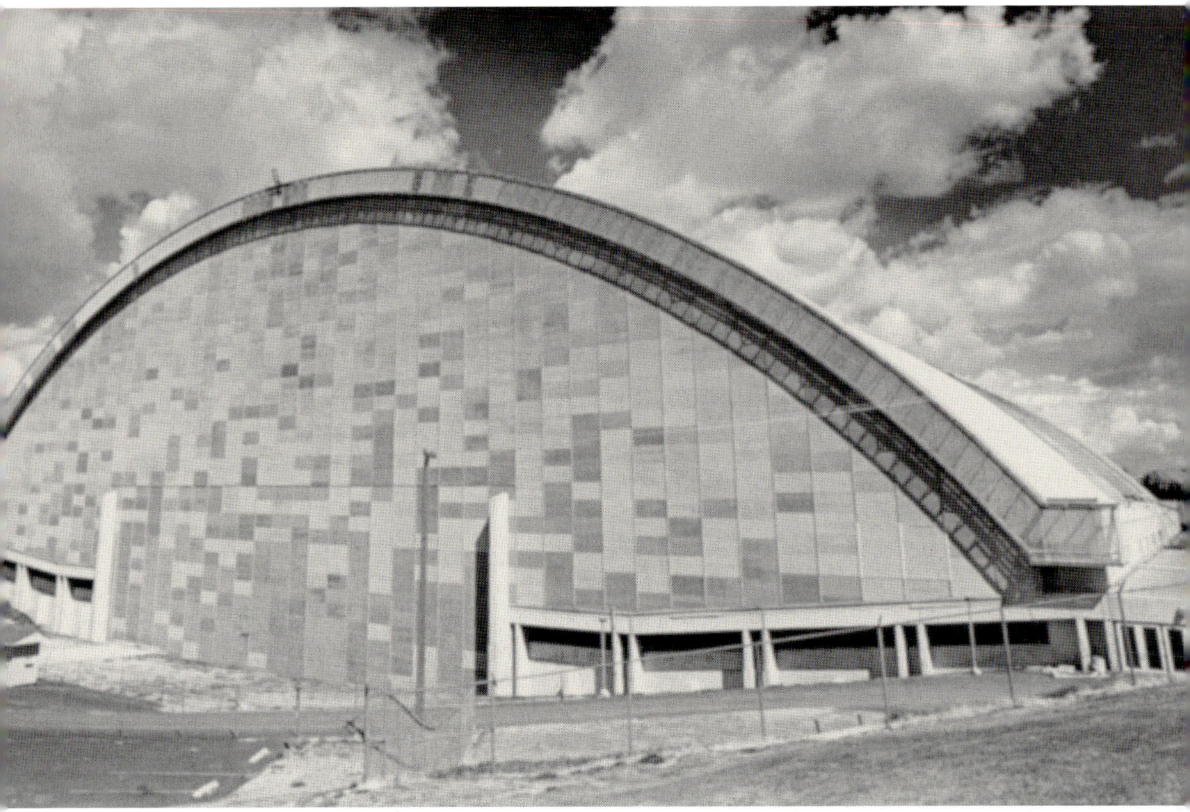

Many University of Idaho sporting and campus events are hosted at the Kibbie Dome, but prior to that, Neale Stadium was the primary venue for games. Designed by architect Glen Cline of Cline, Smull, Hamill & Associates, construction began on the Kibbie Dome in 1971, and it was formally dedicated in September 1975. William H. Kibbie received naming rights after contributing $300,000 to the building fund in 1974. Kibbie attended the university for a short time in 1936.

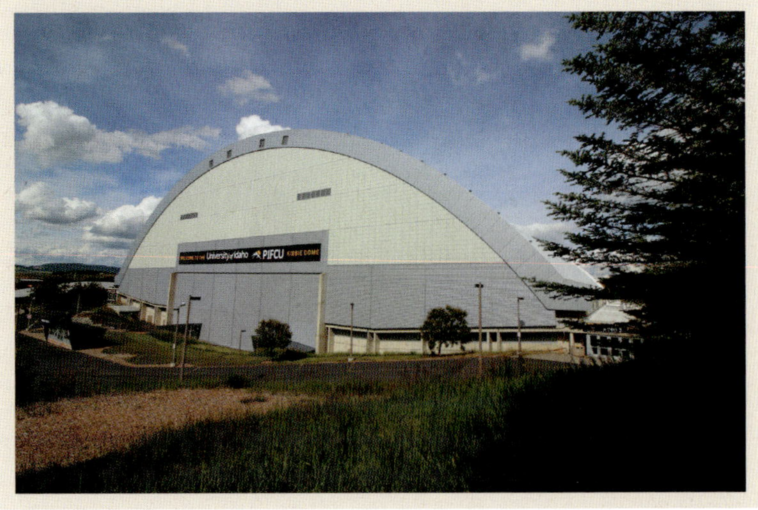

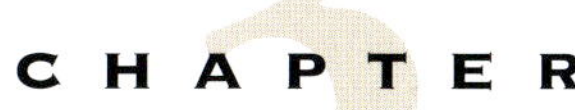

Churches

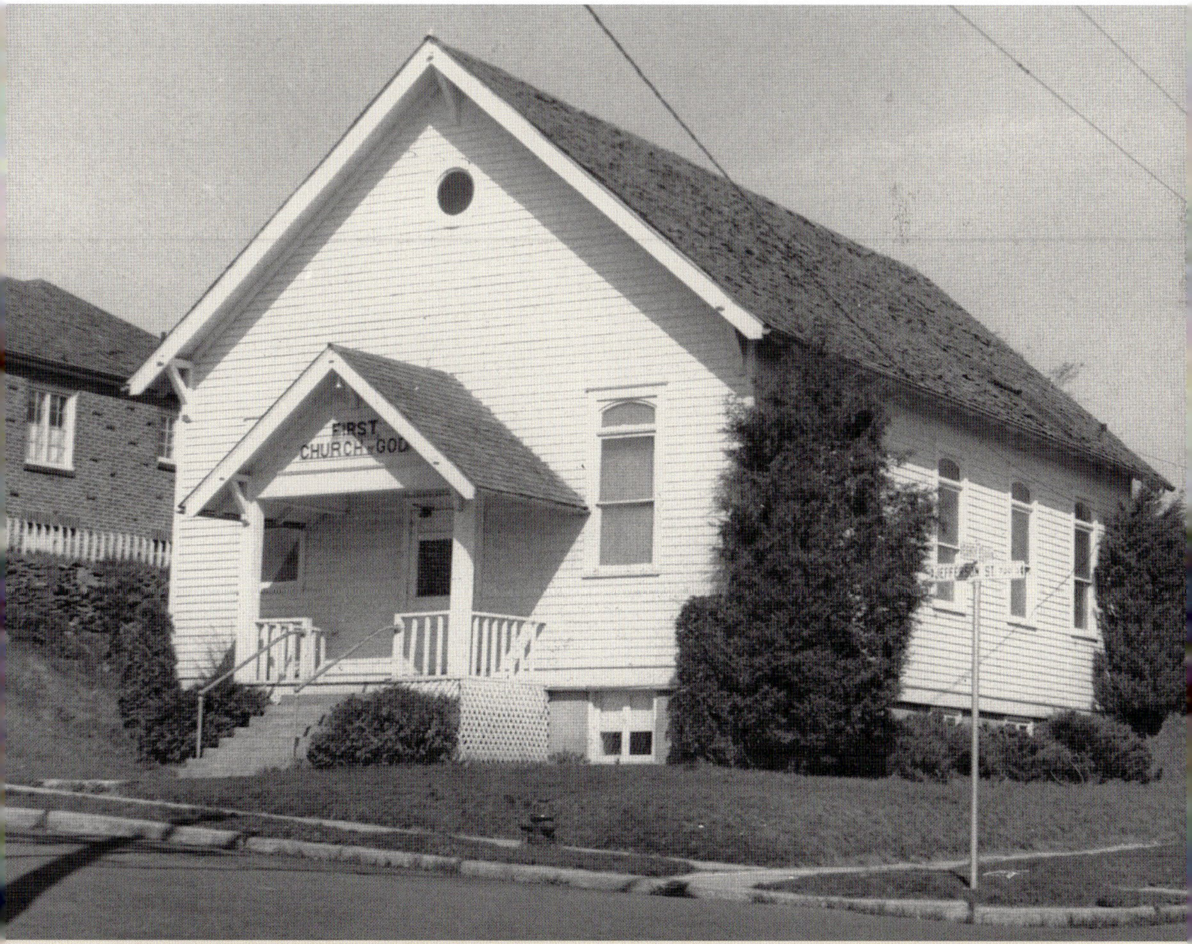

The Church of the Brethren came to Moscow and built their church, located on the corner of Jefferson and Eighth Streets, in 1884. Also referred to as "the Dunkard Church," the Brethren disorganized, and by 1904, the building was empty. In 1909, the First Church of God resided at that location. The building remains relatively unchanged and housed the First Pentecostal Tabernacle in the 1970s. It is now occupied by the White Pine Baptist Church.

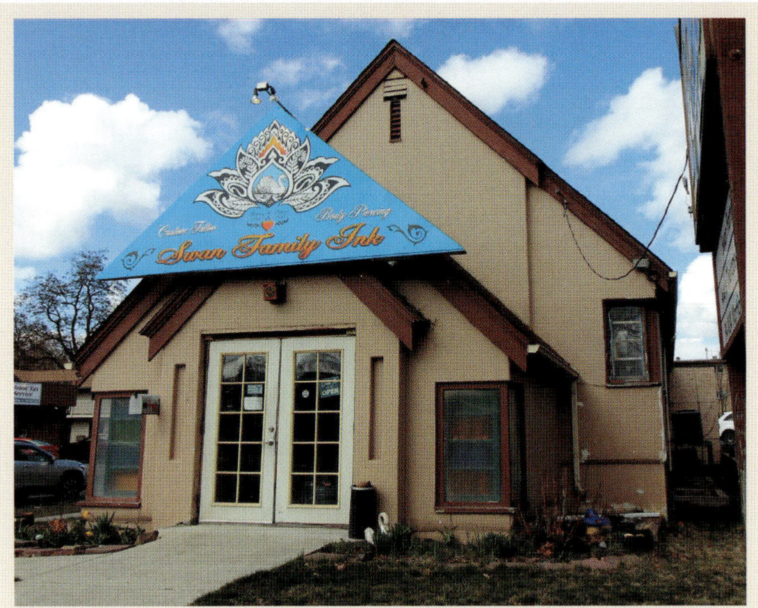

Moscow's early Seventh-day Adventist church was located on the corner of Third and Almon Streets, built in the late 1880s. The Adventists shared the building with the Episcopal and Nazarene congregations. The original building was replaced in 1938 by the existing structure. In 1975, the Adventist church moved to its current location behind the Emmanuel Lutheran Church on West C Street. From 1975 to the 1990s, the building housed the Micro Moviehouse. It is now a tattoo parlor and yoga and massage therapy studio.

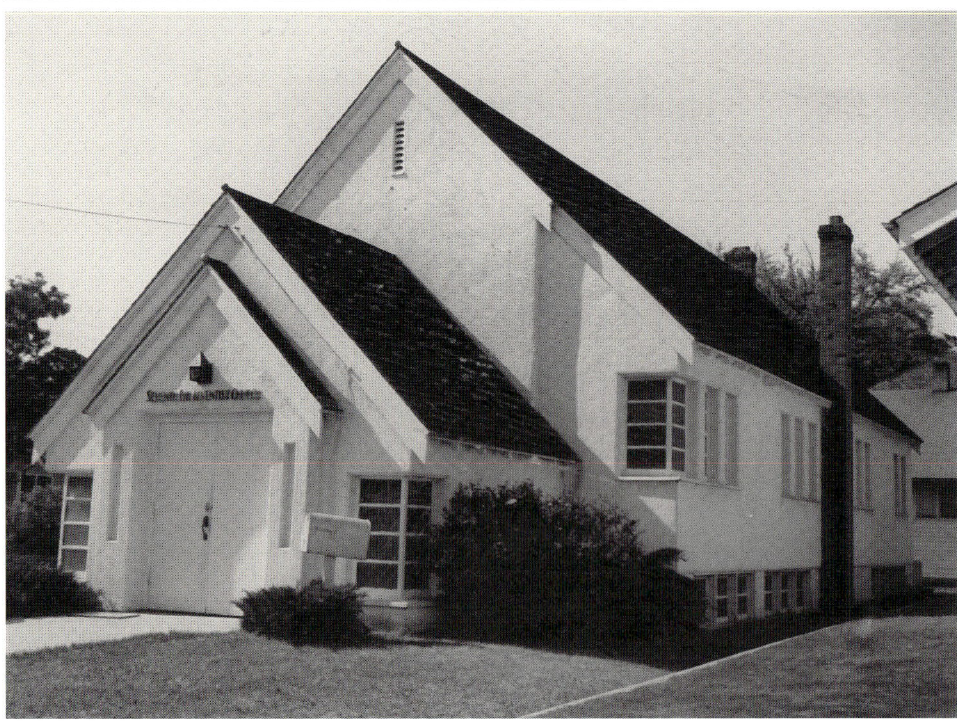

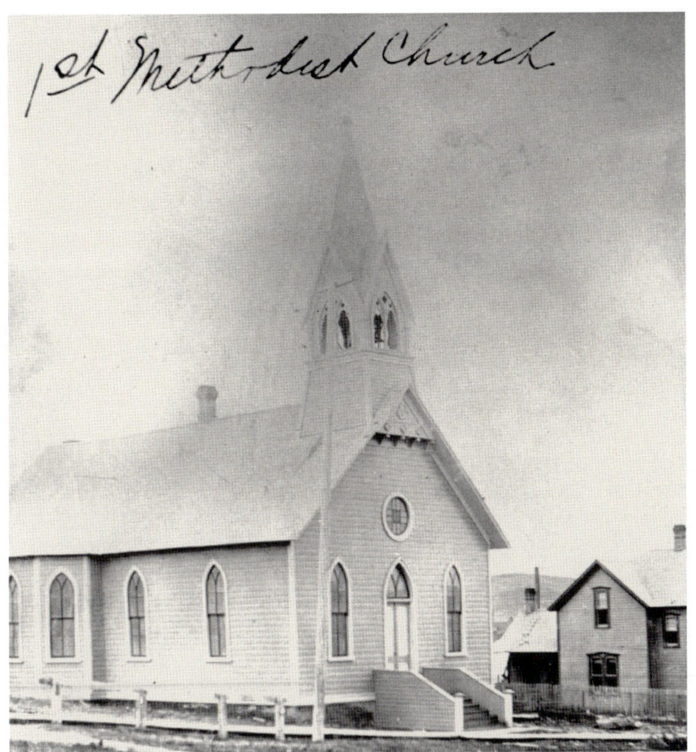

In 1887, the Methodist Episcopal church built this church on Sixth Street before moving to its current building at Third and Adams Streets. In 1904, the Norwegian Lutheran Church took over the building, and it changed the name to Our Savior's Lutheran Church in 1917. After the Lutheran church merger, the building was sold to Grace Baptist Church in 1969, and the Baptists held services there until 2007. In 2008, All Souls Christian Church took ownership of the building.

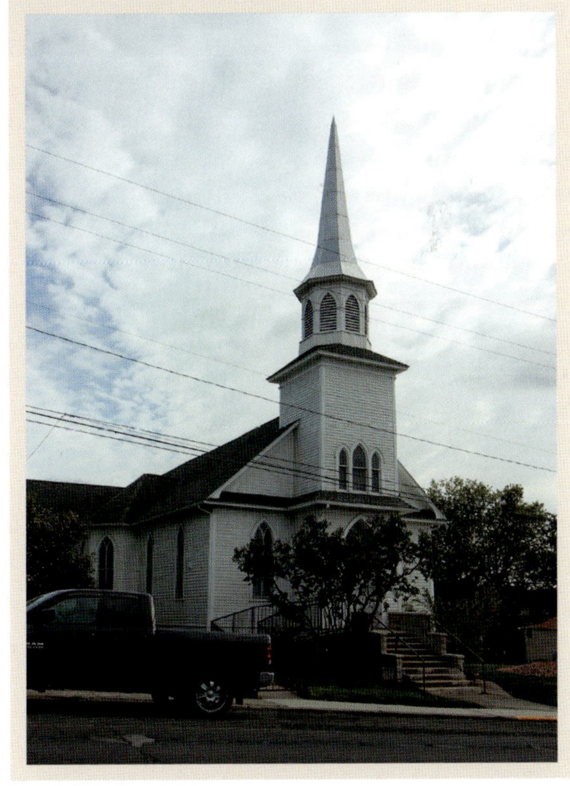

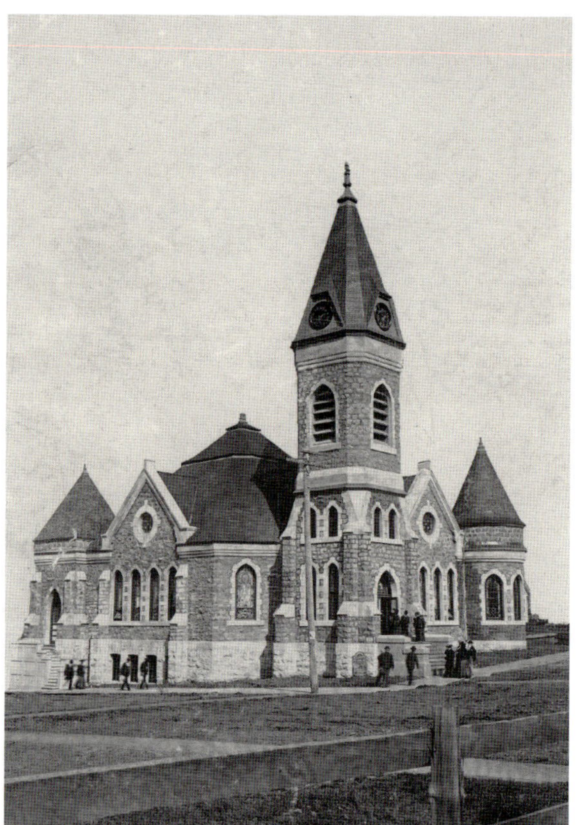

The Methodist Episcopal church at Third and Adams Streets dates from 1904 and was designed by H.N. Black. The dark basalt quarried near Colfax, Washington, gives the building its distinct Romanesque tower and Gothic stained-glass windows. Two additions were added to the building: one in 1923 and a modern education wing on the rear of the church in 1960. The building was listed in the National Register of Historic Places in 1978.

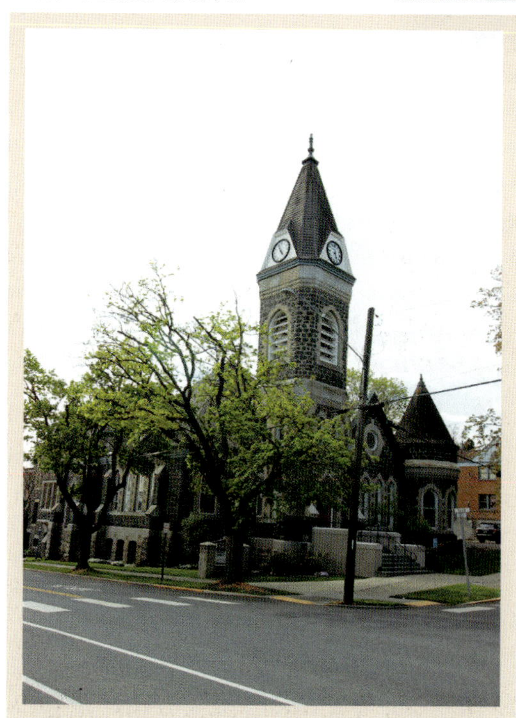

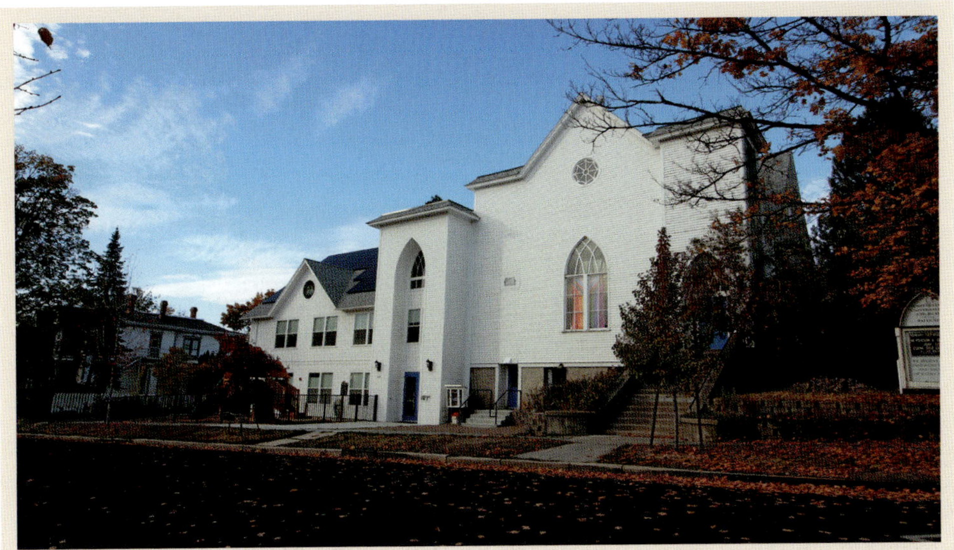

The First Lutheran Church was dedicated in 1890 at the corner of Second and Van Buren Streets. The church continued to grow, and in 1905, a new building was necessary, with the old structure moved. The above church was completed in 1906. The congregation was predominantly Swedish families and was sometimes called the Swedish Lutheran Church. In 1964, the church was sold to the Senior Citizens Club for use as a community space, and in 1985, it was sold again to the Unitarian Universalist Church of the Palouse. Since then, the Unitarians have renovated and remodeled the original 1906 structure, expanding the building several times.

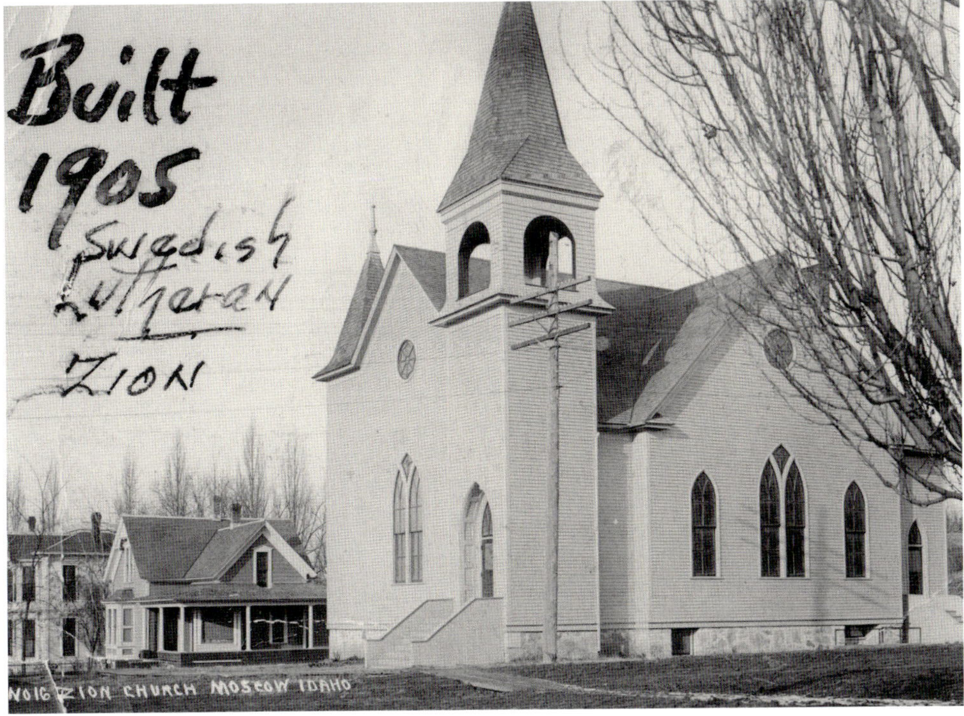

In 1961, the First Lutheran Church and Our Savior's Lutheran Church merged to form Emmanuel Lutheran Church, located on A Street. The spire was constructed from aluminum in Spokane and driven to Moscow for installation. The spire is notable for "singing" when the wind blows from a particular direction. The new building was officially opened with its first service on Easter Sunday in April 1968. Lutherans continue to gather at the church for services and community activities.

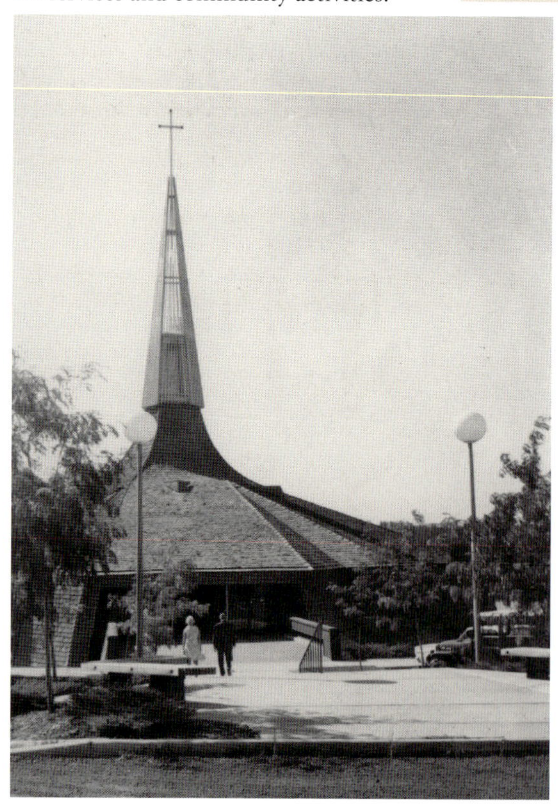

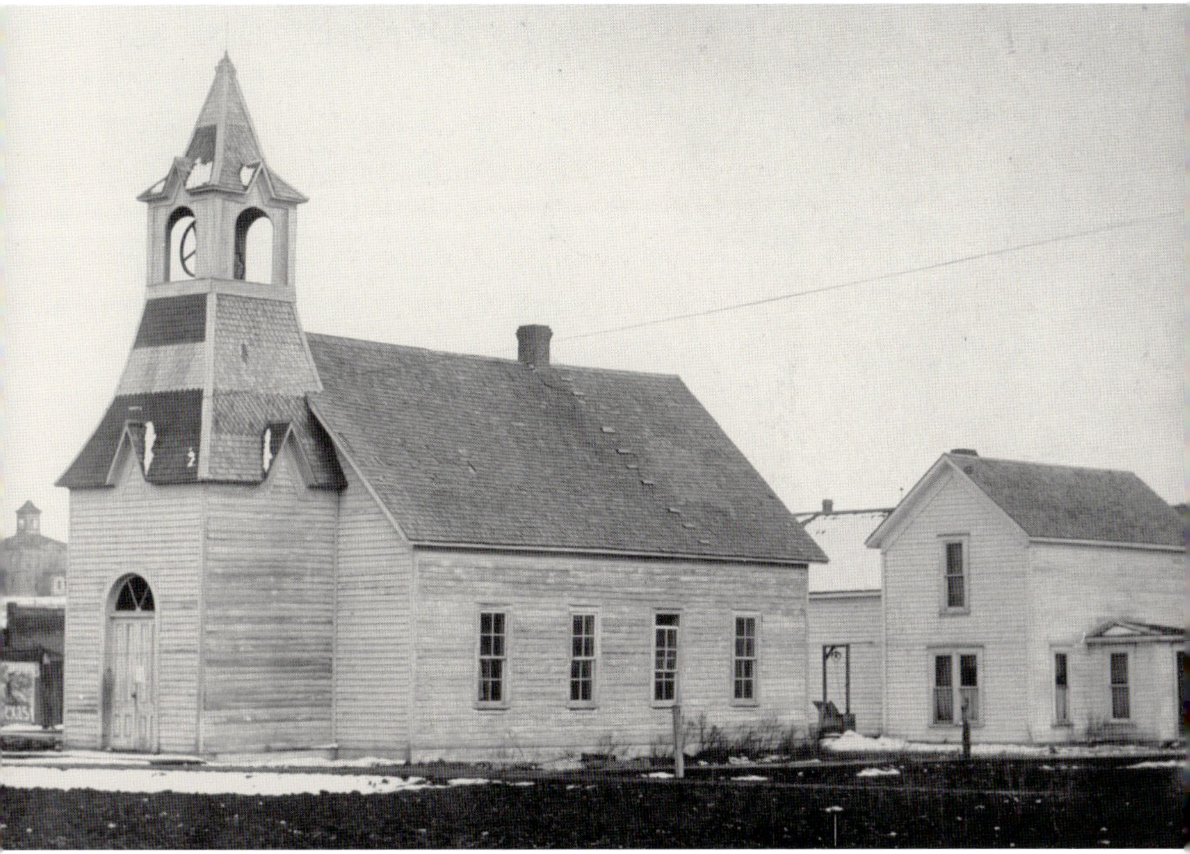

This church was first home to the Zion Baptist congregation, which constructed its original building in 1881 on land donated by Almon Asbury Lieuallen. It is believed to be the first church constructed in Moscow. The name was changed to the First Baptist Church in 1884. The original parsonage house still stands adjacent to the church. The current building was constructed in 1939, with renovations in 1964 and 1976. In 1969, the First Christian Church joined the First Baptist Church to form the United Church of Moscow, which has been worshipping there ever since.

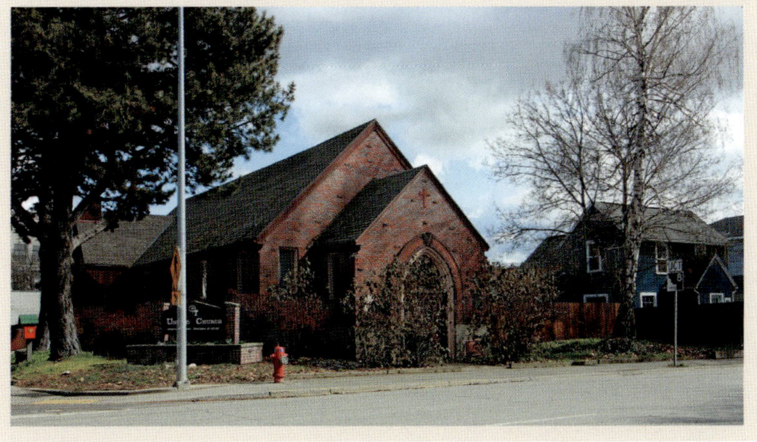

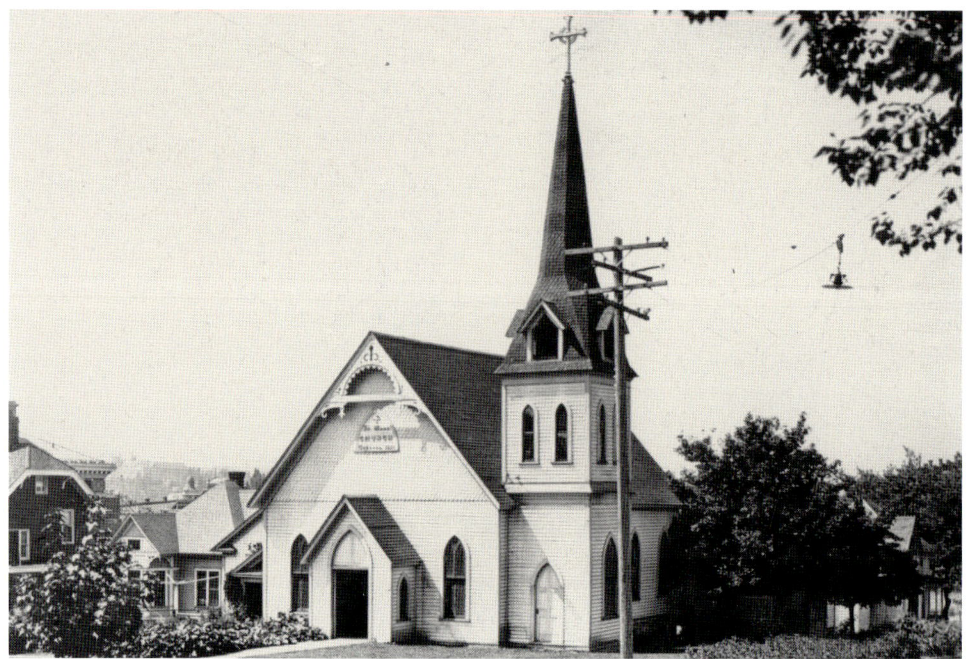

William J. McConnell donated land at the corner of Jefferson and First Streets and St. Mark's Episcopal Church was constructed in 1891. That first church stood until 1937, when a fire destroyed the wooden church, the rectory, and the parish hall. Money was raised, and a new brick church was constructed on the footprint of the old structure and consecrated in 1938. An addition was completed in 1975, but the church remains largely unchanged. The house next door on the corner of Jefferson and Second Streets was purchased in 1956 and is still owned by the church.

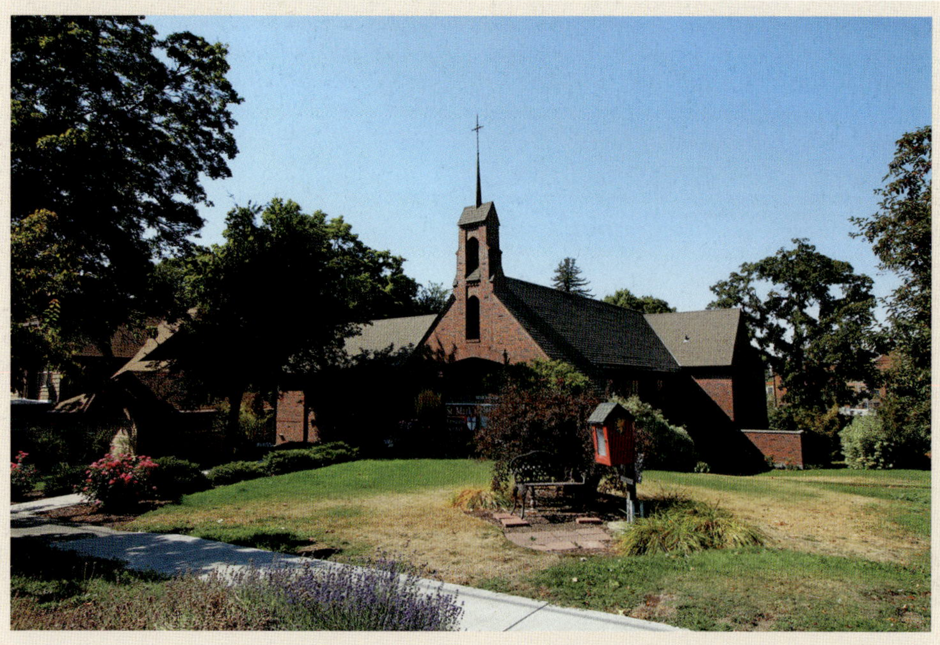

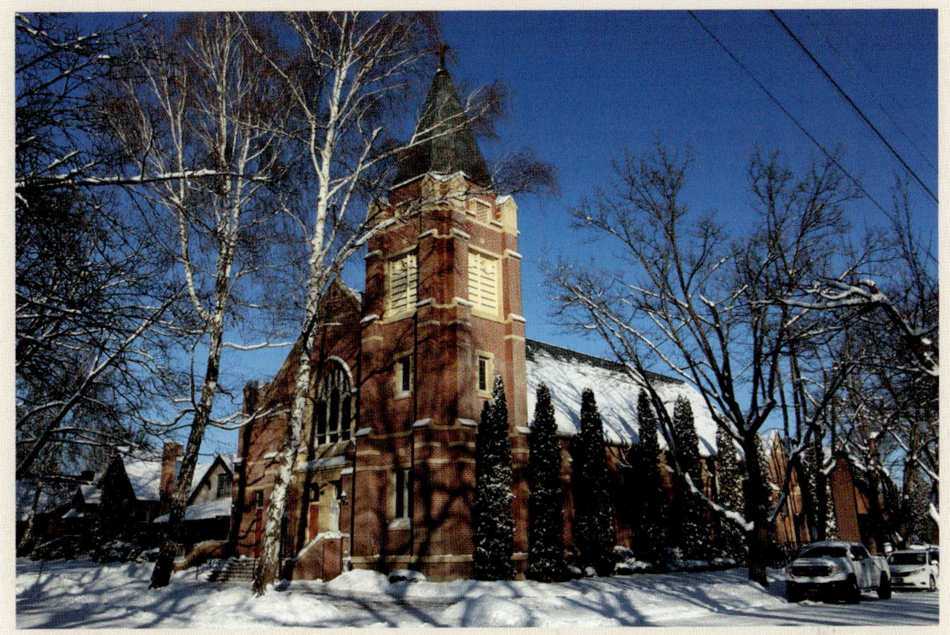

St. Mary's Catholic Church, at the corner of First and North Polk Streets, dates to 1930. Originally known as Holy Trinity, catholic mass was held in various churches throughout Moscow. With the completion of the building, the name was changed to St. Mary's at the request of an anonymous construction donor. The building was renovated in 1968, and a family center was constructed in 1979. The parish acquired land for a school at D and North Monroe Streets and completed St. Mary's Catholic School in 1956.

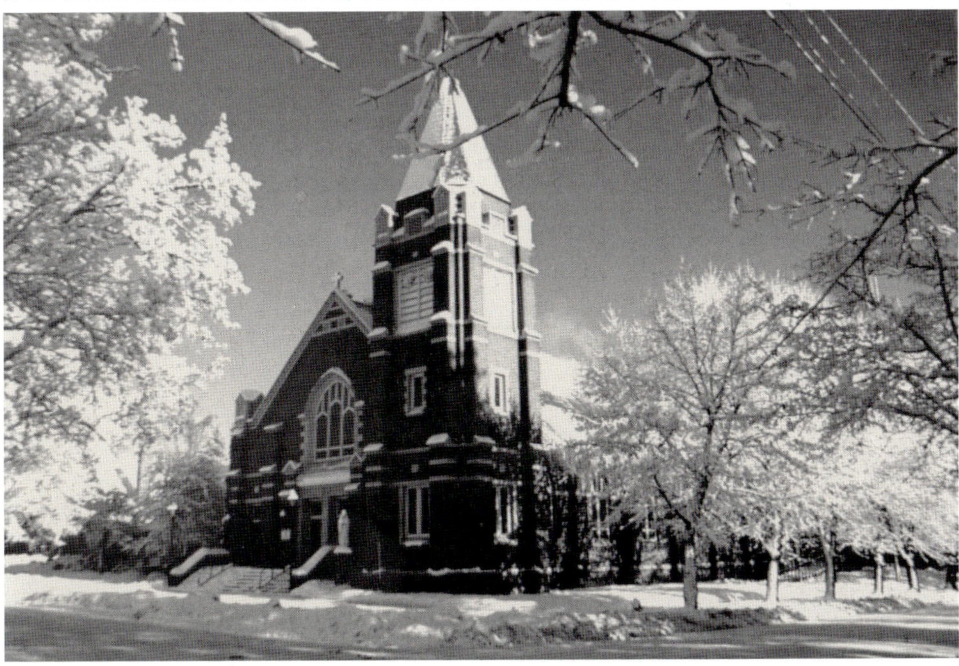

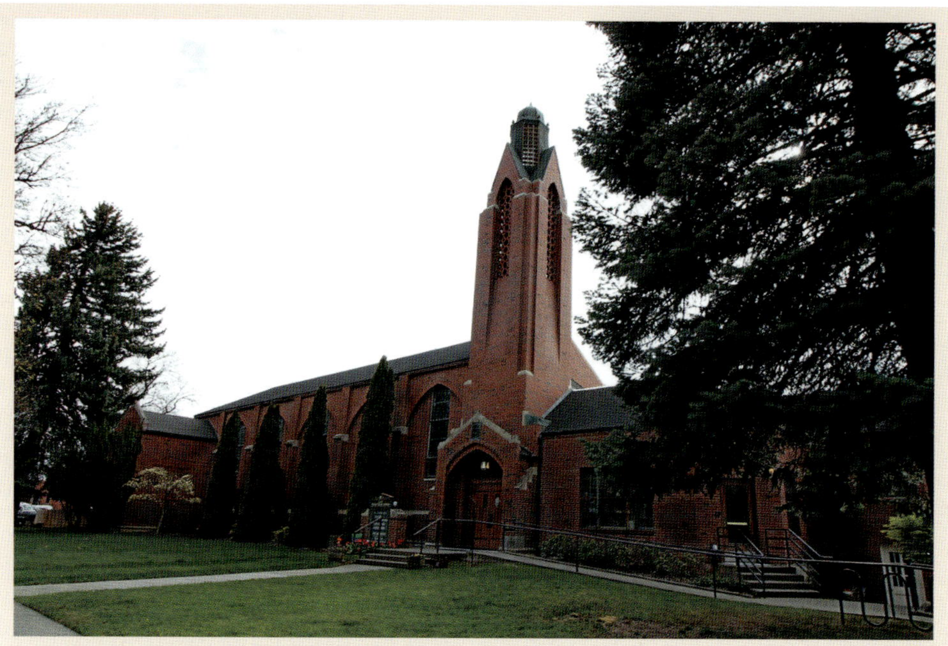

The original First Presbyterian Church was finished in April 1885 at Van Buren and Fifth Streets. This building had several renovations before construction stalled during the Great Depression. The current building was finished as designed by Spokane architects Whitehouse and Price in 1942. Their design repositioned the church to face Van Buren Street and incorporated the Arts and Crafts architectural style with some abstract Gothic Revival elements. The education annex was added in 1966, and further renovations increased accessibility in 1990.

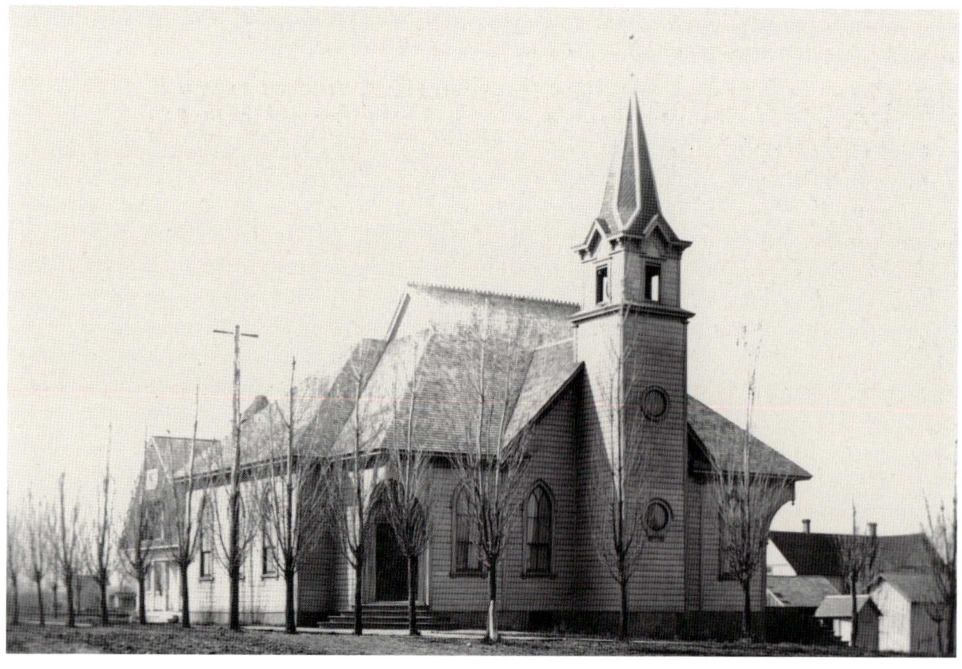

CHAPTER 4

Schools and Public Space

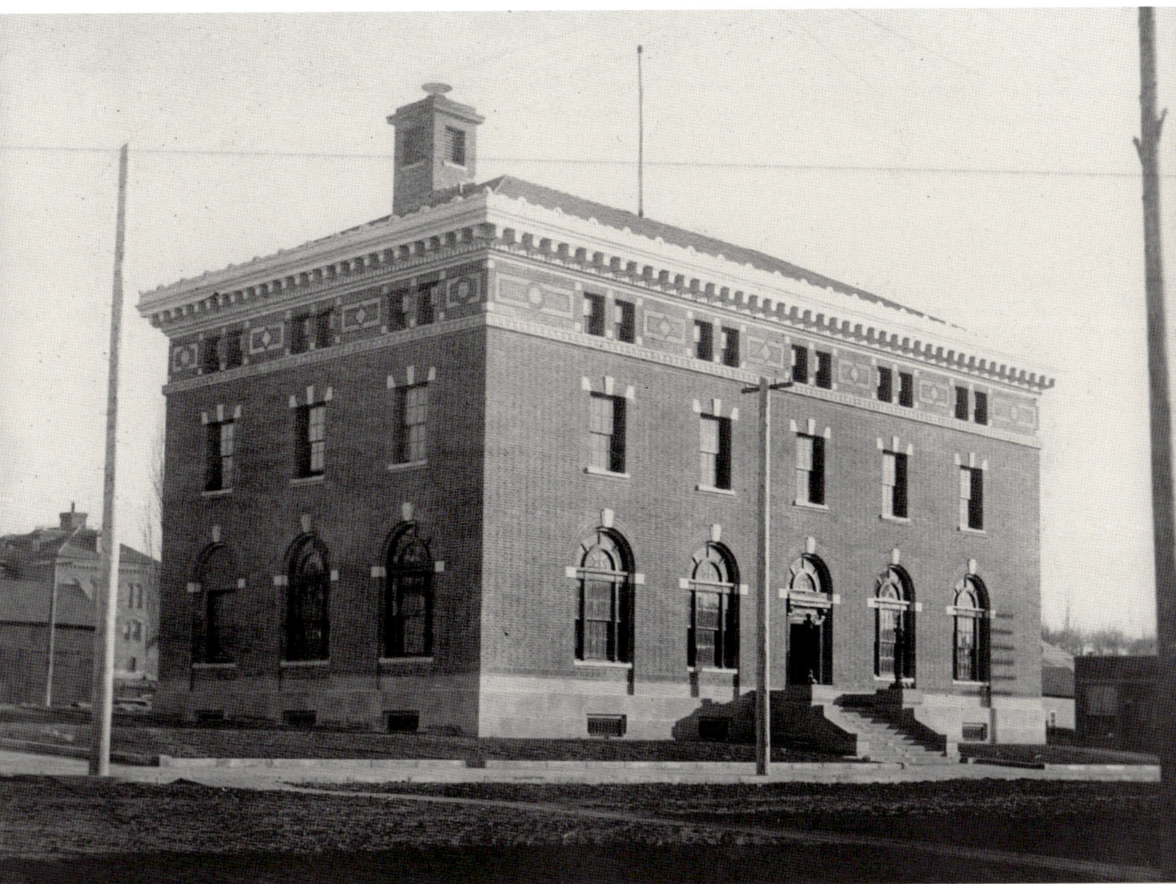

Completed in 1911, this building was known as Moscow's Federal Building, housing the post office and federal courthouse until 1974, when it was vacated and a new federal building was constructed. The City of Moscow purchased the building in 1976, used the space as a community center in the 1980s, and moved city hall from downtown to the building in the early 1990s. The building was placed in the National Register of Historic Places in 1973.

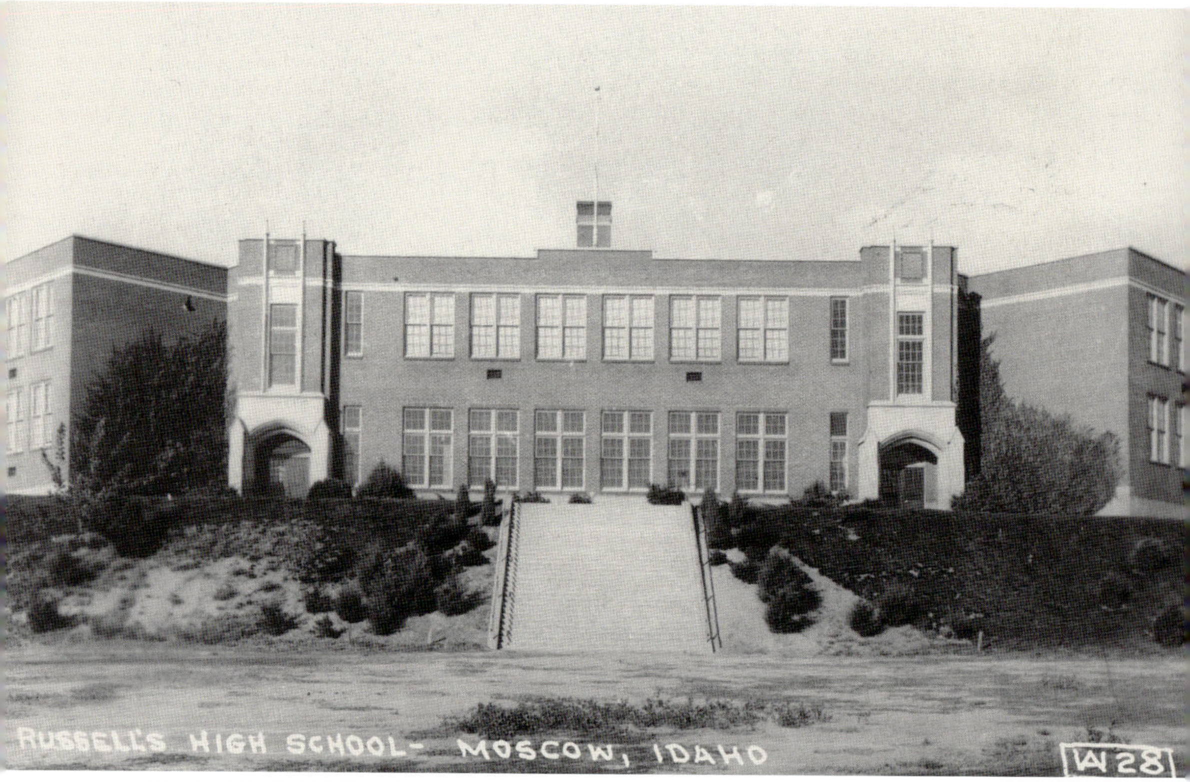

RUSSELL'S HIGH SCHOOL- MOSCOW, IDAHO W28

The Russell School was named for the land donor, John Russell. In 1884, Russell donated this plot of land to the school district for the construction of a school. The first structure was wooden and burned down in 1912. The new school was finished in 1928 and continued to house elementary school students until 2024. A new plan for the building has not been announced.

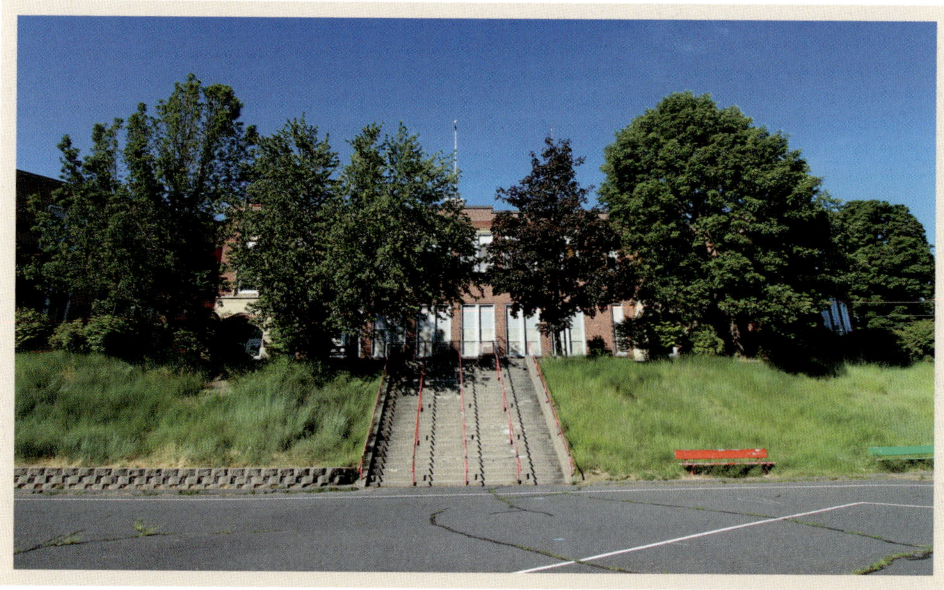

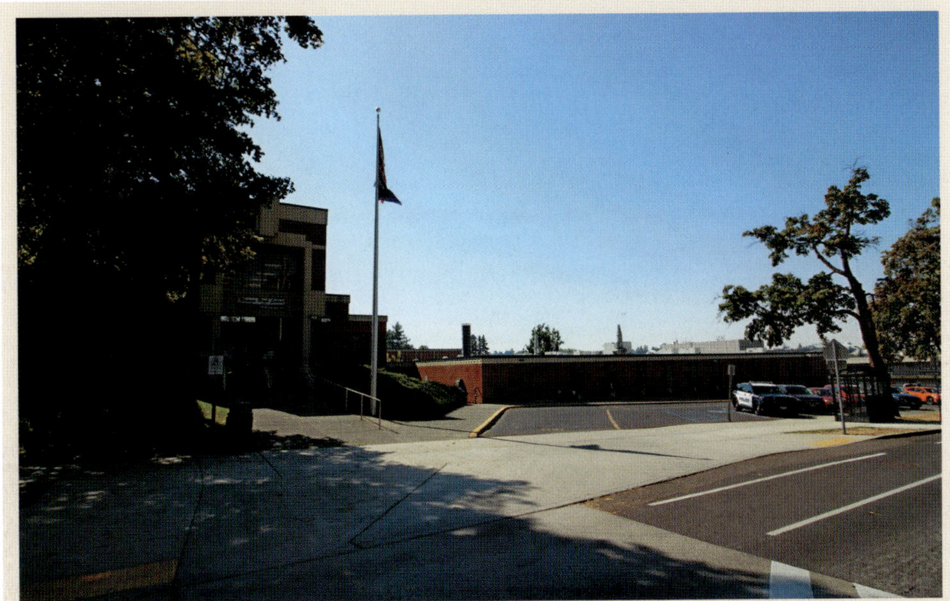

The current high school was not the original high school. Built in 1892, the first school outgrew its space, and classrooms were utilized in the 1912 school built across the street. In 1939, the first high school was razed, and the current high school was constructed. Wings were added in 1968, which covered the original school's footprint, with more renovations in 1991 to accommodate the growing town.

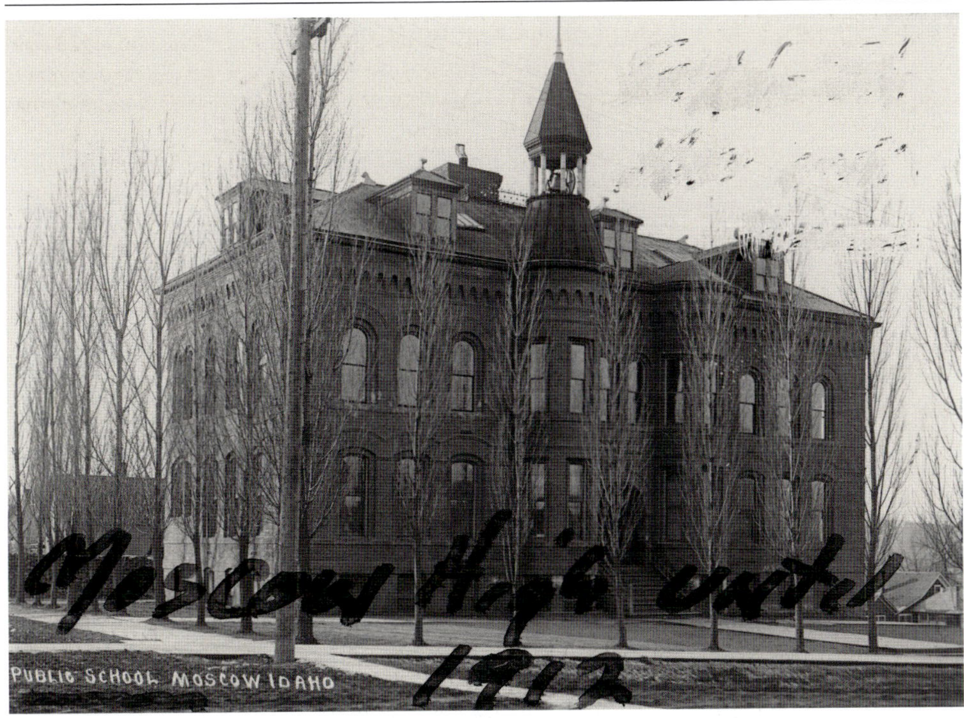

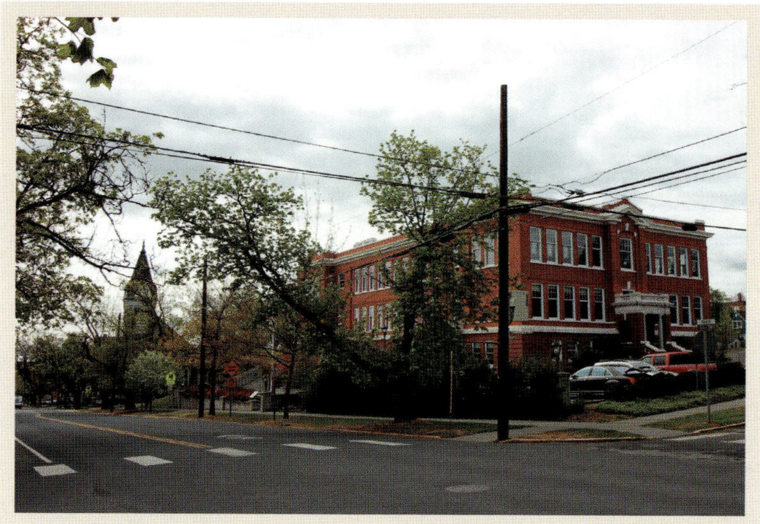

This school was finished in 1912, with high school and elementary students utilizing the building. Over the years, it was also the Moscow Junior High and was referred to as the "Whitworth School." Later, it was used for offices, and in the early 1990s, the building was slated for demolition. In 1997, citizens raised funds for the City of Moscow to purchase the building from the school district. The building first opened to the public in 2001 as a community center and has been undergoing renovations ever since.

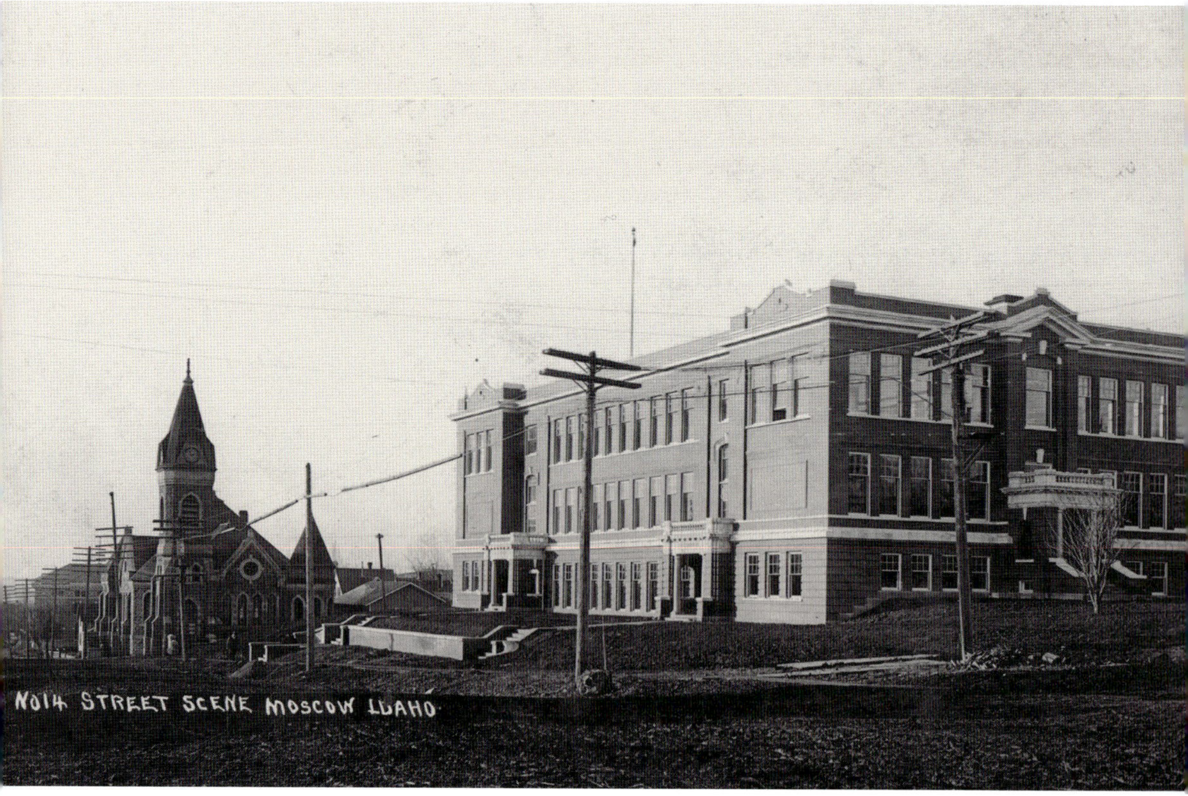

NO14 STREET SCENE MOSCOW IDAHO

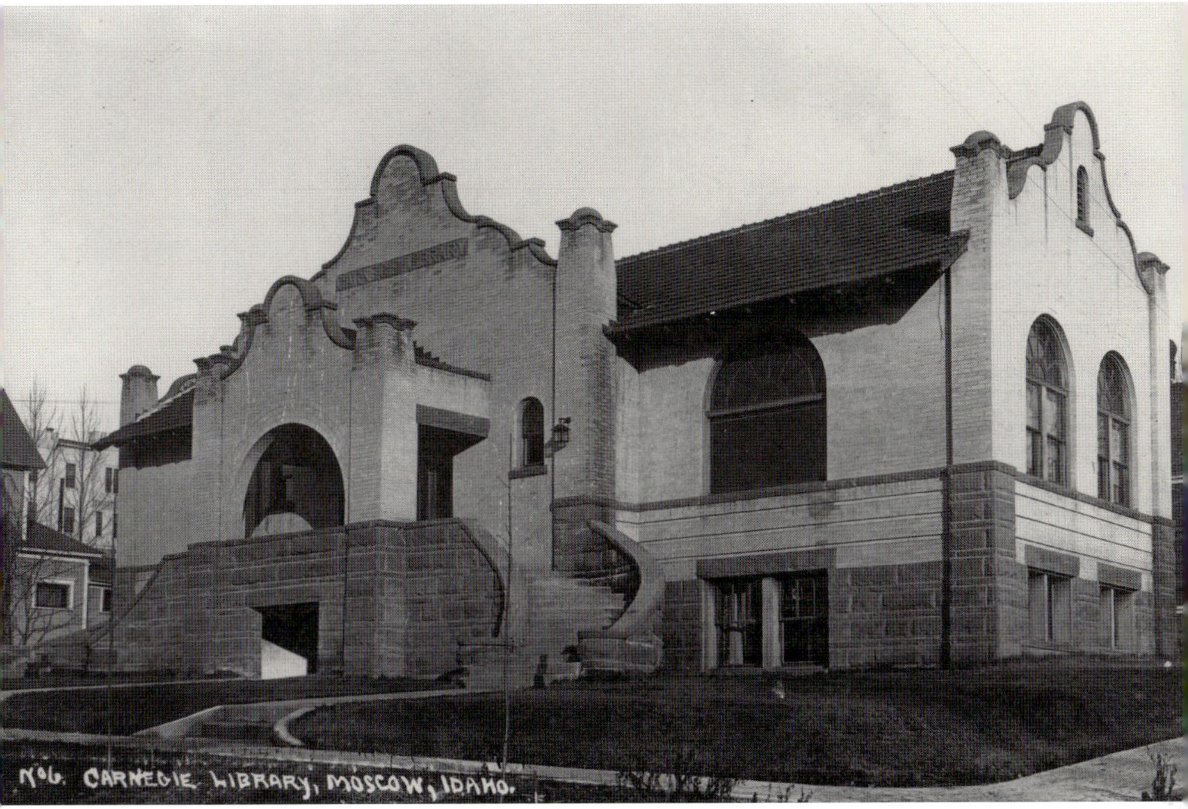

No6. CARNEGIE LIBRARY, MOSCOW, IDAHO.

In 1906, members of the Moscow Historical Club and Pleiades Club successfully raised enough money to open the Moscow Public Library with the help of the Andrew Carnegie Library Endowment. Designed by architect Watson Vernon, the Spanish Mission style is not one commonly seen in northern Idaho. In 1982, the building underwent a significant expansion and more than doubled the space available. At that time, the children's area was designated as the Carol Ryrie Brink Reading Room. The building was placed in the National Register of Historic Places in 1979.

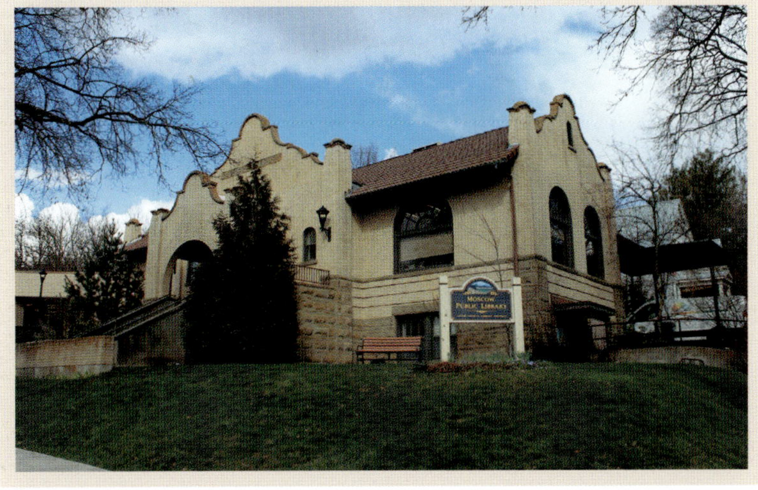

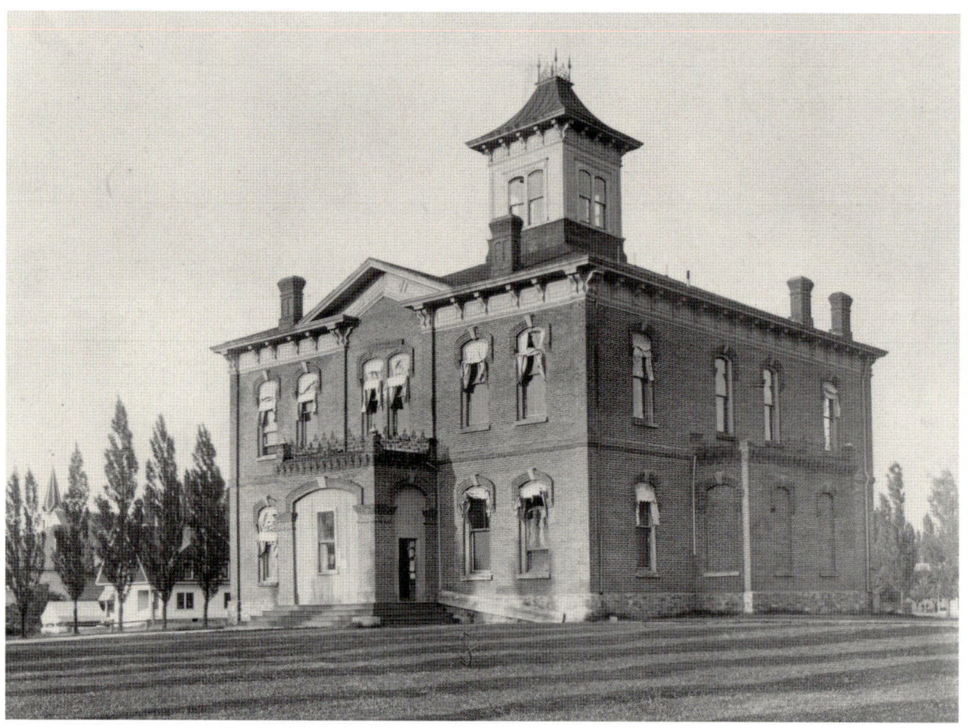

Constructed from 1888 to 1889, the original Latah County Courthouse occupied its place upon the hill overlooking Moscow between Fifth and Sixth Streets. The jail was originally part of the building, but in 1927, a new jail facility was erected behind the courthouse. As Latah County grew, a new facility was needed. The courthouse was demolished in 1958, and a new building was constructed in its place. Then, in 1973, a new jail and law enforcement center was constructed adjacent to the 1958 offices.

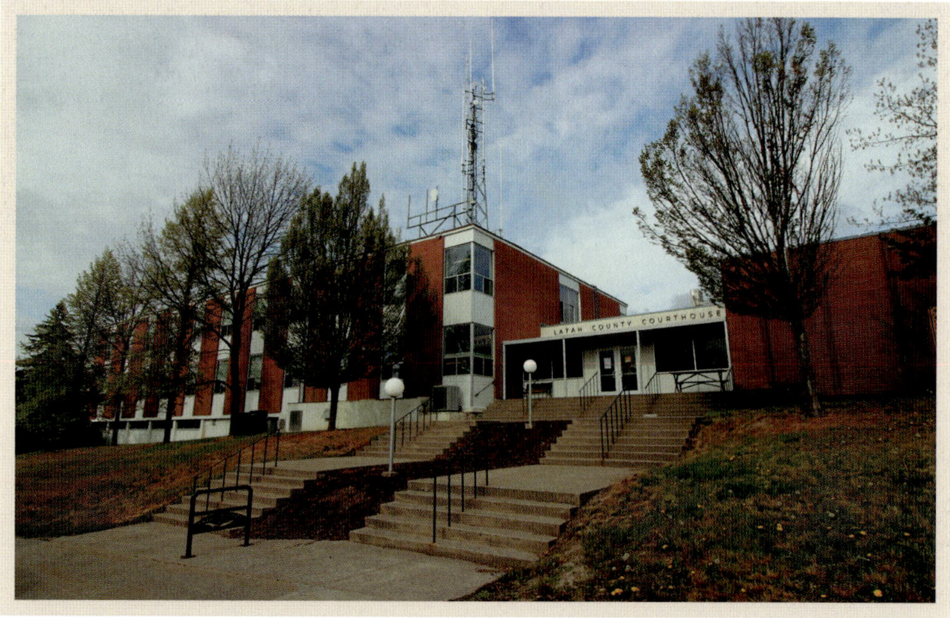

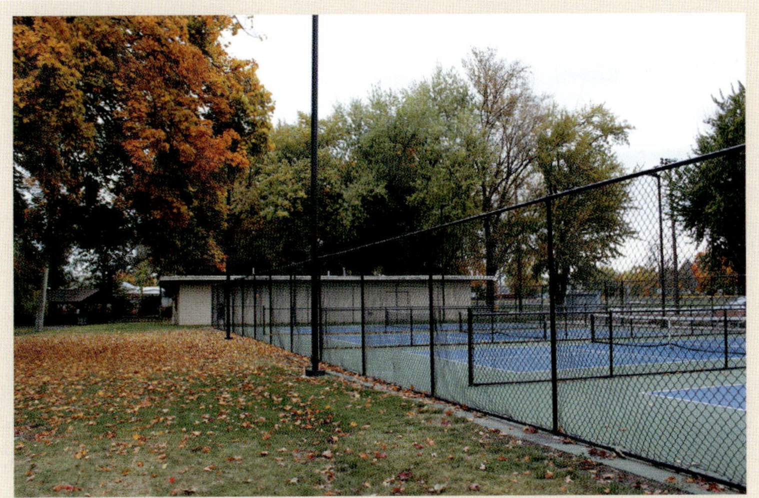

The Latah County Fair Commission purchased an area now referred to as Ghormley Park in 1913. Previously, the area housed a sports field, golf course, and park space. In 1921, the commission donated the land to the City of Moscow for use as a park. In 1933, the city installed a community pool, and in 1942, the pool and adjacent park were dedicated to Moscow Navy veteran Robert L. Ghormley. Ghormley's military career included service in both World War I and II, two Distinguished Service Medals, and Legion of Merit honors. In 1999, the pool was demolished and filled in, adding to the park lawn space and tennis courts.

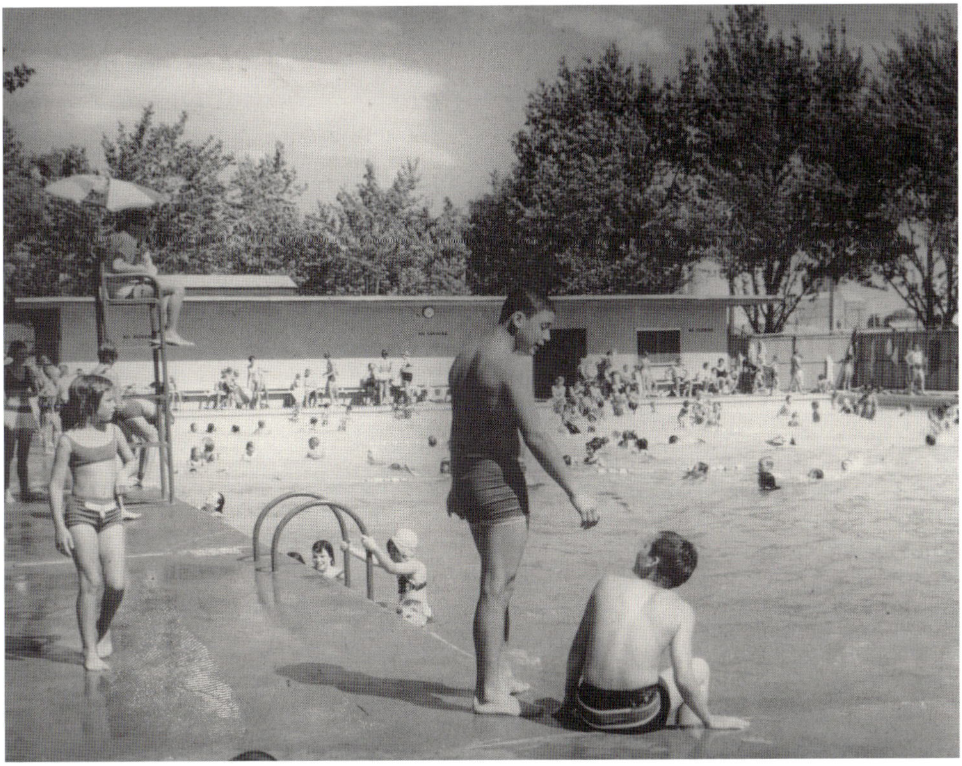

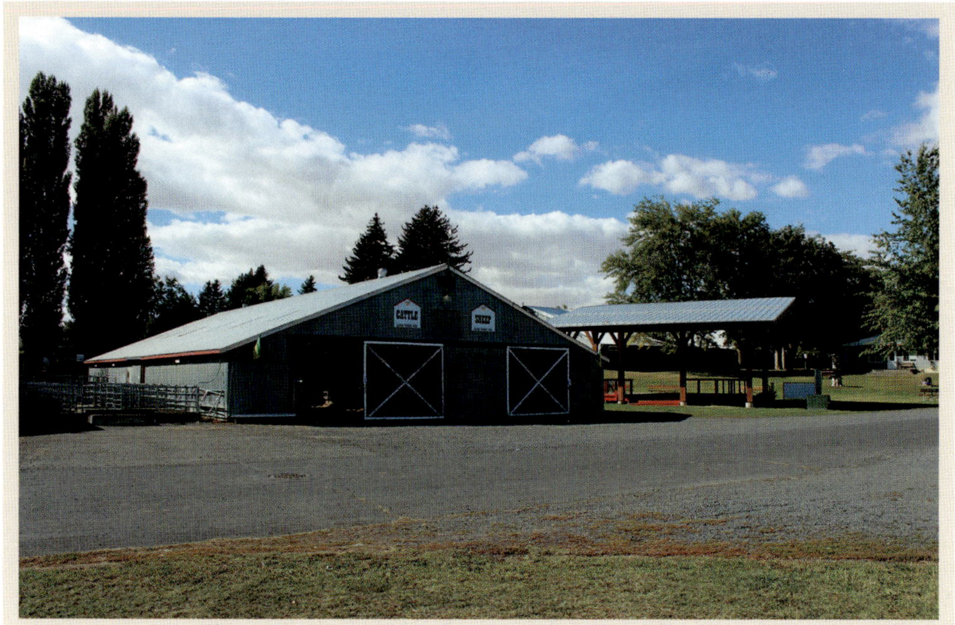

Once considered the edge of town, the current Latah County Fairgrounds was not the original location of the fair. The county's first fairs were held downtown at Nathaniel Williamson's store, at the Grange Hall, and at Ghormley Park. The Latah County Fair Board purchased the current fairgrounds land in 1955, constructing the barns and exhibit buildings over the years. The Latah County Fair continues at this location every September.

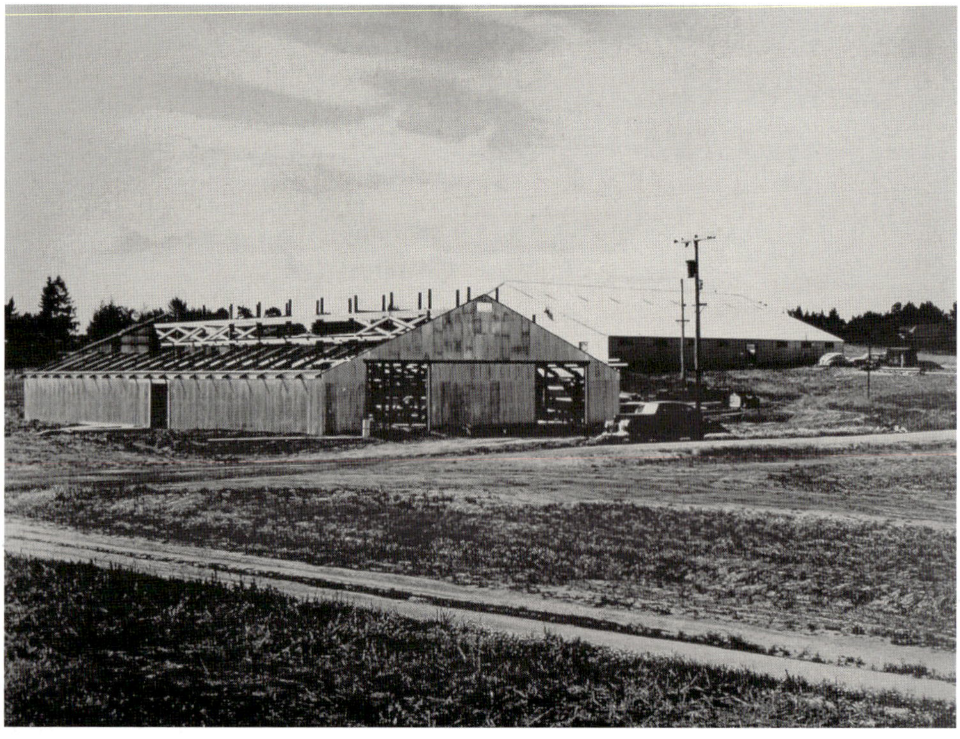

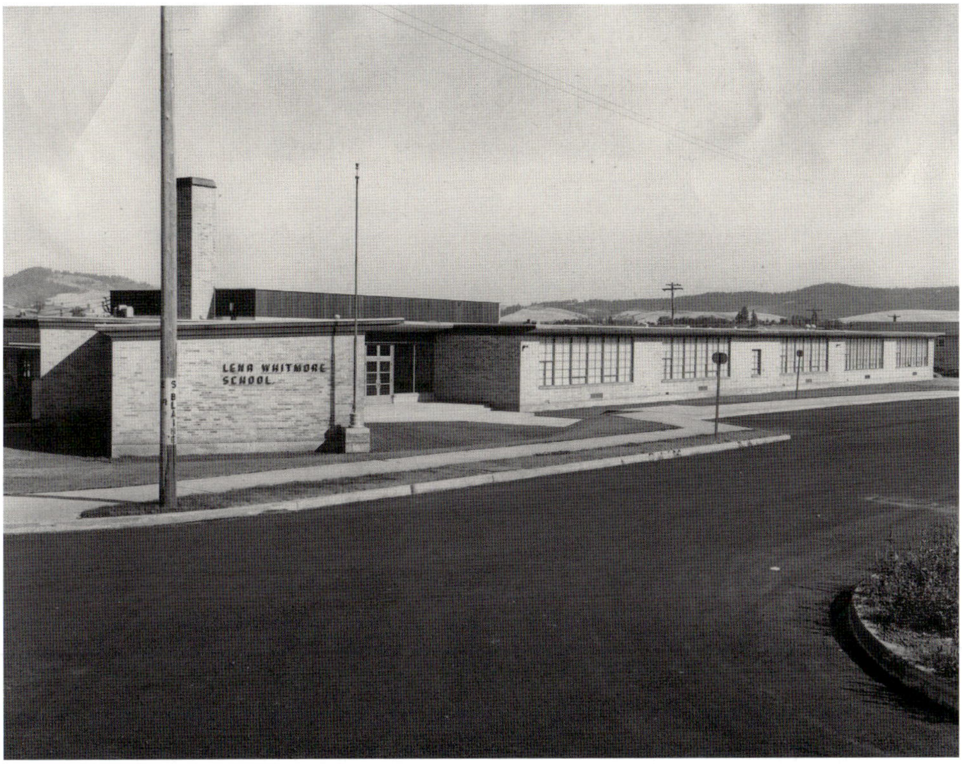

Named for one of Moscow's beloved teachers, Lena Whitmore Elementary School has been serving students since 1952. Lena Whitmore began her teaching career at Russell School and retired in 1950 after 48 years in education. The building was renovated in 1991 to enlarge the gymnasium and add a library. The school continues to serve elementary students today. Behind the school is Lena Whitmore Park, completed in 1976 and maintained by the City of Moscow.

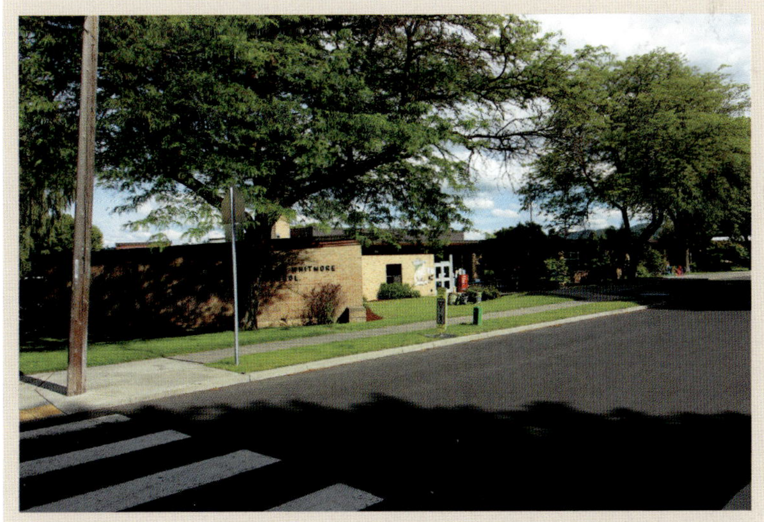

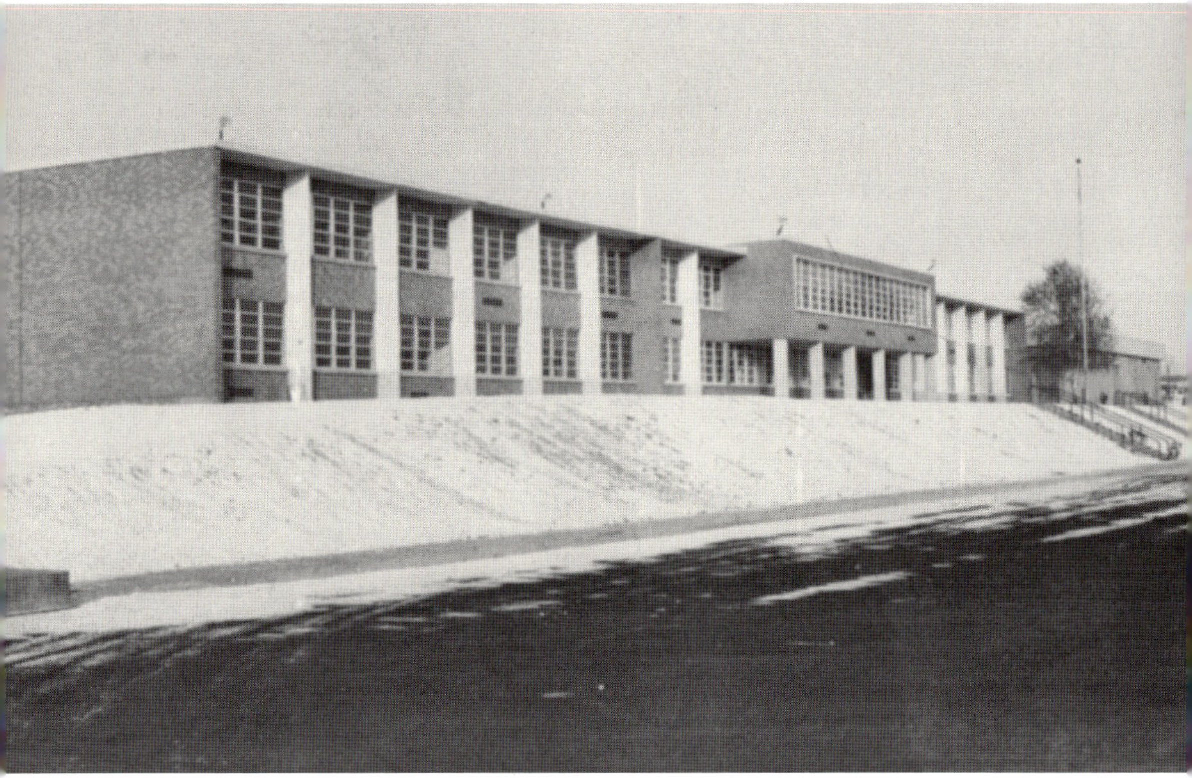

Built in 1959, the Moscow Middle School, between D and F Streets and bordered by Mountain View Road, was once considered the edge of town. Originally called the Moscow Junior High School, this building alleviated crowded classrooms in what is now referred to as the 1912 Center. The extra space for sporting activities means that this school hosts the Moscow High School athletic teams throughout the year, with the school district office nearby. Several renovations expanded the building, the largest of which added another wing in 1990.

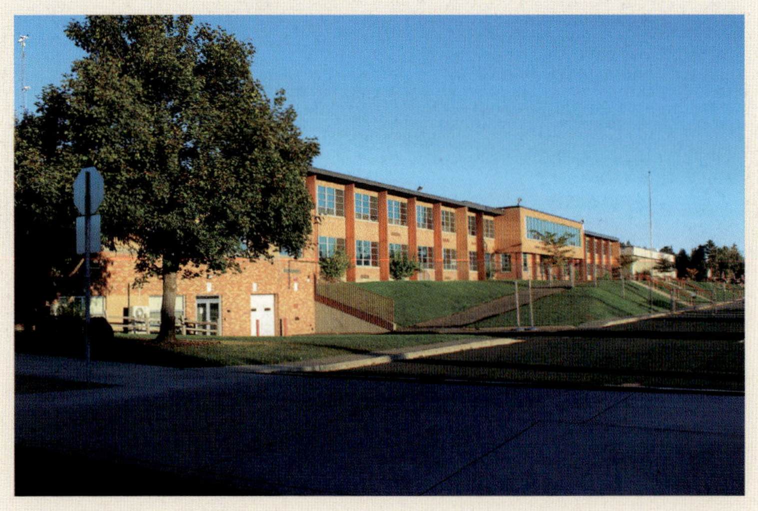

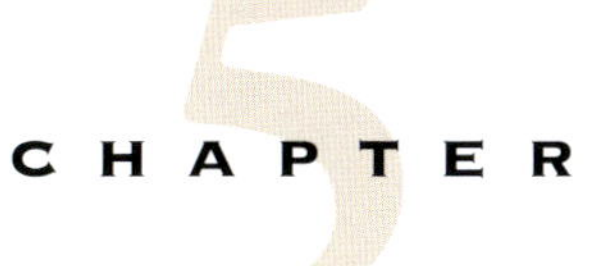

CHAPTER

Residential Scenes

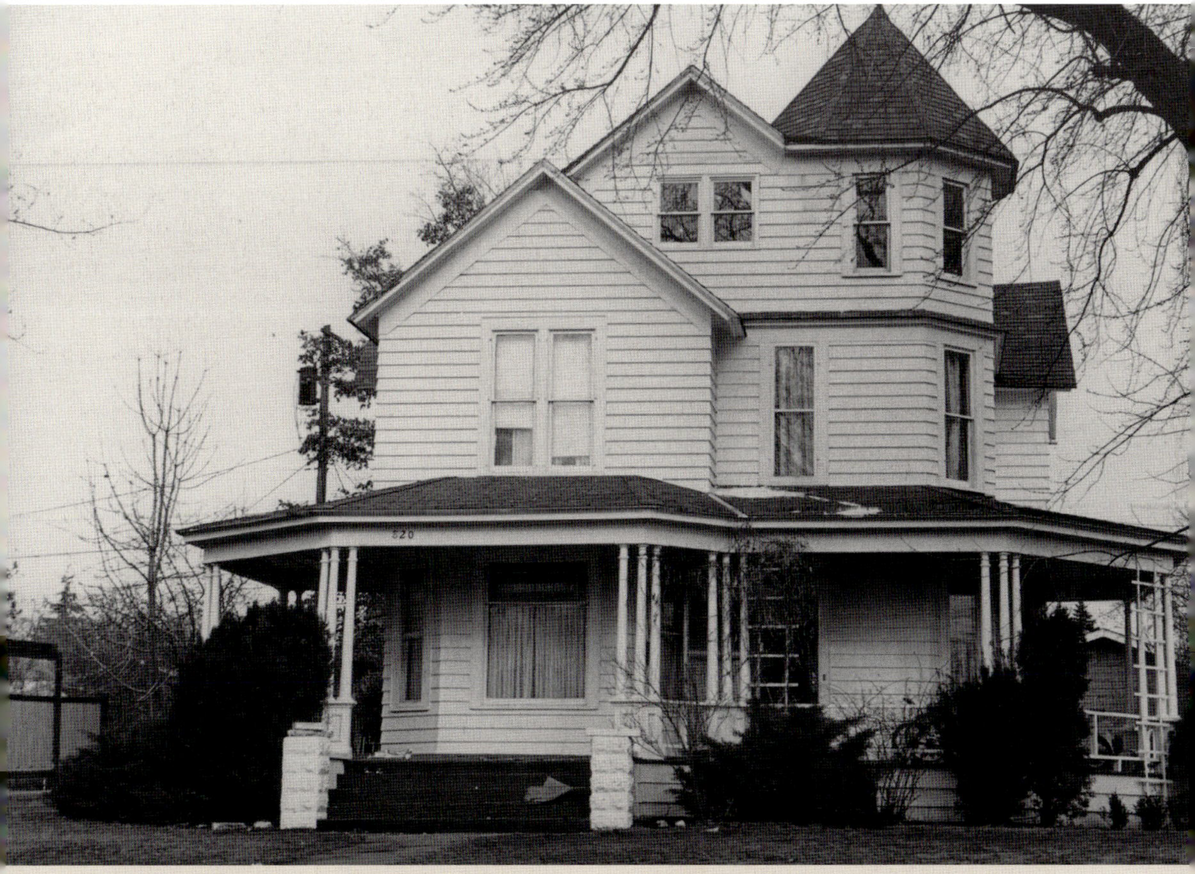

Jesse and Frances Randall built this home around 1904 at the corner of Lincoln and B Streets. Randall made his living as a farmer southeast of Moscow and decided to move into town upon his retirement. The house is now part of the Fort Russell Historic District, which historically has included many of Moscow's early, ornate homes of the wealthy. The original 1980 district boundary did not include this house, but the 2017 boundary change now encompasses the area between Jefferson, D, Hayes, and Third Streets.

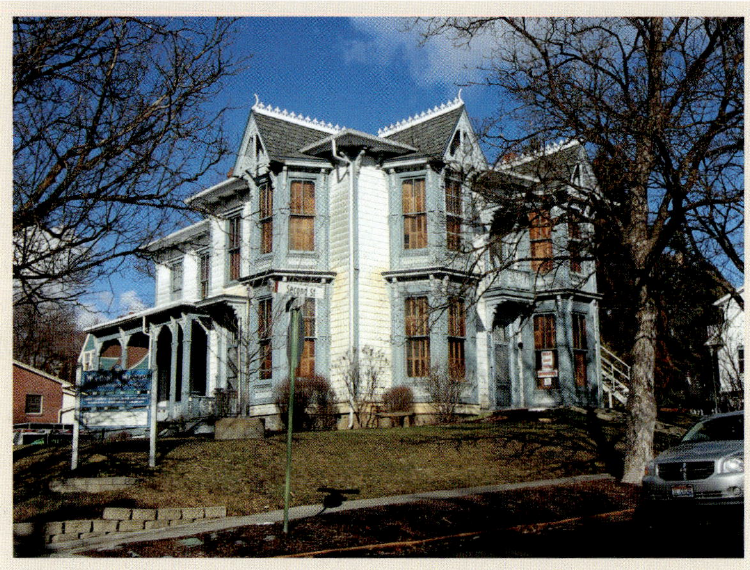

William J. McConnell commissioned this house in 1886, and he and his family moved in on Christmas Eve that year. They lived there until 1897, when an economic depression forced McConnell's business into bankruptcy. The house was then owned by the Adair and Jackson families. The last private owner was Frederic Church, a history professor at the University of Idaho. Upon his death in 1966, he gifted the house to Latah County to use as a meeting place and museum. The Latah County Historical Society has operated the building as a museum since 1970.

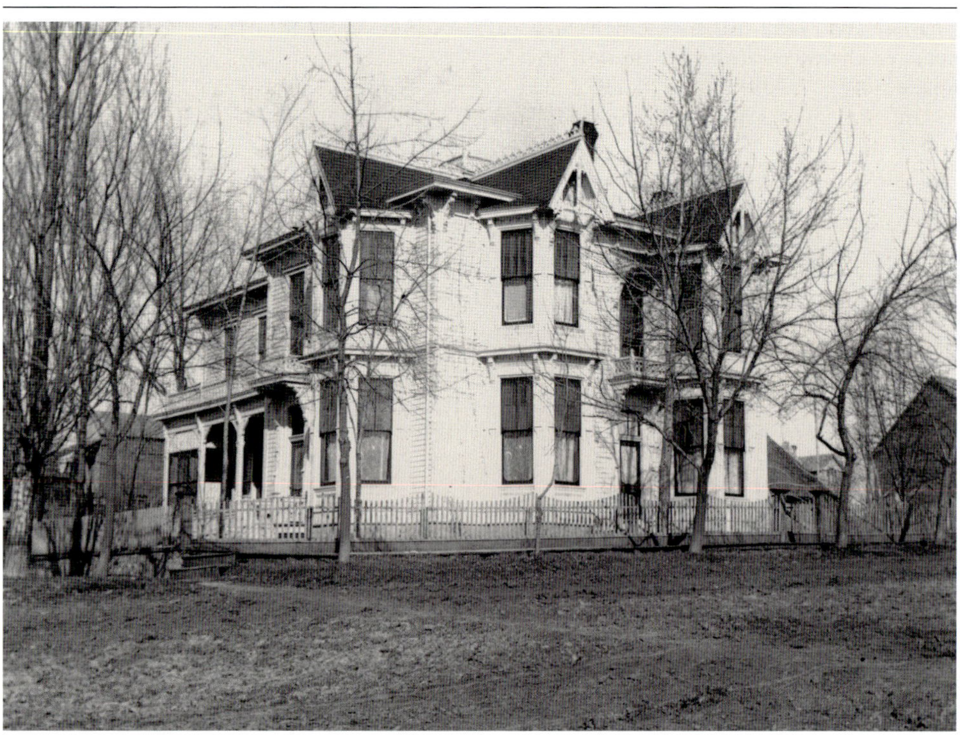

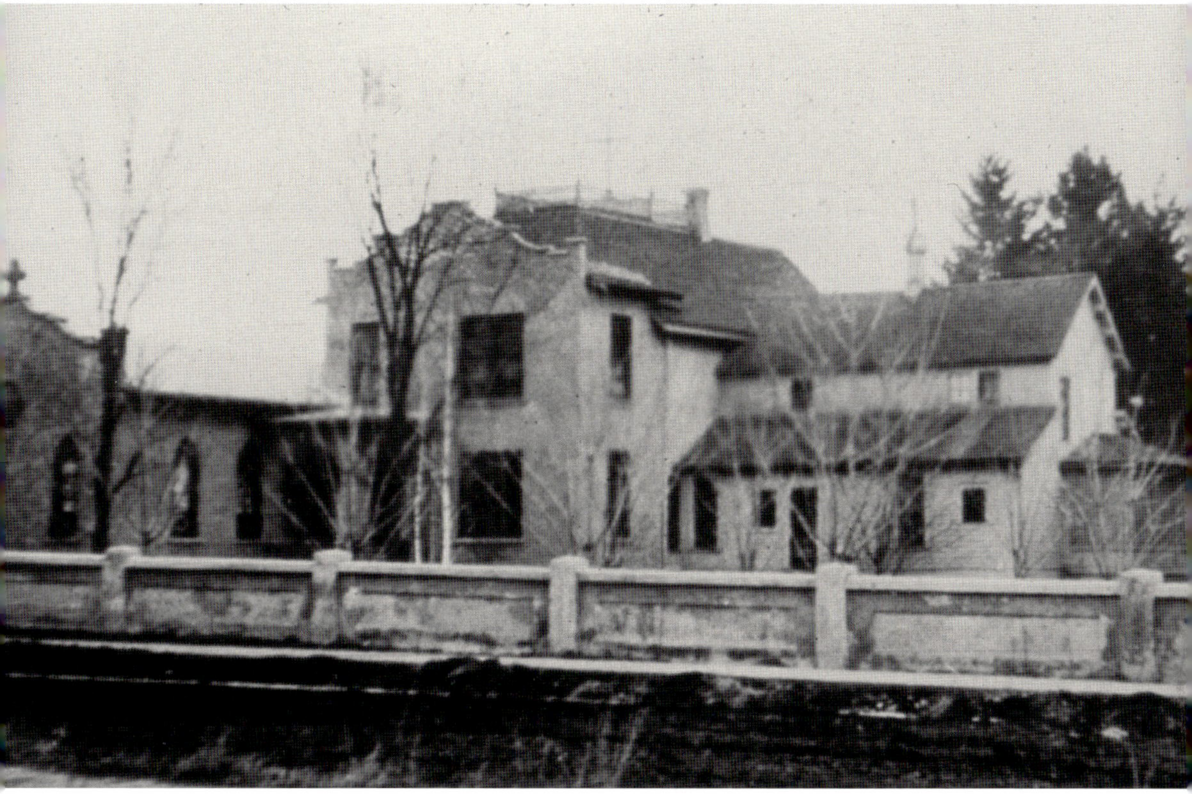

Charles and Julia Moore completed this house on the corner of D and Howard Streets in the 1880s. In 1908, the Ursuline Sisters rented, then purchased, the Moore residence as a Catholic school to house the Ursuline Academy. They used the Moore house as the academy until St. Mary's Catholic School opened across the street in 1956. In 1962, a new convent was constructed on the site of the Moore house. The Sisters lived on-site until they sold the convent building in 2018.

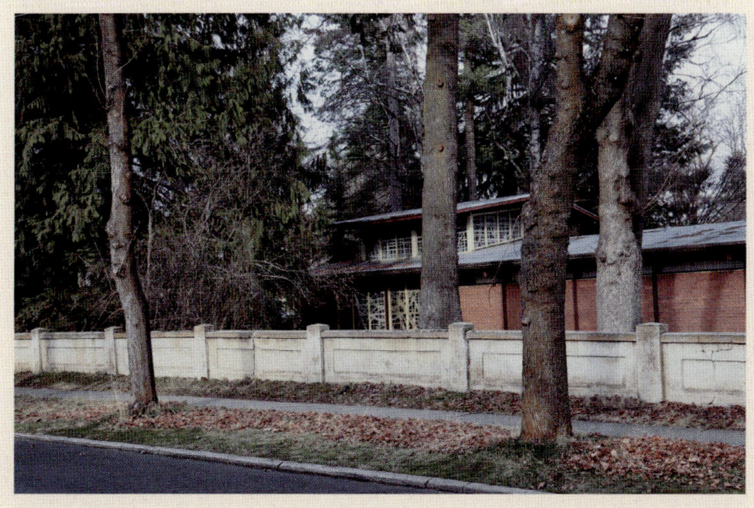

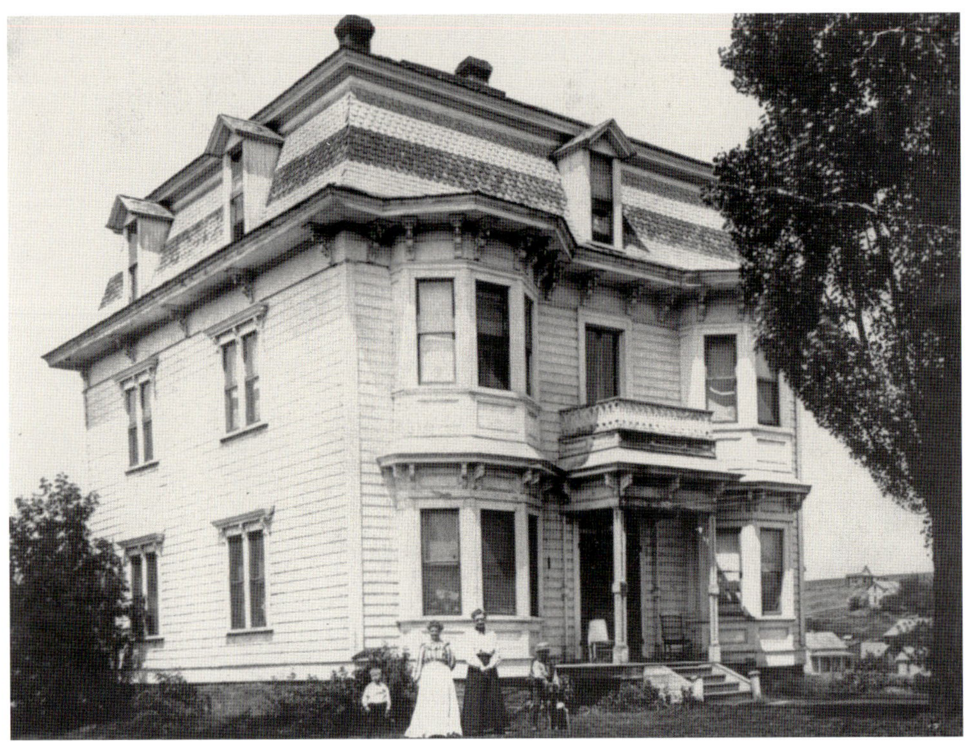

Almon Asbury Lieuallen came to Moscow in the 1870s and was one of the area's first homesteaders. He built this home in 1884 in the middle of a wheat field at what is now the intersection of First and Almon Streets. Local lore recounts that the Lieuallen children used the top undivided floor as a roller rink. University of Idaho faculty and the Kappa Sigma fraternity lodged here before Lieuallen's daughter Lillie converted the house into six apartments in 1917. The house was placed in the National Register of Historic Places in 1978.

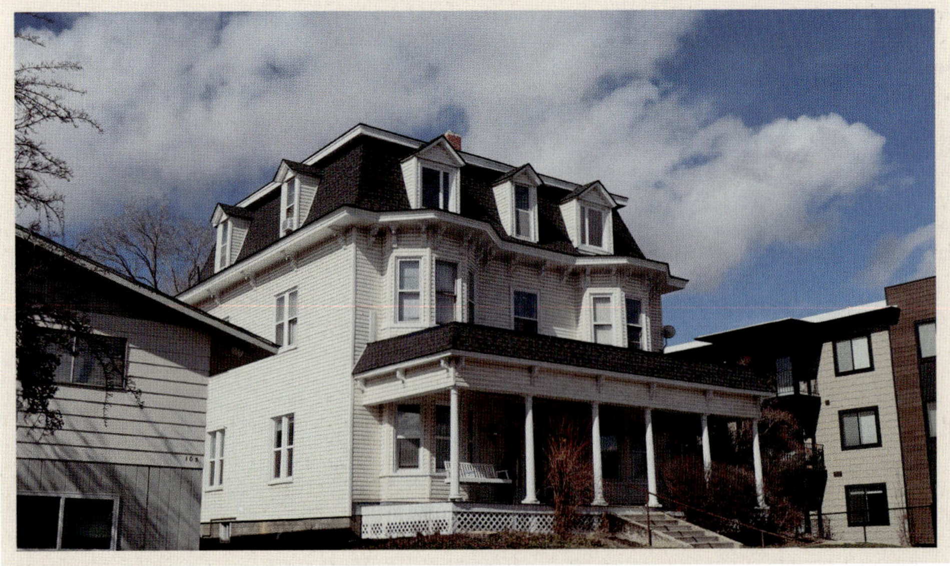

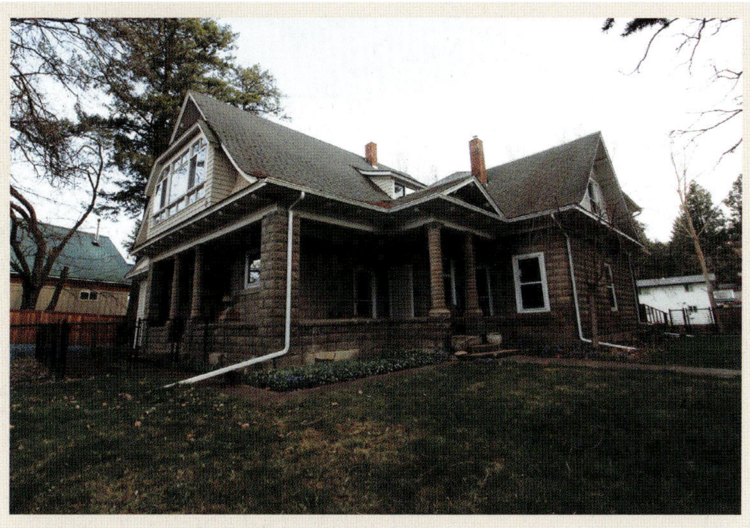

Wylie and Minnie Lauder lived on Van Buren Street before constructing this house near the University of Idaho campus at 1320 South Deakin Extension around 1907. Lauder partnered with his brother-in-law Tom Taylor to form a construction and brick company. They built many of Moscow's early downtown and university structures. At the time of its construction, this house was relatively secluded, but as the campus has expanded, more houses and apartments surround the property. Adjacent street names honor both the Taylor and Lauder families.

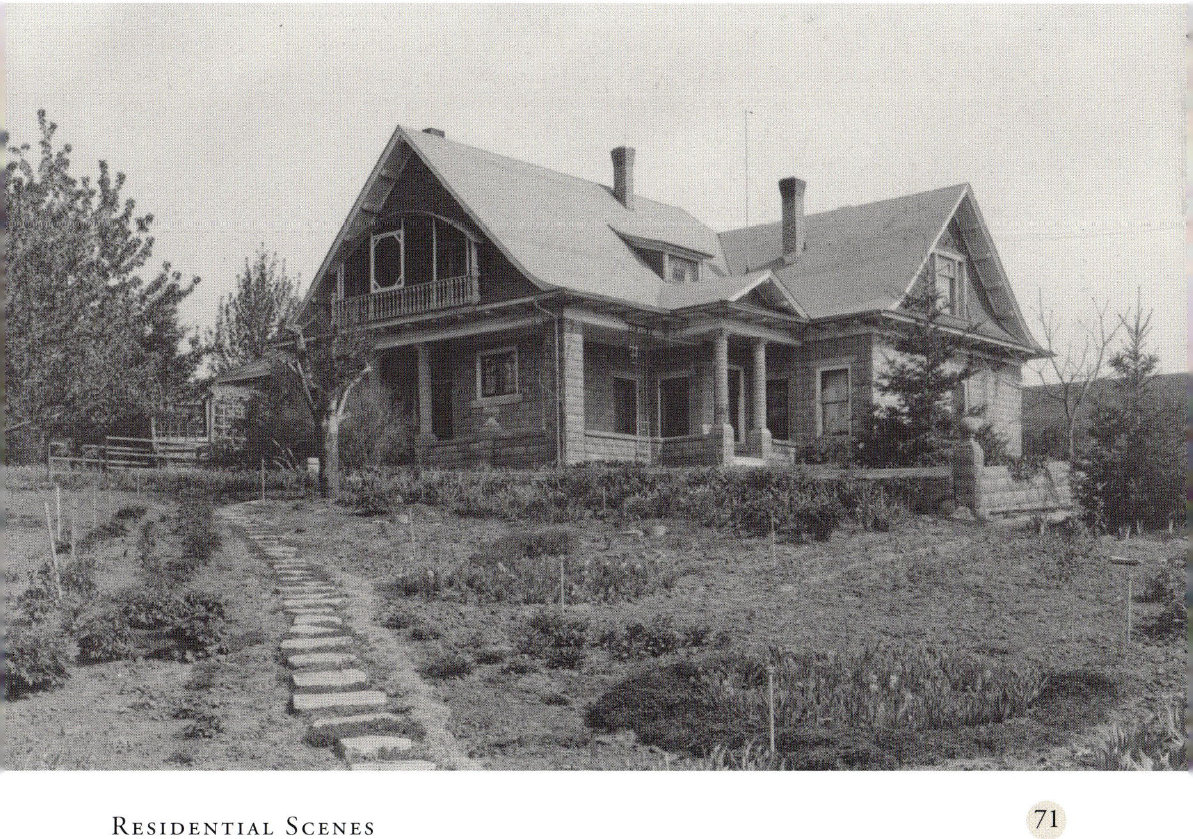

Jerome Day made his fortune in the mines of Coeur d'Alene and built this stately house in 1904, complete with a carriage house and 24 rooms. A banker and politician, Day helped create Latah County in 1888 and served on the University of Idaho Board of Regents for many years. The family's prominence made this home a popular social gathering place. Much of the house's exterior remains unchanged. The interior was divided into apartments, and a library wing was added at some point.

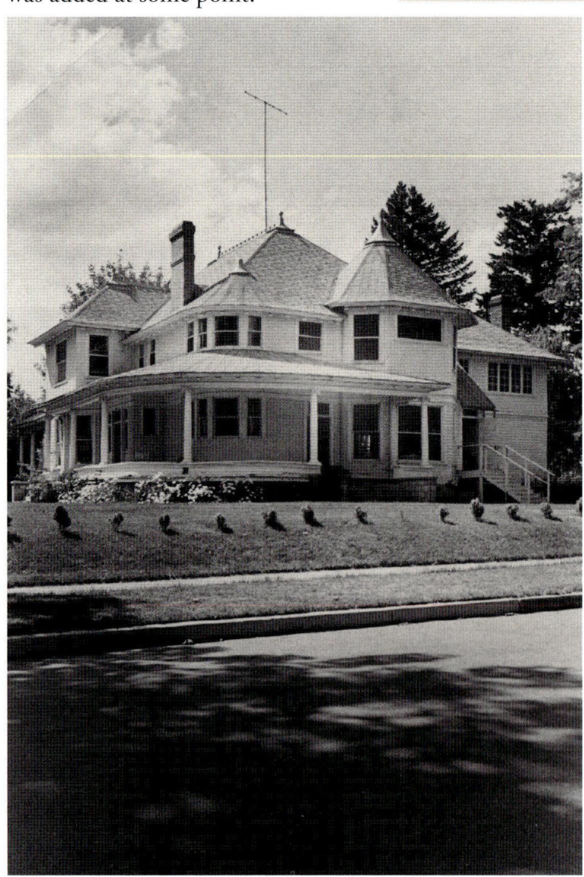

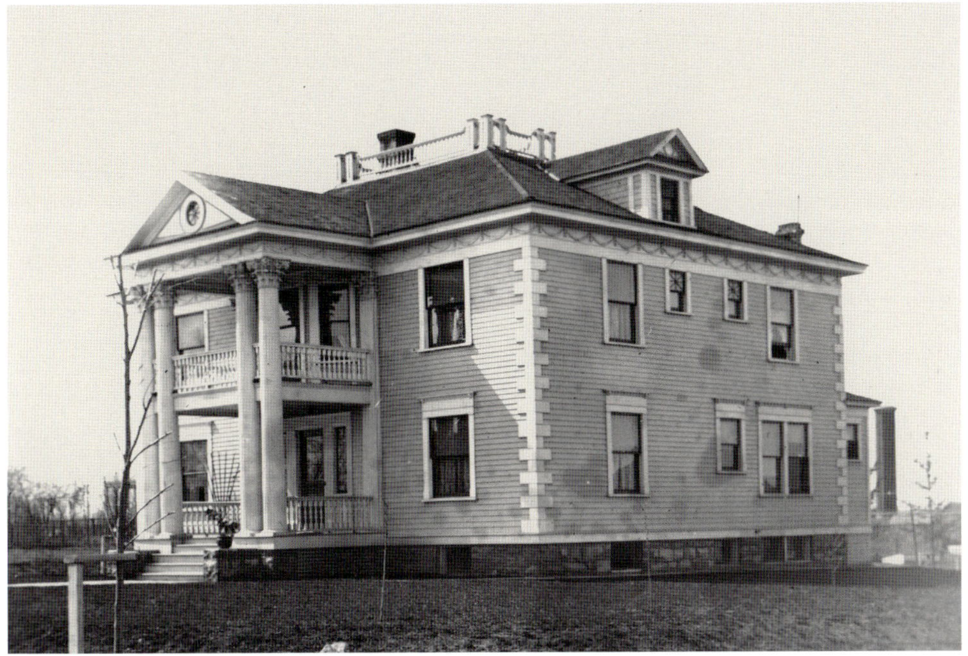

A local businessman, Charles Butterfield, built this home at 403 North Polk Street in 1902. It is one of the few examples of Greek Revival architecture in Moscow, complete with Corinthian columns on the front porch. In 2024, the house is now broken up into apartments, a visible fireplace was added, and the widow's walk on the roof is no longer there. This house is part of the Fort Russell Historic District, placed in the National Register of Historic Places in 1980.

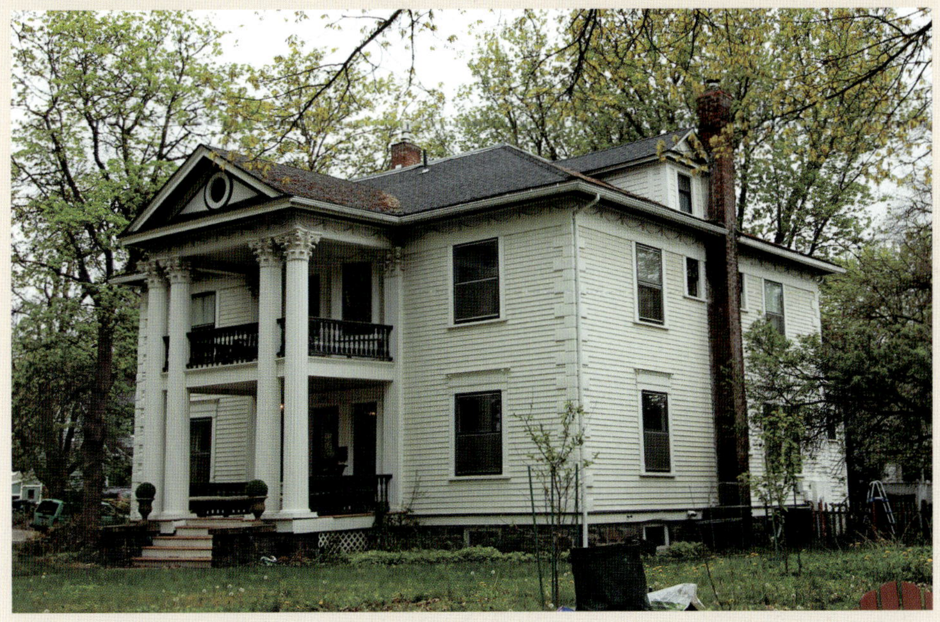

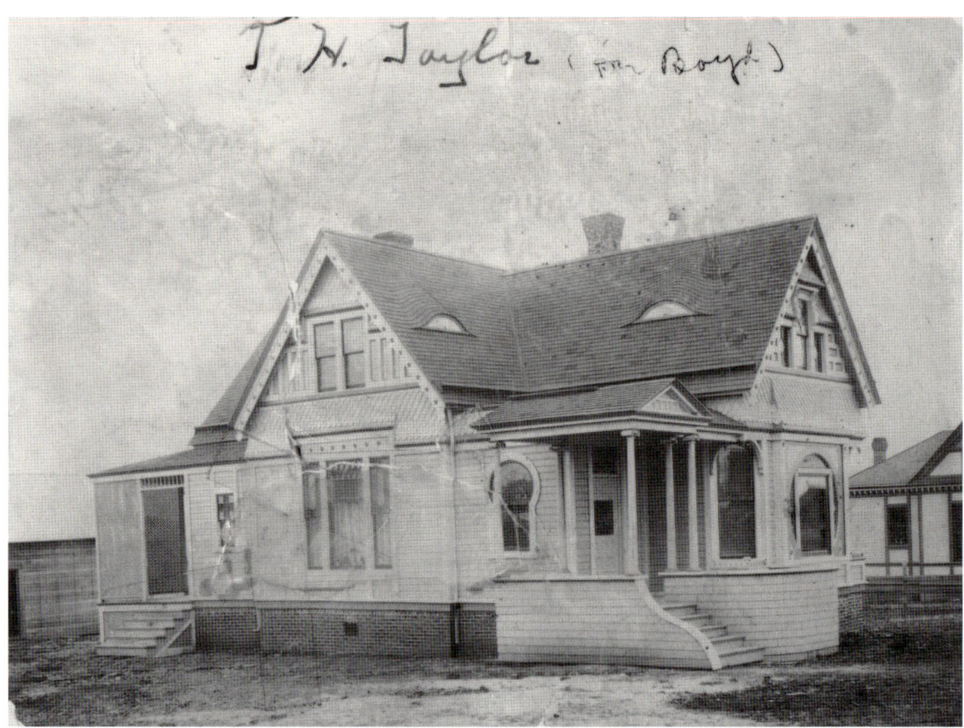

Alexander Ryrie built this small Queen Anne cottage at the corner of A and Polk Streets in 1893. Ryrie was one of Moscow's early mayors and the father of celebrated author Carol Ryrie Brink. A plaque on the front porch notes this house as the birthplace of Brink. Tom Taylor, a partner in the Taylor and Lauder brickyard and construction company, bought the house from Ryrie. The house has been painted pink for the last 20 years, which accentuates the intricate ornamentation and distinctive front round window.

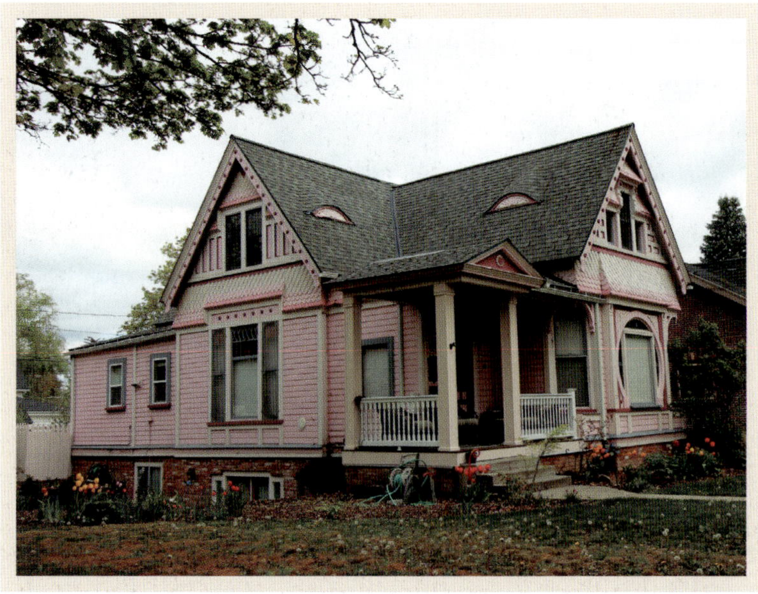

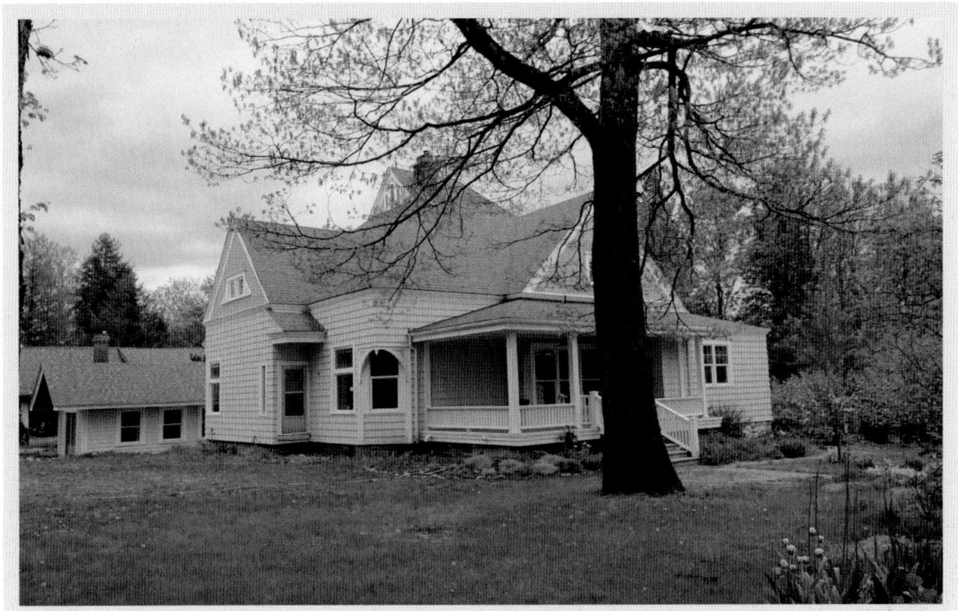

At the corner of A and Van Buren Streets, Alfred and Maggie Spotswood completed this house in the early 1890s. Spotswood operated a real estate business downtown during Moscow's early growth. His friend Fred Veatch lived with the family here until his own marriage. A nearby street bears Spotswood's name, recognizing him as an important businessman in Moscow's infancy.

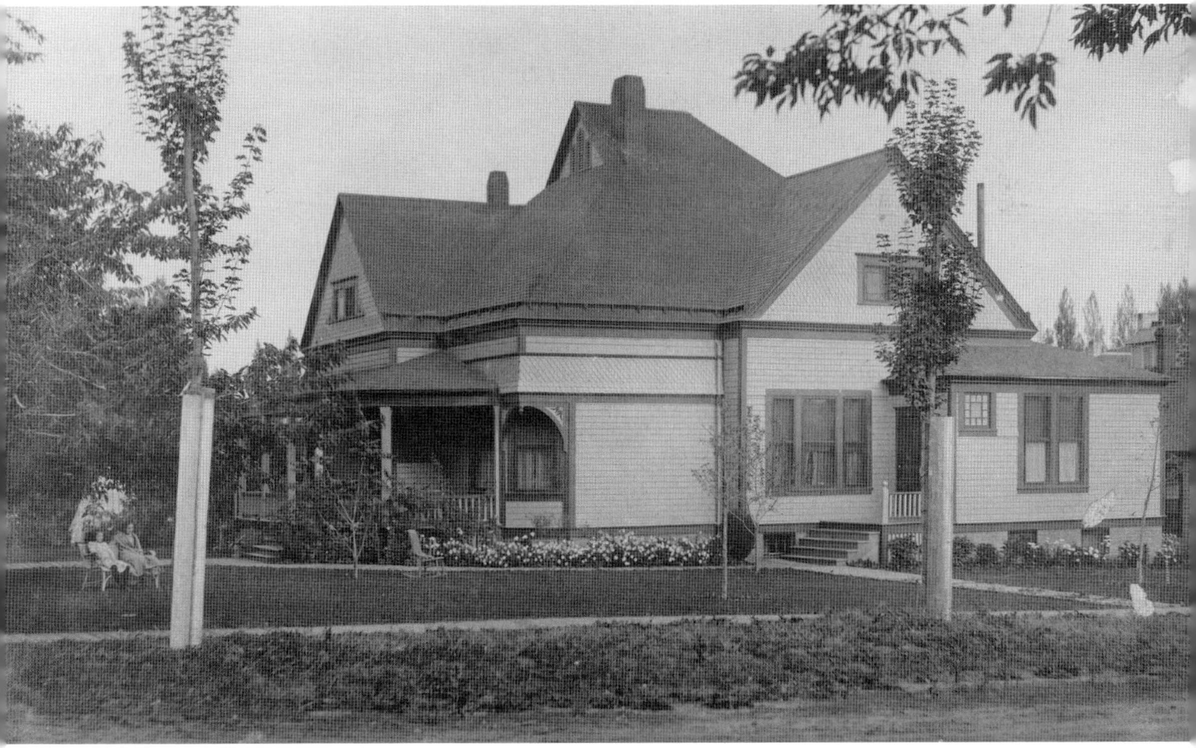

This home is located at 803 East Seventh Street, in area of Moscow referred to as "Swede Town" due to the numerous Scandinavian families that lived here in the early 1900s. Victor Ramstedt built this home in 1904 using earnings from his job at George Creighton's Store. Ramstedt began working with Creighton in 1894 and purchased Creighton's in 1923. Ramstedt's son Allen and son-in-law Milford Peterson purchased the store in 1962. Creighton's Department Store closed in the 1980s, and Cactus Computers opened in the 1990s.

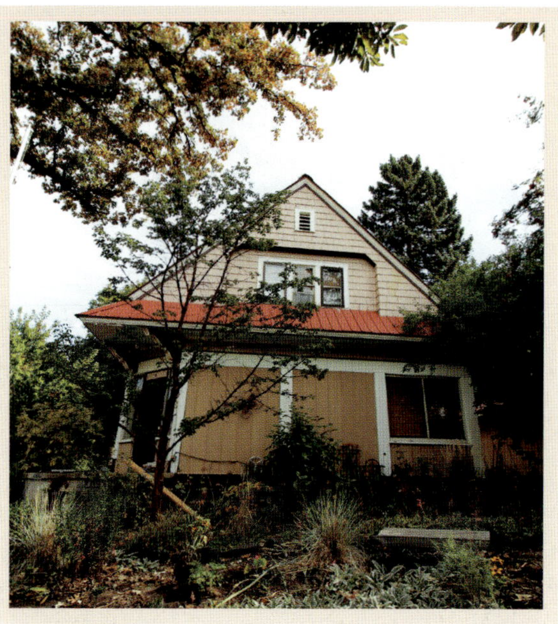

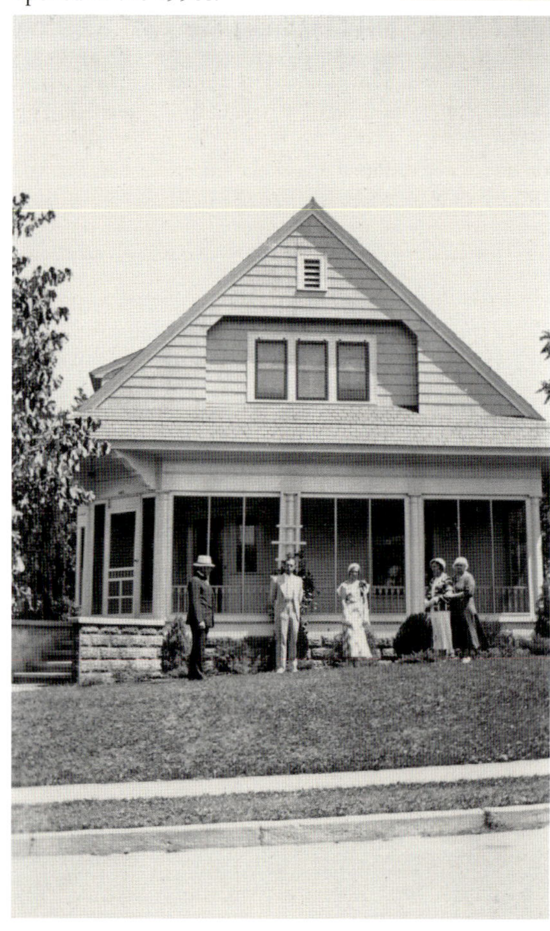

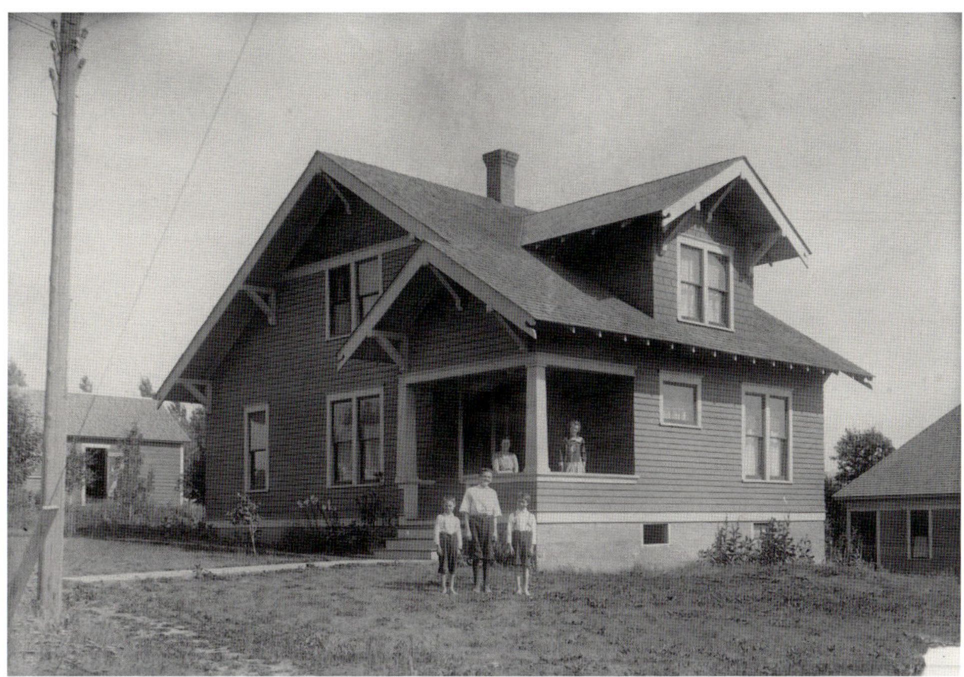

Otto Charles and Rhoda Belle Carssow built this home at 503 Spotswood Street shortly before his death in 1913. Belle continued to live in this house until her death in 1964. Otto is noted in Moscow's history for establishing Moscow's Leading Grocery store in the early 1900s. Their son Eugene later took over the business. The Carssows were early supporters of the Latah County Pioneer Association, the predecessor of the Latah County Historical Society.

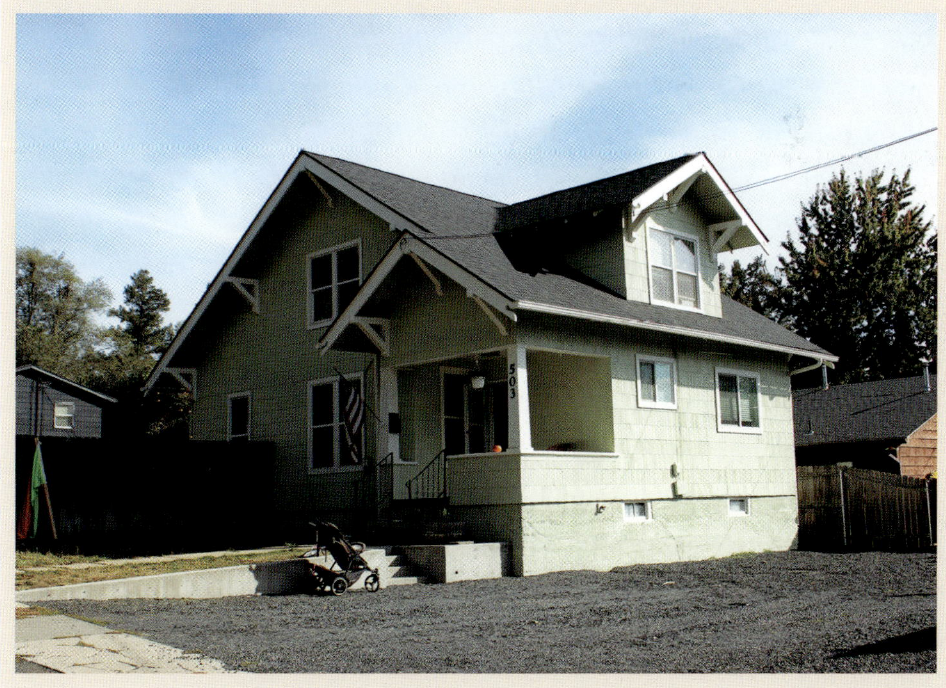

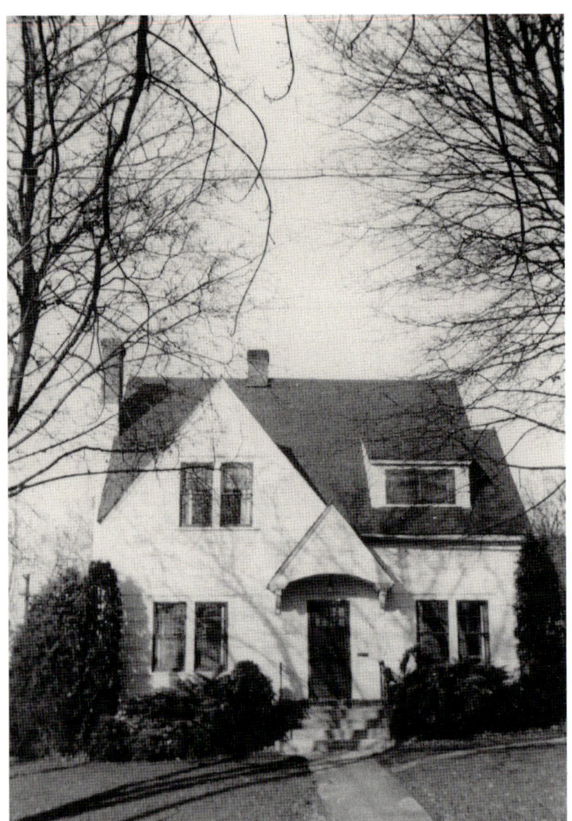

Mi and Marie Lew owned this home while they operated the Grill Café at 214 South Main Street. Marie's father purchased Huff's Café in 1926 and changed the name to the Grill Café. Mi and Marie took over the business in 1931 and operated the restaurant until 1970. The home is now subdivided into apartments, but the property is owned by Mi and Marie's grandchildren.

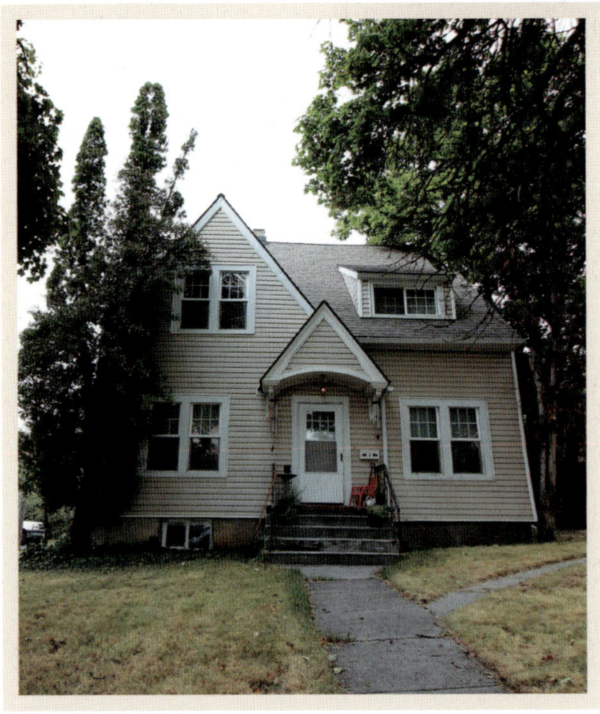

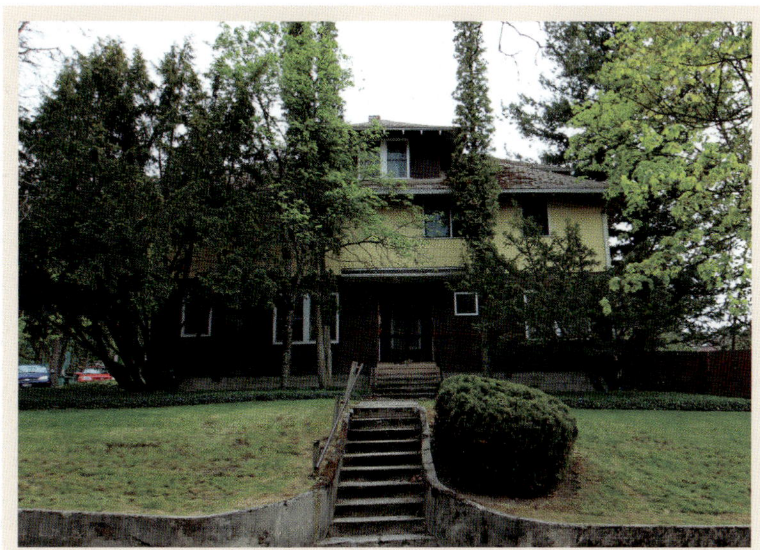

This house, built at the corner of Van Buren and East Third Streets in 1911, was a rooming house run by Emma Edmundson. Many university faculty members and undergraduates called the house home by the 1920s. The structure was later renovated into apartments, with the upstairs porch closed in. Today, the building is still used as apartments.

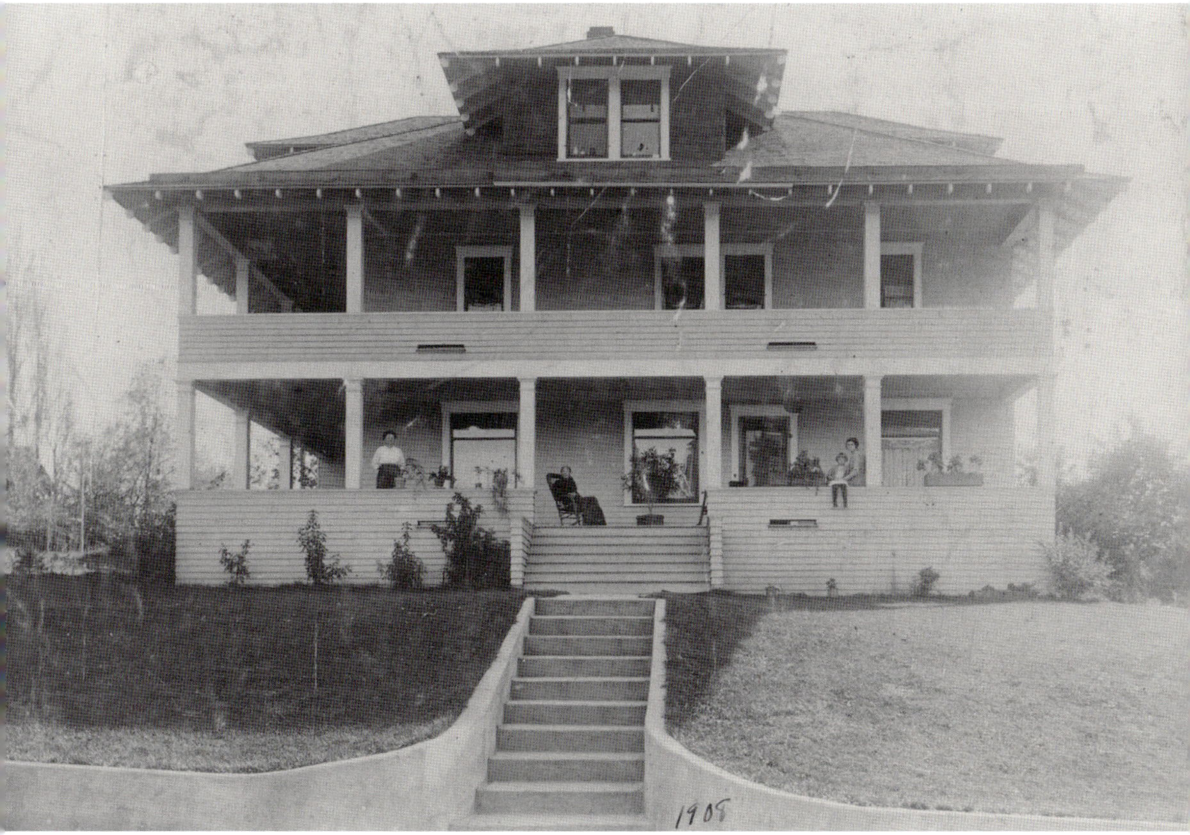

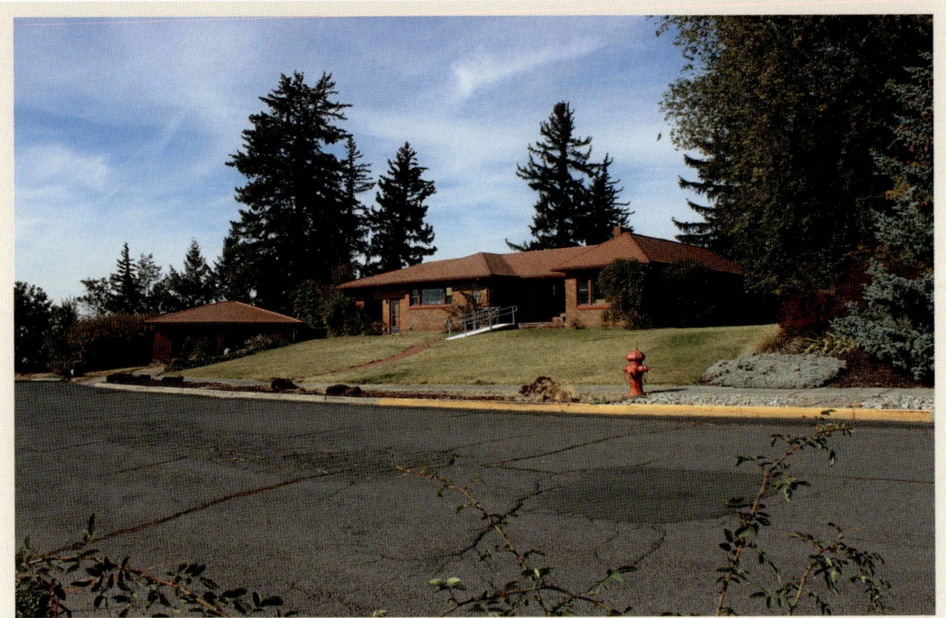

Julia Moore originally owned the land where the Loehr Addition was constructed. Doyle Loehr purchased the land from her estate in 1938 and built this house at 928 West C Street in 1940. Ranch-style houses like this one gained popularity in the 1940s and 1950s for their open floor plans and affordability by the middle class. Today, the mature landscaping has drastically changed the stark look of the house in the 1940s.

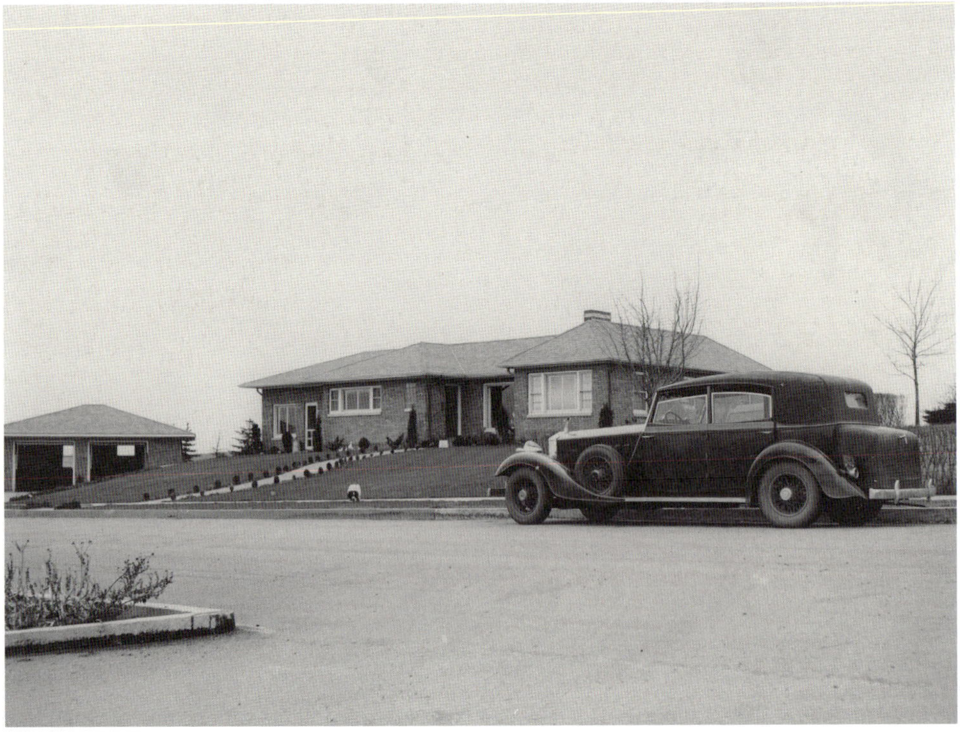

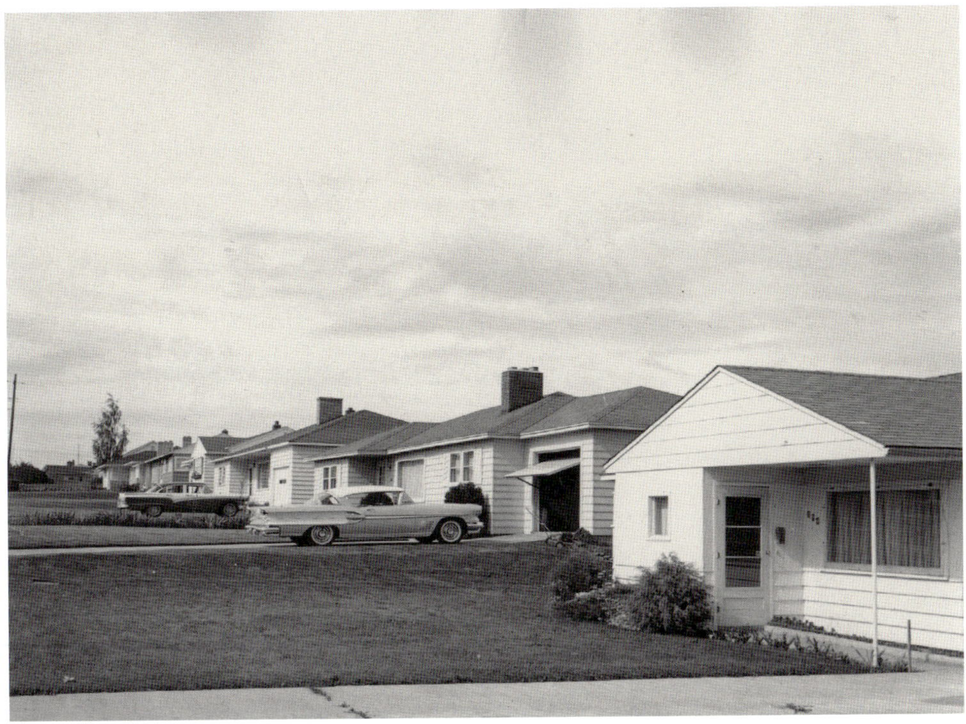

These houses along Blaine Street next to Lena Whitmore Elementary School were constructed in the early 1950s. As Moscow continued to grow, so too did its need for modest single-family homes. The house farthest on the right once belonged to Theodore Carlson, who owned Ted's Burgers from 1968 to his death in 1996. The burger joint was located where Dutch Brothers currently serves coffee.

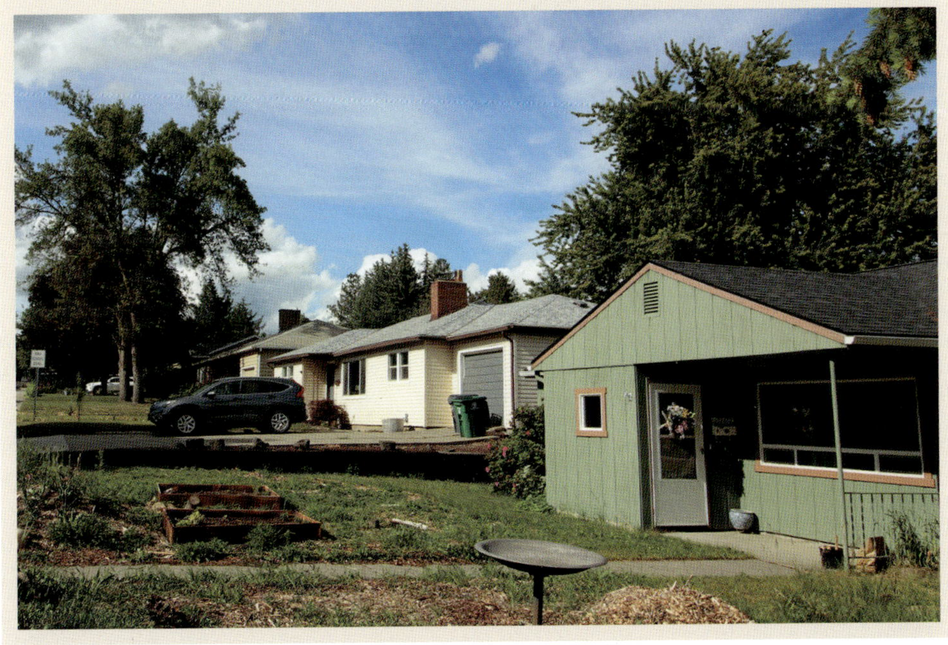

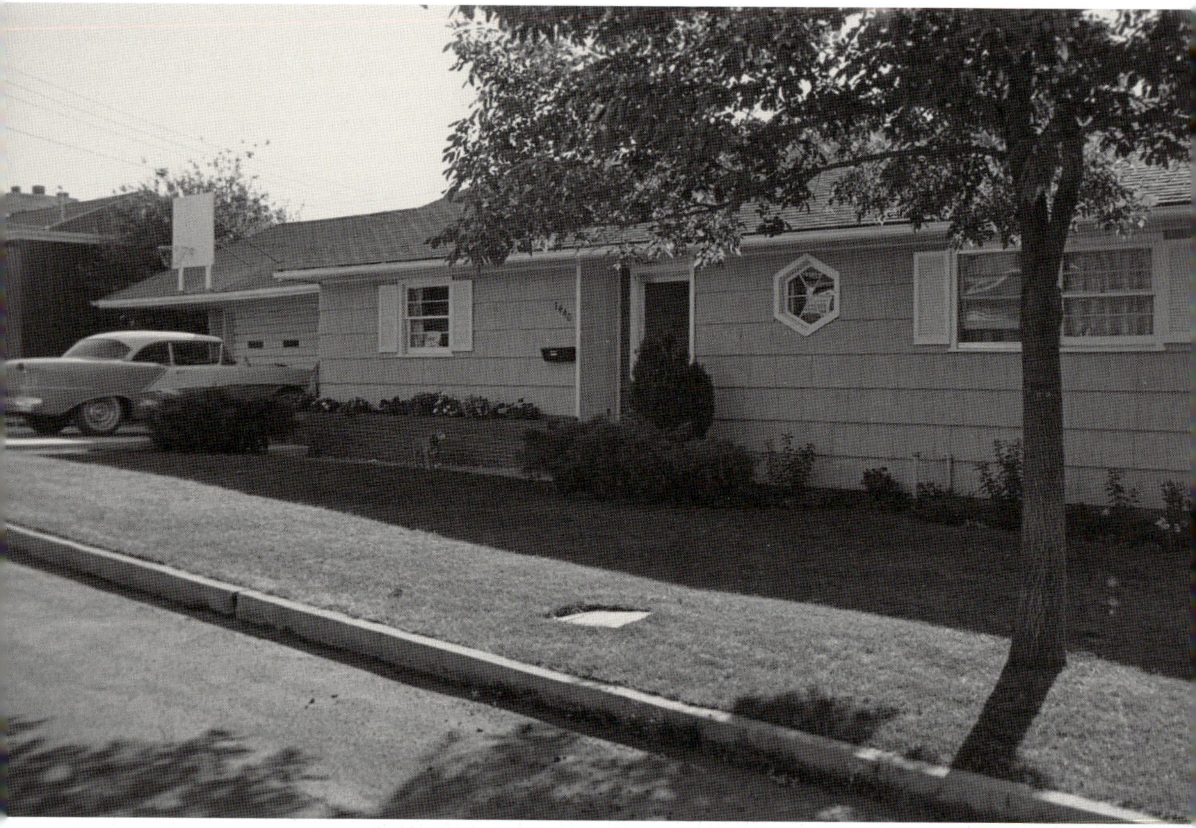

This house at 1440 Borah Avenue is located south of the University of Idaho campus. It was constructed in the early 1950s as part of the University Heights neighborhood, noteworthy for the fact that private citizens, not professional developers, built the neighborhood as a response to the housing shortage following World War II. The population boom following the war and increased enrollment at the University of Idaho meant that both students and faculty struggled to find housing in Moscow. The houses in this neighborhood resulted from their community's pooled resources.

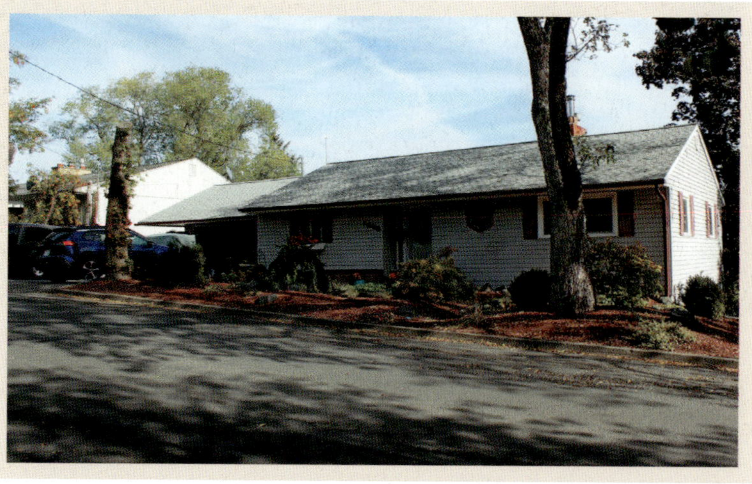

CHAPTER 6

AROUND TOWN

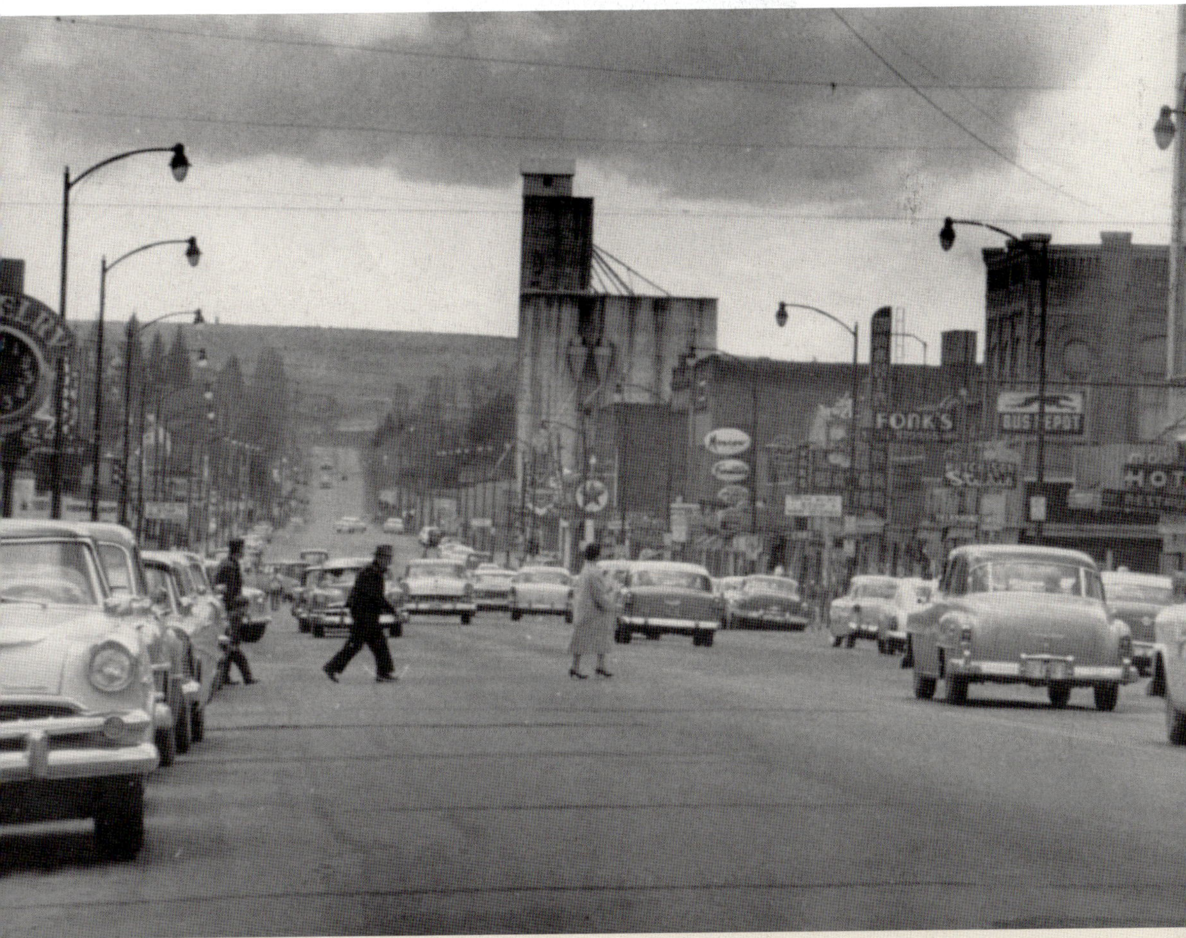

Moscow underwent significant changes when north-south Highway 95 was rerouted in the early 1980s. Prior to this, Main Street accommodated four lanes of traffic and was not pedestrian-friendly. Northbound traffic was rerouted, traveling down Washington Street as a one-way street, with southbound traffic detouring to Jackson Street, also as a one-way. Without the heavy traffic on Main Street, Moscow is more suited for pedestrians, outdoor dining, street fairs, and other local events.

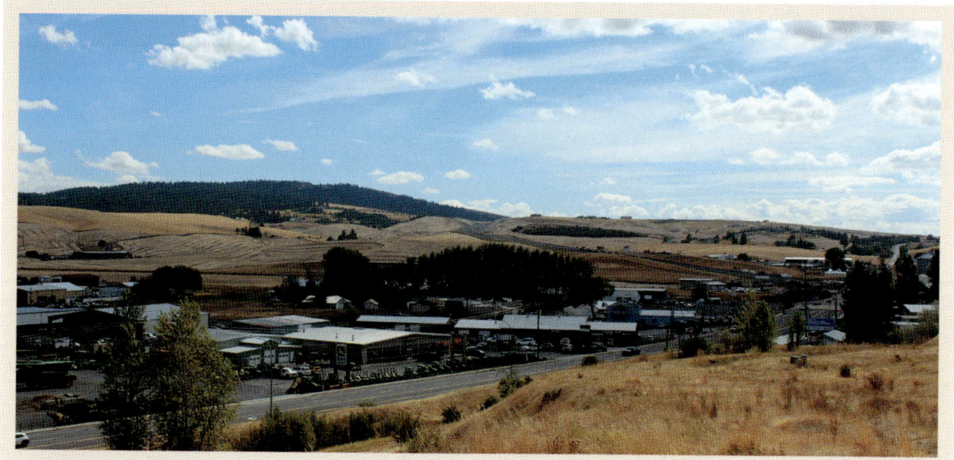

This 1937 view south of Moscow on Highway 95 shows the Civilian Conservation Corps camp that provided manual labor jobs to men during the Depression. Many of the men worked as regional farm laborers and stayed in the barracks shown in the photograph. The program ended in 1942. Now, Moscow has grown south of the town center with businesses occupying the land that the corps camp used.

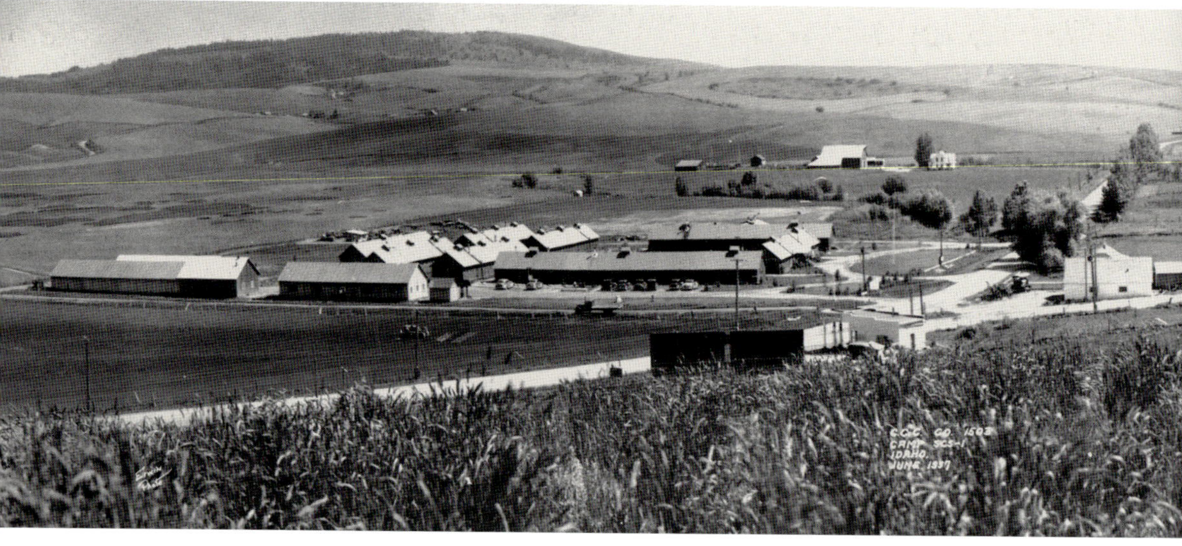

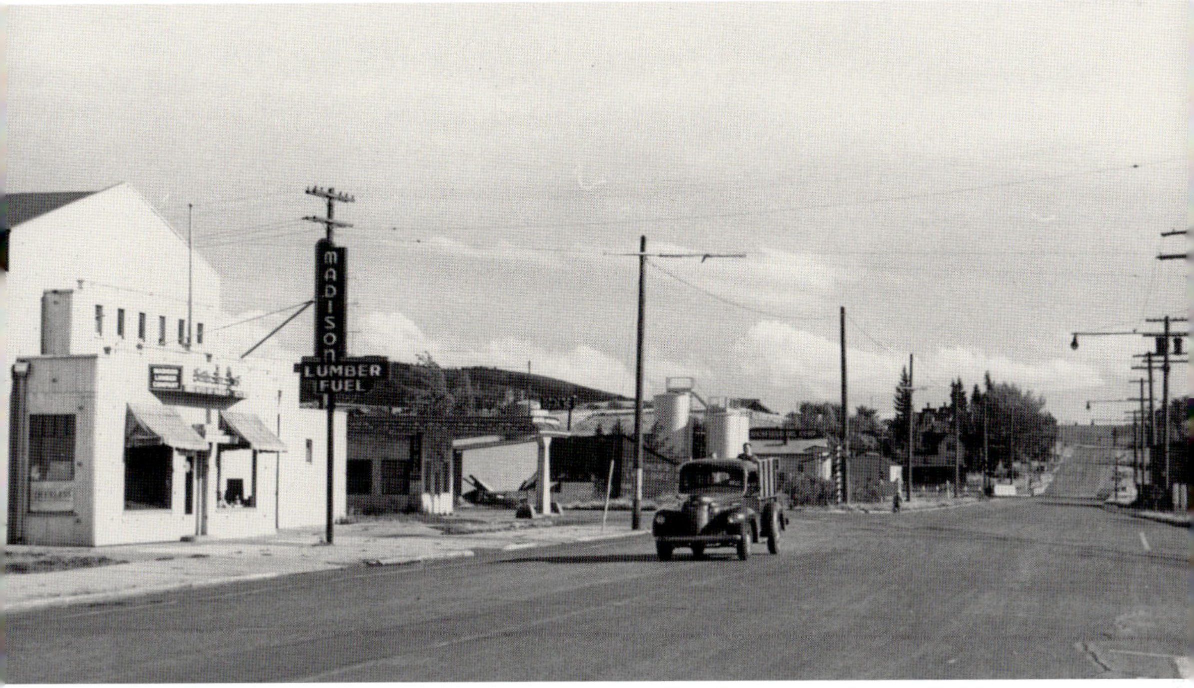

This view of south Main Street shows several businesses and buildings that no longer exist. In 1944, Madison Lumber and Fuel, as well as Richfield Oil Corporation, operated along south Main Street. When Highway 95 was rerouted to bypass Main Street and the railroad tracks were pulled up, this area of town drastically changed. The need for student housing close to campus resulted in an apartment building with a Pizza Hut next door and a bridge over Paradise Creek that is no longer used.

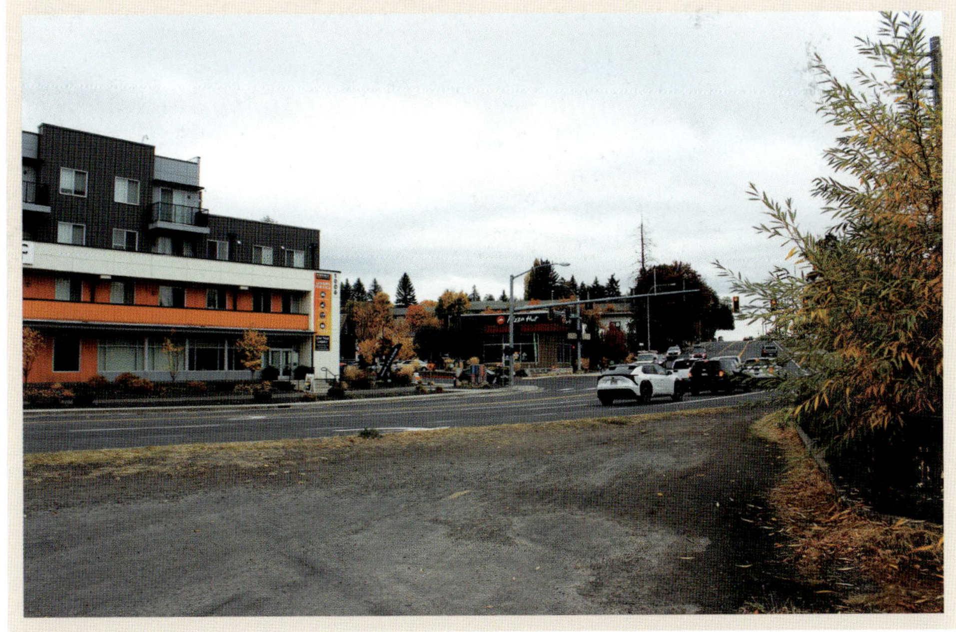

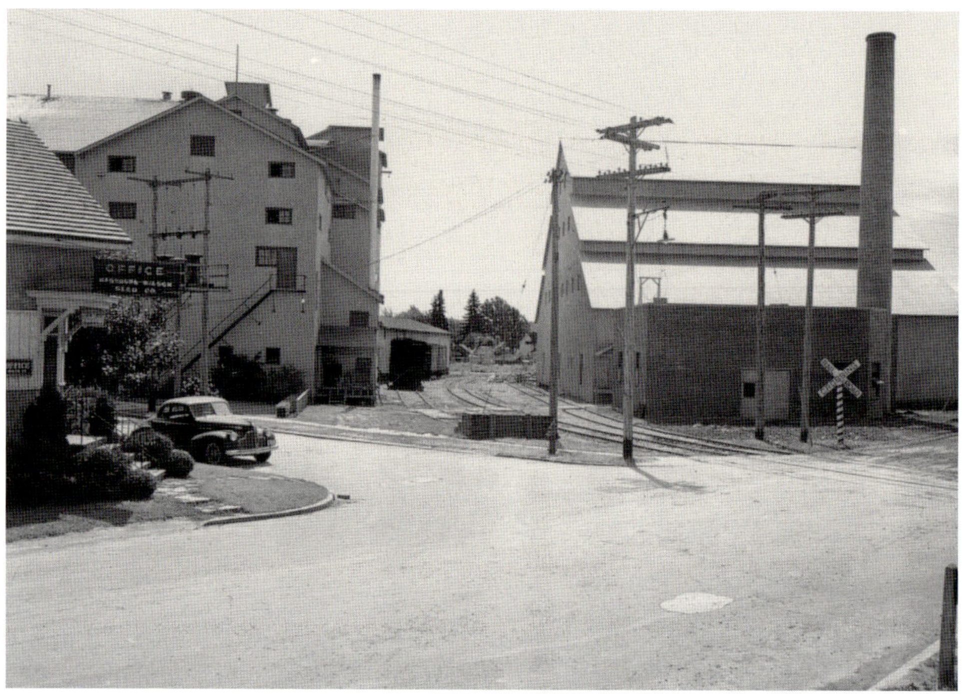

Melvin Washburn and Herman Wilson created the Washburn-Wilson Seed Company and constructed their pea processing plant and warehouse at the corner of A and Almon Streets around 1916. Adjacent to the railroad tracks, this processing plant could easily transport peas across the country. A 1945 fire and renovations changed the buildings over the years, and the company expanded to include barley. In the late 2000s, the railroad tracks were pulled up and the buildings were razed. The chimney and the former office building on the left are all that remain of the structures.

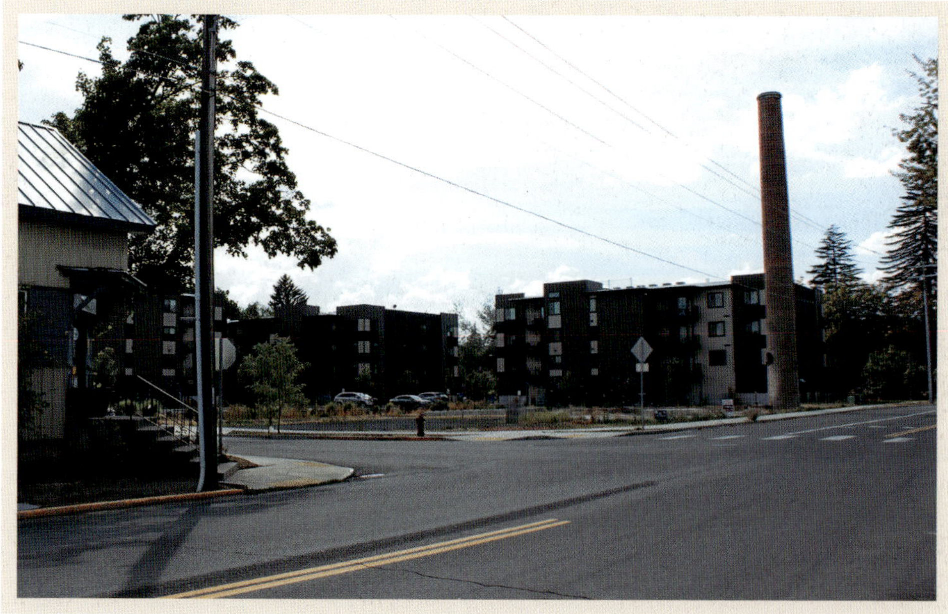

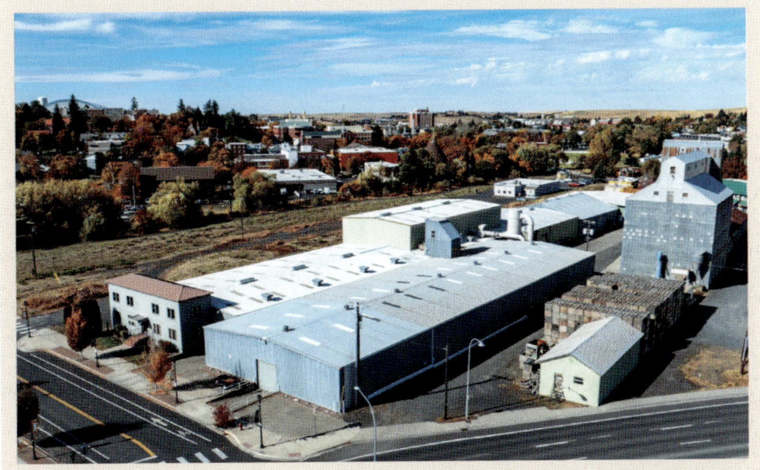

This area along Highway 95 where Eighth Street turns into College Street shows Moscow's continued reliance on agriculture with facilities from the 1930s. Companies like Crites Seed still utilize these structures to store and transport wheat, legumes, and other crops from the Palouse all over the country. The photograph illustrates where the railroad used to stop in town to transport these crops. Now, the railroad is no longer there, and the expansion of the University of Idaho campus behind these buildings is apparent. (Present, courtesy of B.J. Swanson.)

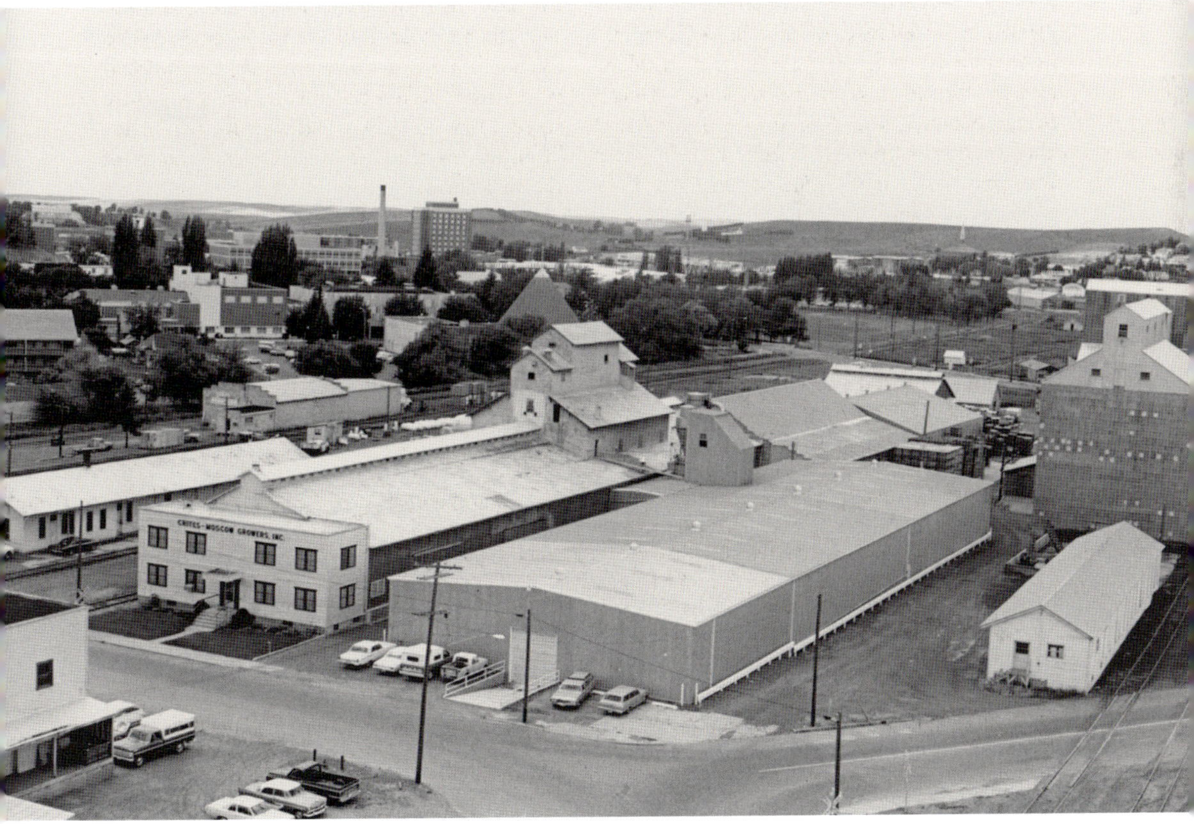

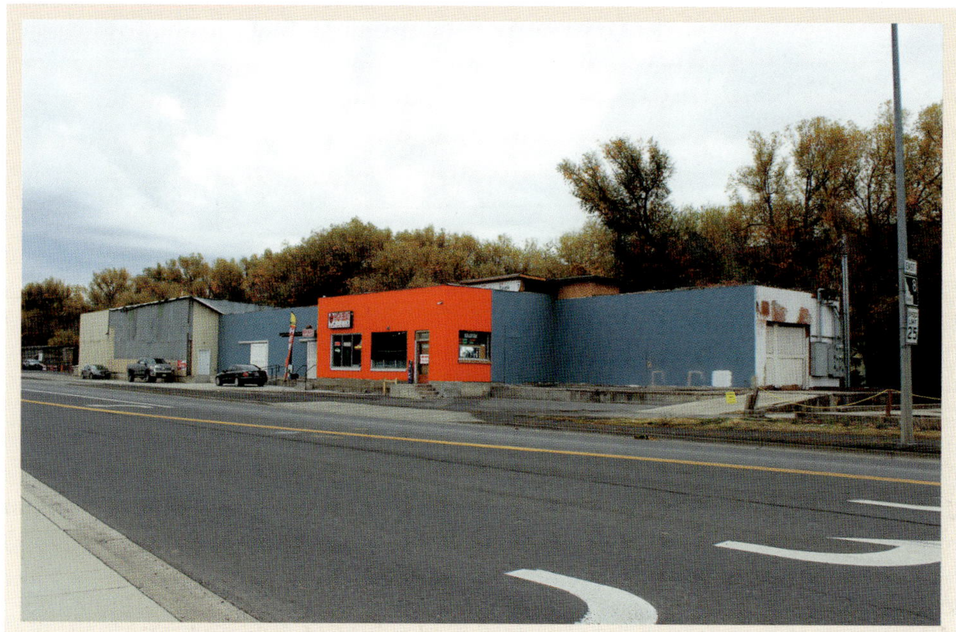

Like Crites Seed, Stubbs Seed Services was an extension of the industrial area that paralleled the railroad. Merle Stubbs opened this facility at the corner of Troy Road and Highway 95 after starting his career with Crites as the founder of their research program. Ronald Robinson purchased the business from the Stubbs family in 1965. The company closed in 2001. Today, High Beast Vape and Smoke Shop occupies the old crop storage office building.

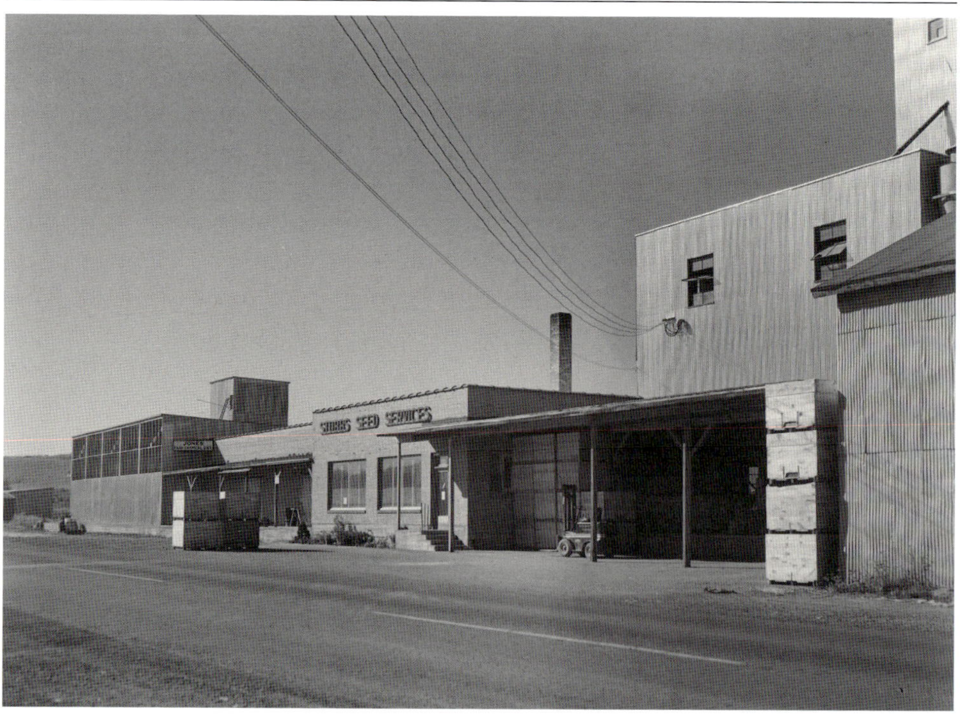

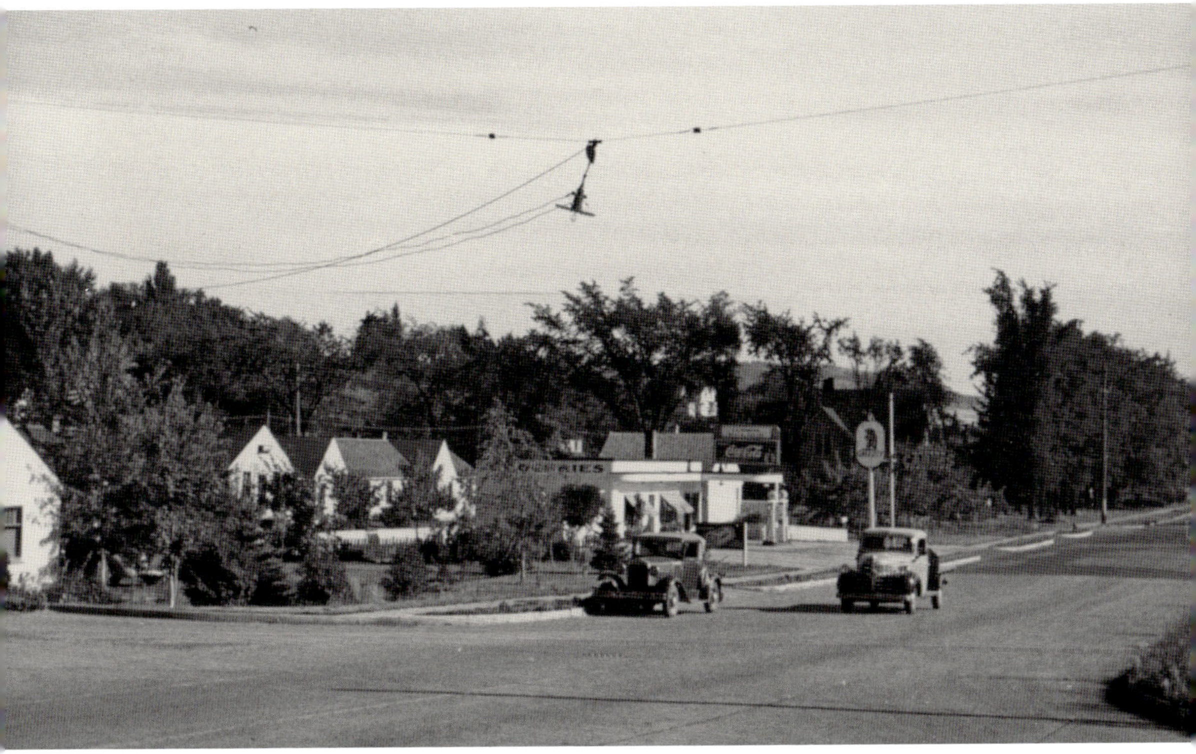

This 1944 view of the intersection at Main and E Streets shows rental cabins, a small grocery store, and a service station. Sam Fountain operated this grocery store and service station for many years. North Main Street has changed significantly, with few of the original buildings remaining. Now, that corner is home to Anytime Fitness gym and a Walgreens drugstore.

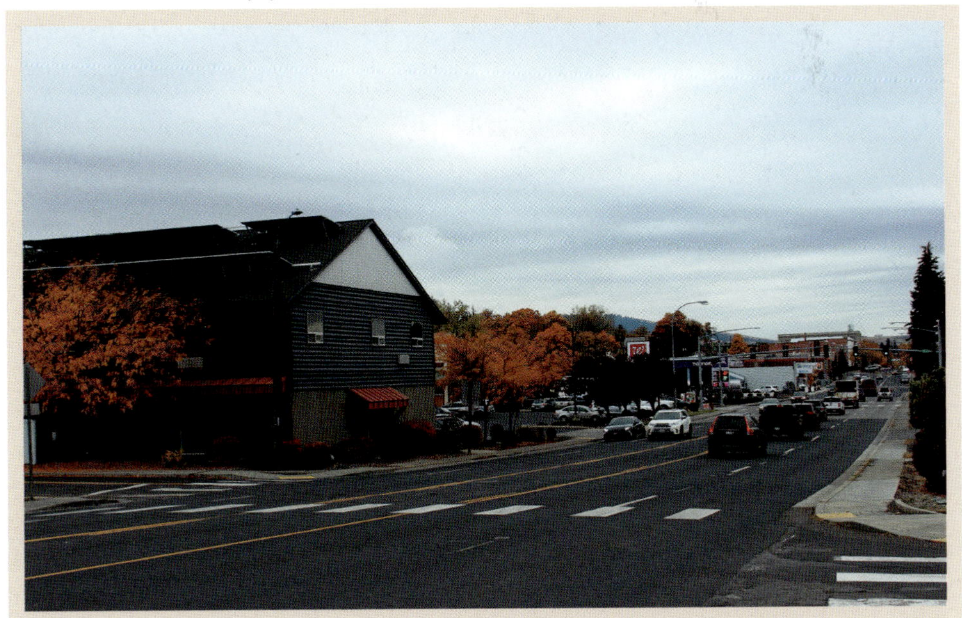

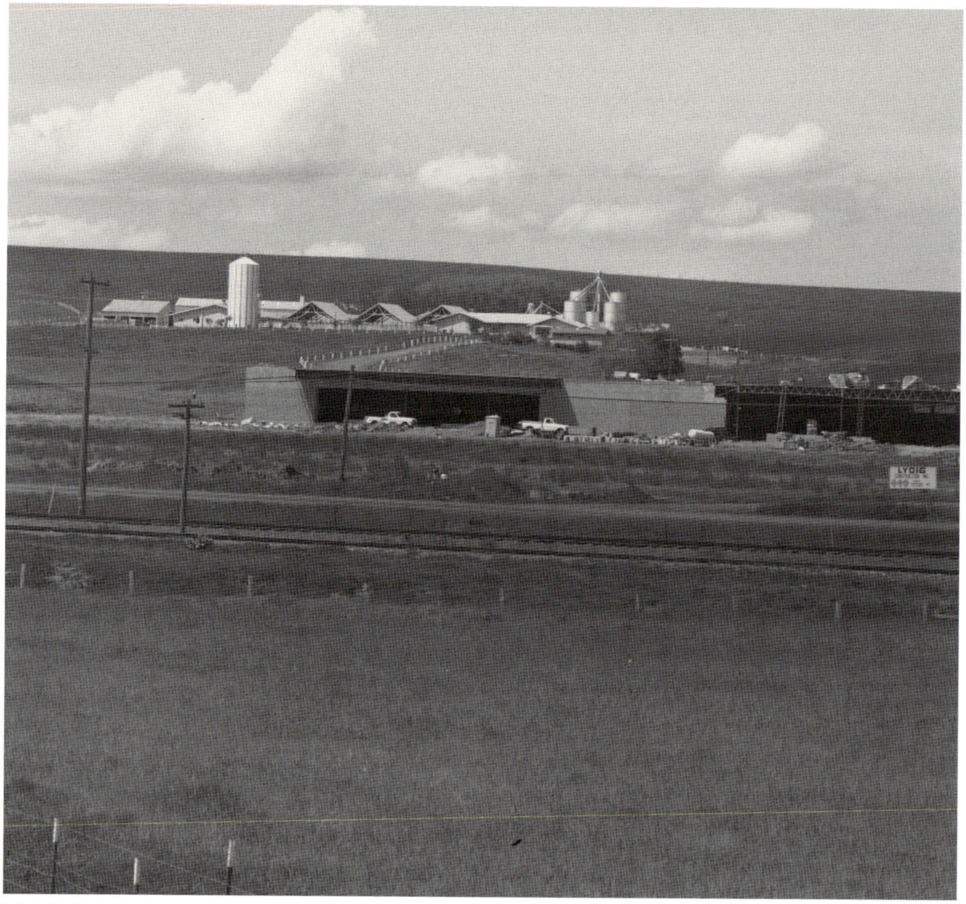

The Palouse Empire Mall opened in 1976. The land was leased from the University of Idaho and, prior to that, had been owned and farmed by the Mix family. Since 1976, the stores have changed, and the mall underwent several renovations, notably in 1997. More recently, the mall was rebranded as Palouse Place, and construction is currently being completed on a future Home Depot on the hillside behind the mall. (Past, courtesy of the University of Idaho Special Collections and Archives; present, courtesy of B.J. Swanson.)

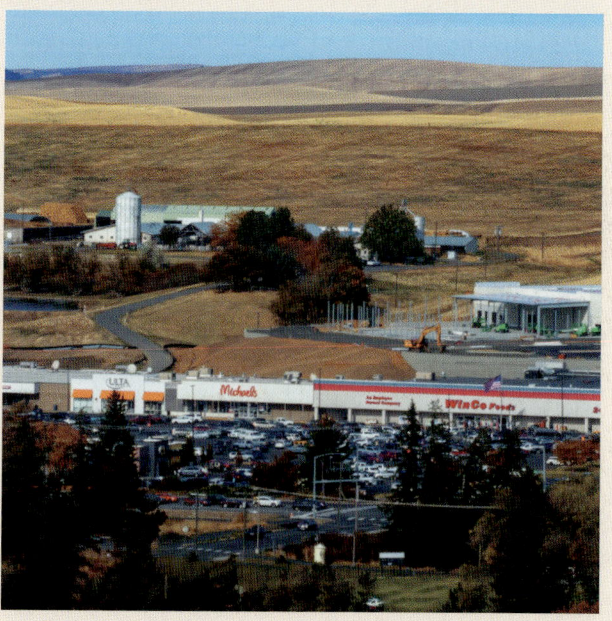

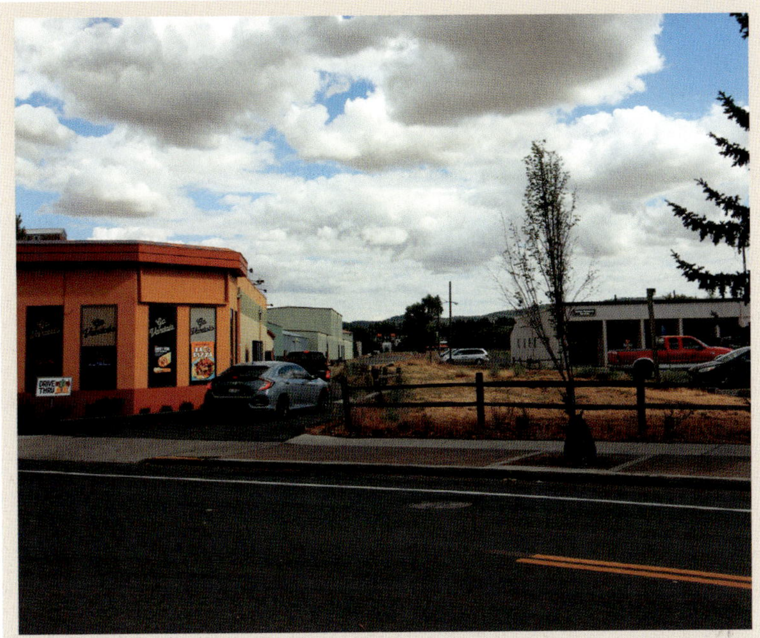

The railroad first came to Moscow in 1885 and became essential in the transportation of people and agricultural products. The agricultural buildings from this 1970s view were razed, leaving an empty field. The railroad tracks were removed from this area along Sixth Street near Asbury Street in the late 2000s. The building on the left is now home to a Taco Time.

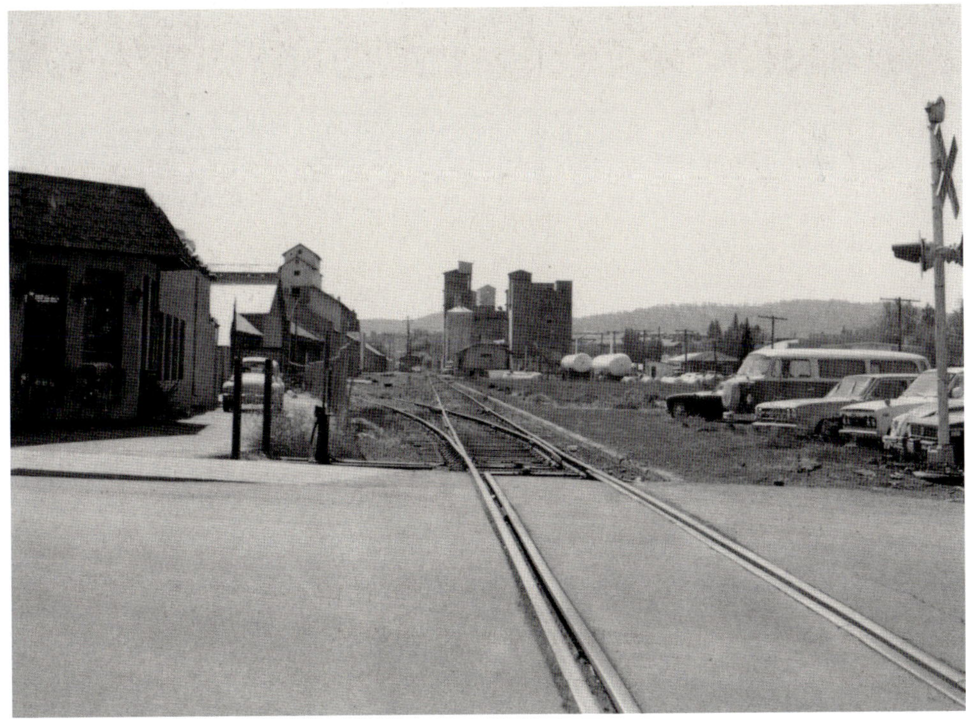

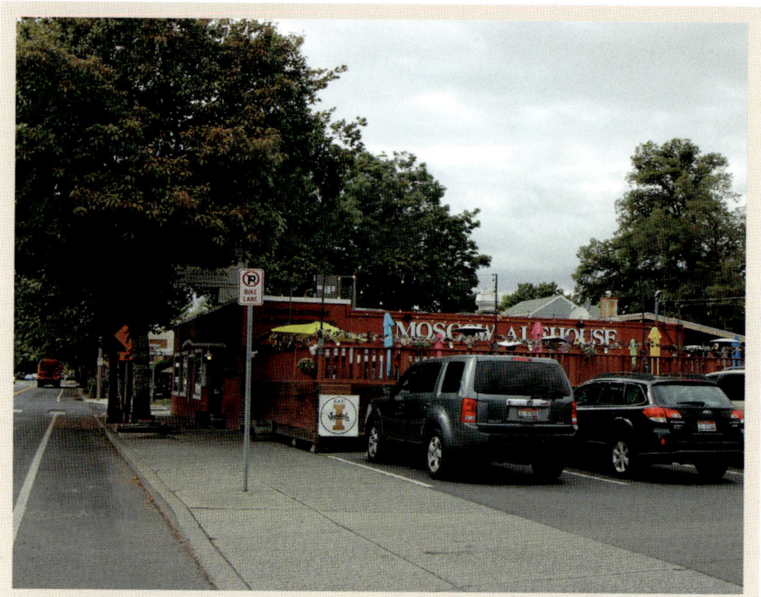

Johnnie's Café opened in the 1940s at the corner of Sixth and Almon Streets as a classic soda fountain and burger shop. Then, renovations in the 1970s and a new name, Johnnie's Restaurant, advertised pool tables and home-style meals. In 1999, the Alehouse, owned by the Coeur d'Alene Brewing Company, opened its doors. The current iteration of the restaurant came in 2013, when the business sold again and became the Moscow Alehouse.

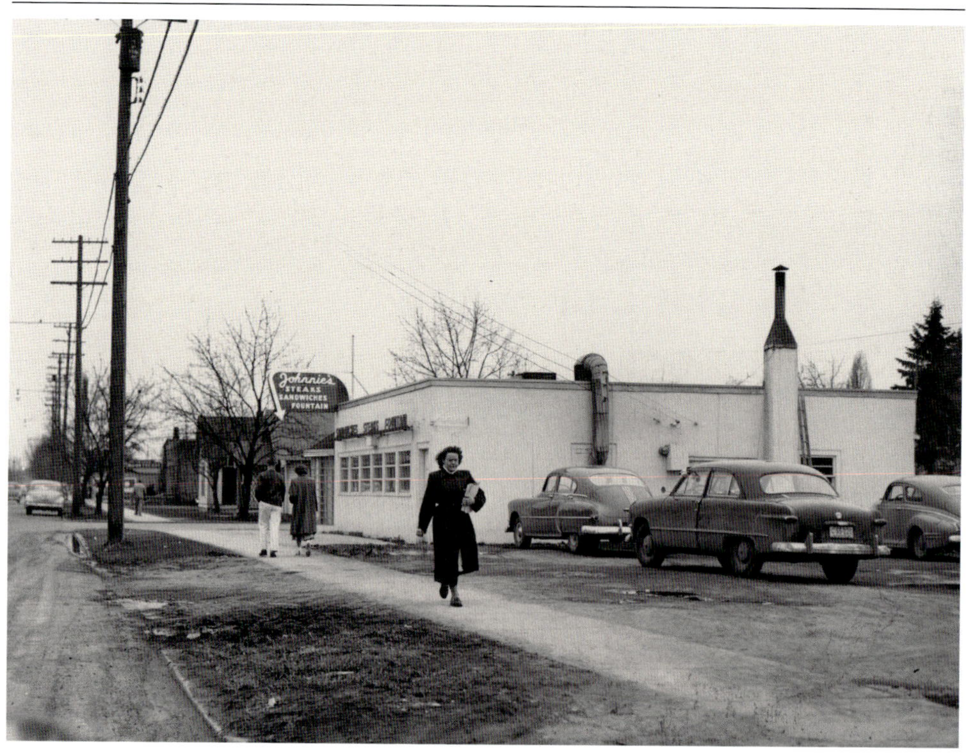

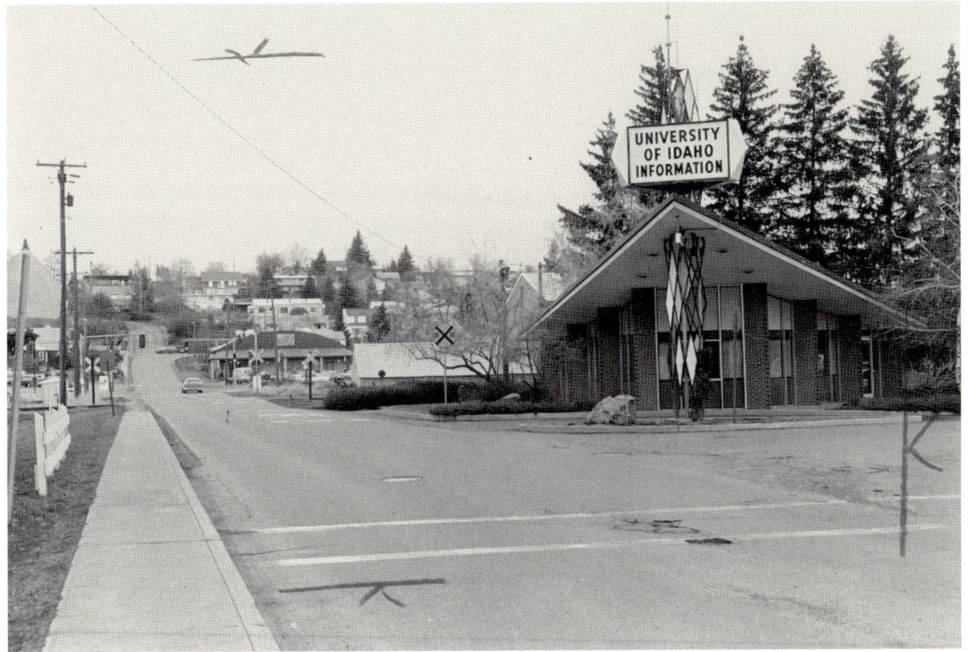

The University of Idaho previously welcomed visitors to campus from this location at the intersection of Line and Third Streets. Reminiscent of its mid-century construction in 1962, the building featured a hyperbolic paraboloid roof and decorative glass pillar. The university demolished this building in 2015 and constructed a parking lot. Line Street used to cross A Street and continue north up the hill, but today, Line Street ends at A Street, with a retaining wall blocking access.

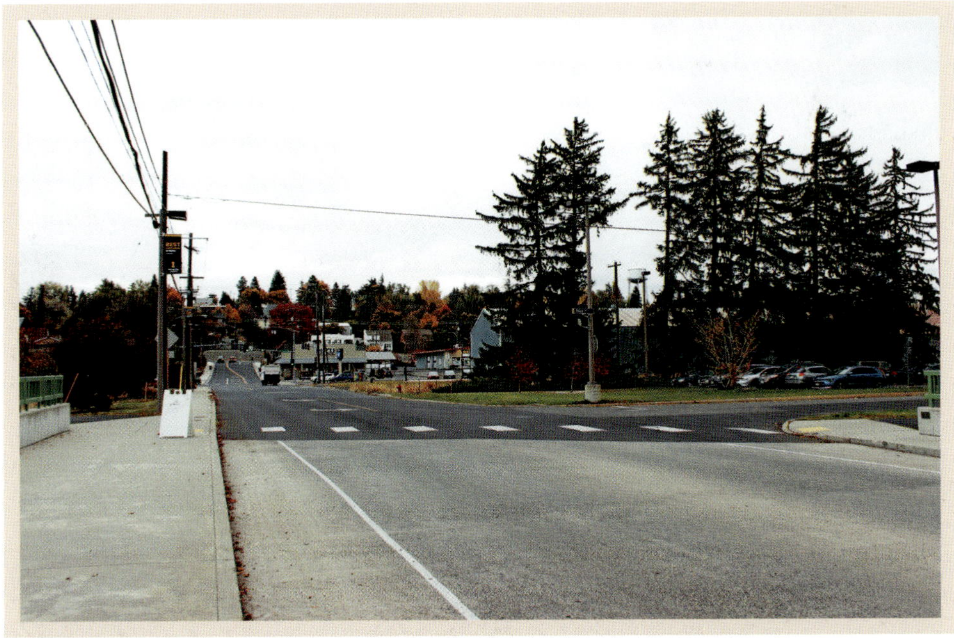

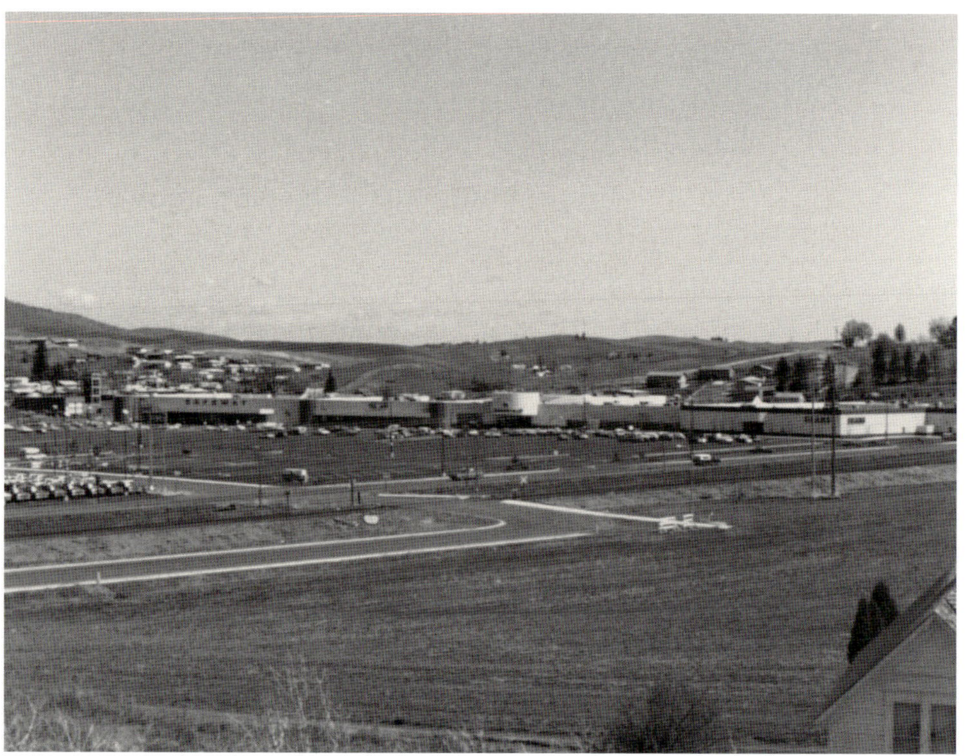

The Moscow Mall opened its doors in 1978 to serve Moscow's east side of town, which did not want to venture to the other side of town to Palouse Empire Mall. Sears, Safeway, and Thrifty Discount Drug Center were the first tenants, although many stores have occupied the mall over the years. Through the 1980s, the space was neglected, but new owners revitalized the mall and changed the name to Eastside Marketplace in 1994. Safeway remains, but renovations and the addition of a movie theater and new stores make the mall hardly recognizable. (Present, courtesy of B.J. Swanson.)

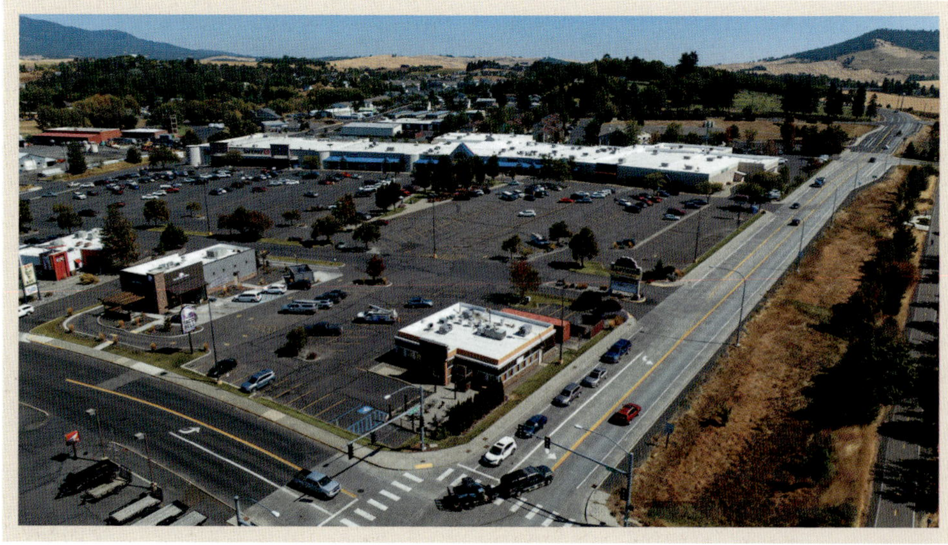

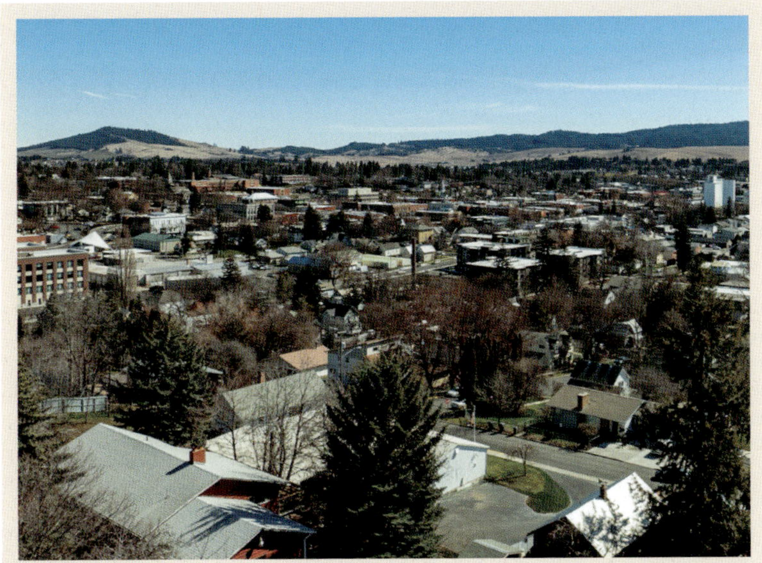

This view, dating from around 1980 and looking east over Moscow from the water tower in Almon Asbury Lieuallen Park, shows how much Moscow has grown in just 40 years. The McConnell Building, the old Post Office and Federal Building, and Moscow High School are shown in the center of the photograph. Tomer Butte looms over the town on the left, with Paradise Ridge to the right. (Present, courtesy of B.J. Swanson.)

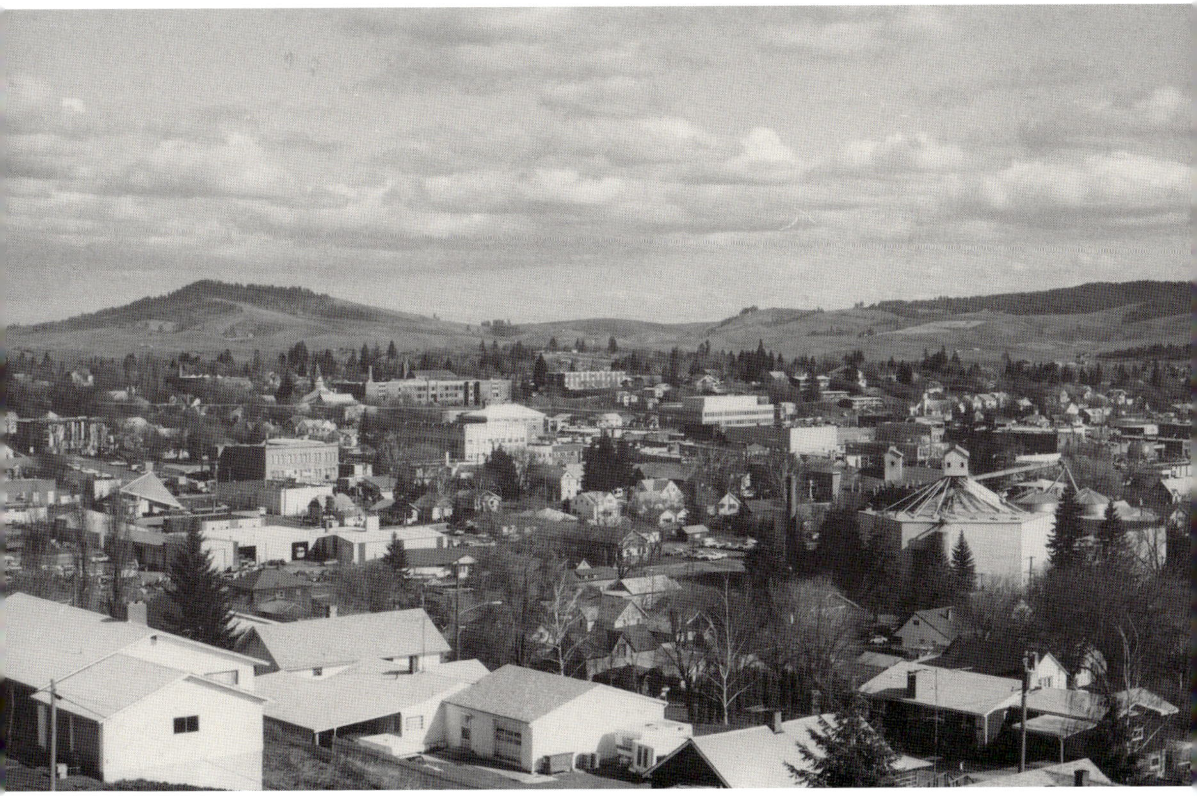

DISCOVER THOUSANDS OF LOCAL HISTORY BOOKS FEATURING MILLIONS OF VINTAGE IMAGES

Arcadia Publishing, the leading local history publisher in the United States, is committed to making history accessible and meaningful through publishing books that celebrate and preserve the heritage of America's people and places.

Find more books like this at
www.arcadiapublishing.com

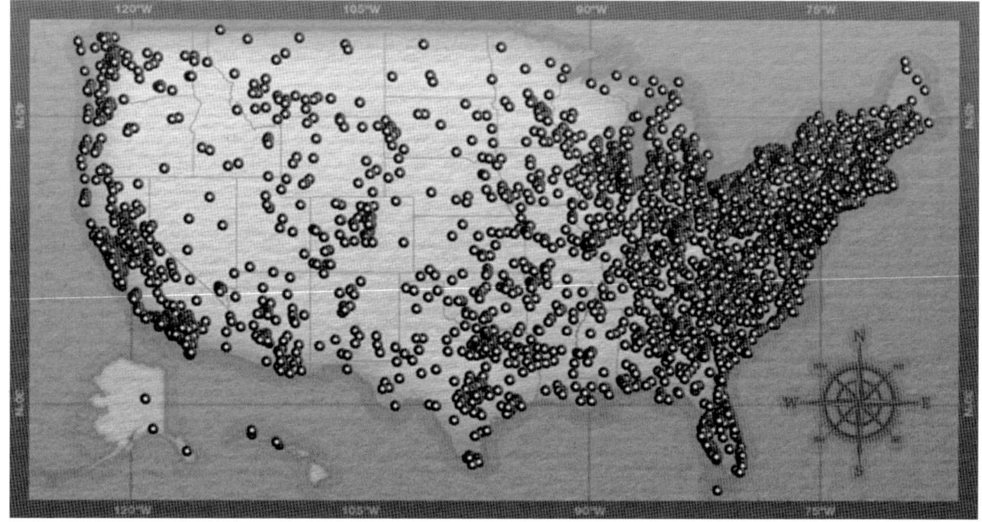

Search for your hometown history, your old stomping grounds, and even your favorite sports team.

Consistent with our mission to preserve history on a local level, this book was printed in South Carolina on American-made paper and manufactured entirely in the United States. Products carrying the accredited Forest Stewardship Council (FSC) label are printed on 100 percent FSC-certified paper.

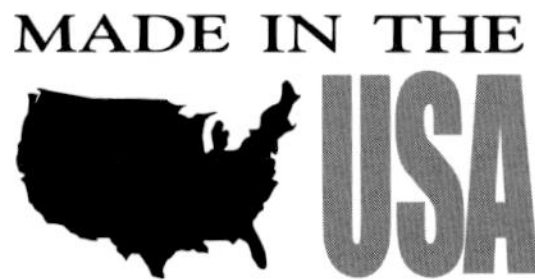